Khushwant Singh was born in 1915 in Hadali, Punjab. He was educated at Government College, Lahore and at King's College and the Inner Temple in London. He practised at the Lahore High Court for several years before joining the Indian Ministry of External Affairs in 1947. He began a distinguished career as a journalist with All India Radio in 1951. Since then he has been founder-editor of *Yojna* (1951-1953), editor of the *Illustrated Weekly of India* (1979-1980), chief editor of *New Delhi* (1979-1980), and editor of the *Hindustan Times* (1980-1983). Today he is India's best-known columnist and journalist.

Khushwant Singh has also had an extremely successful career as a writer. Among the works he has published are a classic two-volume history of the Sikhs, several novels (the best known of which are *Delhi*, *Train to Pakistan* and *The Company of Women*), and a number of translated works and non-fiction books on Delhi, nature and current affairs.

Khushwant Singh was Member of Parliament from 1980 to 1986. Among other honours he was awarded the Padma Bhushan in 1974 by the President of India (he returned the decoration in 1984 in protest against the Union Government's siege of the Golden Temple, Amritsar).

1. MAHARAJA RANJIT SINGH
(Photo: Victoria & Albert Museum)

RANJIT SINGH

MAHARAJA OF THE PUNJAB

KHUSHWANT SINGH

PENGUIN BOOKS

Penguin Books India (P) Ltd., 11 Community Centre, Panchsheel Park, New Delhi 110 017, India
Penguin Books Ltd., 80 Strand, London WC2R 0RL, UK
Penguin Putnam Inc., 375 Hudson Street, New York, NY 10014, USA
Penguin Books Australia Ltd., Ringwood, Victoria, Australia
Penguin Books Canada Ltd., 10 Alcorn Avenue, Suite 300, Toronto, Ontario, M4V 3B2, Canada
Penguin Books (NZ) Ltd., Cnr Rosedale and Airborne Roads, Albany, Auckland, New Zealand

First published by George Allen Unwin Ltd. 1962
Published by Penguin Books India 2001

Copyright © Khushwant Singh 1962, 2001

10 9 8 7 6 5 4 3 2

Typeset in *Sabon* by S.R. Enterprises, New Delhi
Printed at Chaman Offset Printers, New Delhi

FOR

KAVAL

CONTENTS

The wise man neglects not his duty towards his master; but taking his seat in the hall of obedience, remembers that humility and faithfulness bring exaltation. Falsehood brings a man to shame, and lying lips dishonour their possessor. Be then contented with the fortune that has been poured on your head; be faithful, honest and true, and mankind will praise you, and my favour will follow you; think of your end, and oppress not the poor; so shall your name remain when all else of you is gone.

Maharaja Ranjit Singh's
message to an officer

ILLUSTRATIONS

The author and the publisher wish to thank
Mr. W.G. Archer of the Victoria and Albert
Museum for his kindness and co-operation
in furnishing the illustrations

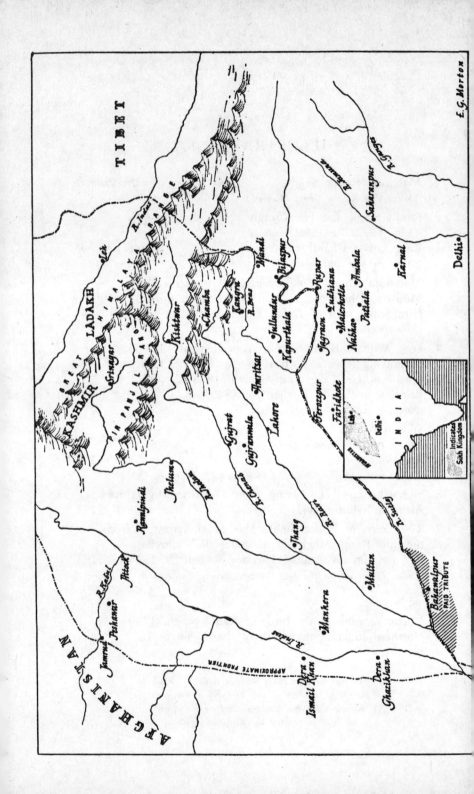

INTRODUCTION

A CALLIGRAPHIST who had spent many years making a copy of the Koran and had failed to get any of the Muslim princes of Hindustan to give him an adequate price for his labours turned up at Lahore to try and sell it to the Foreign Minister, Fakeer Azizuddin. The Fakeer praised the work but expressed his inability to pay for it. The argument was overheard by Ranjit Singh who summoned the calligraphist to his presence. The Maharaja respectfully pressed the holy book against his forehead and then scrutinized the writing with his single eye. He was impressed with the excellence of the work and bought the Koran for his private collection. Some time later Fakeer Azizuddin asked him why he had paid such a high price for a book for which he, as a Sikh, would have no use. Ranjit Singh replied: 'God intended me to look upon all religions with one eye; that is why he took away the light from the other.'

The story is apocryphal. But it continues to be told by the Punjabis to this day because it has the answer to the question why Ranjit Singh was able to unite Punjabi Mussulmans, Hindus and Sikhs and create the one and only independent kingdom in the history of the Punjab. Another anecdote, equally apocryphal and even more popular, illustrates the second reason why Ranjit Singh succeeded in the face of heavy odds: his single-minded pursuit of power. It is said that once his Muslim wife, Mohran, remarked on his ugliness—he was dark, pitted with small-pox and blind of one eye ('exactly like an old mouse with Grey whiskers and one eye'— Emily Eden), 'Where was your Highness when God was distributing beauty?' 'I had gone to find myself a kingdom,' replied the monarch.

Ranjit Singh has been poorly served by his biographers. Hindu and Sikh admirers deified him as a virtuous man and a selfless patriot. This academic apotheosis reduced a full-blooded man and an astute politician to an anaemic saint and a simple-minded nationalist. Muslim historians were unduly harsh in describing him as an avaricious freebooter. English writers, who took their material largely from Muslim sources, portrayed him as a cunning man (the cliché often used is 'wily oriental'), devoid of moral considerations, whose only redeeming feature was his friendship with the English. They were not only not averse to picking up any gossip they could (every oriental court has always been a whispering gallery of rumours), but also gave them currency by incorporating them in works of history. In recent years monographs on different aspects of Ranjit Singh's government have been produced under the auspices of departments of history in some Indian universities. These are mostly catalogues of known facts put in chronological order without any attempt to explain them in terms of historical movements. This method of treatment makes the meteoric rise of Ranjit Singh and the equally meteoric collapse of his kingdom appear as freaks of history instead of as the culmination of an important historical movement. Just as a tide seems deceptively still to those who watch it from the shore, so did the swift undercurrent of Punjabi nationalism pass unnoticed by people who did not fathom the depths beneath the swell on which the Sikhs led by Ranjit Singh rode to power. In the same way, the fall of the Sikh kingdom was not simply due to misfortune in the field of battle but, as a wave spends itself on the sands when its driving force is gone, it was the petering out of a movement whose life force was spent and which had lost its leader.

Ranjit Singh was neither a selfless patriot nor an avaricious freebooter. He was neither a model of virtue nor a lascivious sensualist. Above all, he was too warm and lively a character to have his life-story told in a lifeless catalogue of facts, figures and footnotes. As a political figure Ranjit Singh was in every way as remarkable a man as his two famous contemporaries, Napoleon Bonaparte of France and Mohammed Ali of Egypt. He rose from the status of petty chieftain to become the most powerful Indian ruler of his time. He was the first Indian in a thousand years to stem the tides of invasions from whence they had come across the North-West frontiers of Hindustan. Although he dispossessed hundreds of feudal landholders to consolidate his kingdom, he succeeded in winning their affections and converting them into faithful courtiers. In the history of the world, it would be hard to find another despot who never took life in cold blood, yet built as large an empire as Ranjit's. He persuaded the turbulent Sikhs and Mussulmans of the Punjab to become the willing instruments of an expansionist policy which brought the Kashmiris and the Pathans of the North-West Frontier under his subjection and extended his sphere of influence from the borders of China and Afghanistan in the north to the deserts of Sindh in the south. His success was undoubtedly due to his ability to arouse the nascent sense of nationalism amongst his people and make them conscious that more important than being Muslim, Hindu or Sikh was the fact of being Punjabi. His Sikh and Hindu troops subdued the Sikh and Hindu Rajas of the Punjab. His Mussulman Najibs rejected the appeals of their Hindustani, Afghan and Pathan co-religionists to crusade against the 'infidel' and instead helped to liquidate the crusaders. The year Ranjit Singh died, it was his Muslim troops led by Colonel Sheikh Basawan that forced the Khyber pass and carried Ranjit's colours through the streets of Kabul in the victory parade. And a couple of years later Zorawar Singh, a Dogra Hindu, planted the Sikh flag in the heart of Tibet. These events were the high water mark of Punjabi imperialism which had carried Ranjit Singh to the heights of power and which subsided soon after his death.

The personal life of Ranjit Singh was as colourful as his political career. Although an ugly man himself, he loved to surround himself with handsome men and beautiful women. He was small of stature and slight of build, but he was full of daring. In many campaigns, he led his troops himself and fought sword in hand. He lived the life of a soldier and like a soldier drank hard. But after the bacchanalian feasts were over, he sat up till the early hours dictating letters and memoranda to a relay of writers. Although he calculated his political moves, he was known to provoke hostilities just to acquire a horse that had caught his fancy: for horses he loved even more than human beings. Kipling's lines are apt for Ranjit Singh:

> Four things greater than all things are
> Women and Horses and Power and War.

This work is largely based on the following sources:

(a) The diary of Sohan Lal Suri which forms part of his larger work *Umdat-ut-Tawarikh*. Vidya Sagar Suri, Director of the Punjab Government Archives, who has translated this work, was kind enough to place the relevant volumes at my disposal.

(b) Newsletters of agents of Indian princes accredited to the Lahore Court.

(c) Correspondence between English agents and their government in Calcutta.

(d) Accounts of European officers in the service of Ranjit Singh, travellers and visitors to the Lahore Court. Their works are listed in the bibliography.

Some of the material in this book is used in Volume I of the Sikhs (1469-1839) published by Princeton University Press.

I would like to express my gratitude to Miss Yvonne Le Rougetel who collaborated with me in the research; to Serbjeet Singh for making the two maps; to Mr. M. L. Ahluwalia, Archivist, National Archives of India, New Delhi; Susheila Lall, and Miss Janet Ward for reading the manuscript.

I would also like to place on record my deep sense of gratitude to the Rockefeller Foundation, which by its munificence made it possible for me to devote myself to the study of records of Sikh history.

KHUSHWANT SINGH

THE SIKHS

IN THE SUMMER of A.D. 1499, a man who had spent the best part of his life wandering over the Punjab countryside, decided to proclaim a new creed. He did this after many years of pondering upon the plight of his countrymen. As far back as human memory could go, the Punjab had been subjected to foreign invasions. On many occasions the invaders had been invited by the rulers of Hindustan to settle internal disputes. At other times they had come because India was rich and, being disunited, easy to conquer. Since the Punjab was the first Indian province in which the invaders set foot, it was the Punjab that suffered most at their hands. The land once lush with vegetation had been flattened out to a treeless, wind-blown desert with dust-pillars spiralling across the waste. Its temples had been destroyed in the name of religion, its granaries looted to feed foreign armies, its villages pillaged and burnt in sadistic orgies, its women ravished to appease the lust of violent men. But Punjabis had not learnt their lesson. They continued to be divided amongst themselves and when the invader gave them respite they turned their hands against each other.

Since A.D. 1000, all the invaders had been Muslims and had by the end of the fifteenth century converted half the population of the Punjab to their faith; the other half continued to subscribe to Hinduism. This not only led to constant friction between them but also gave the Punjabi Muslim a dual loyalty, the stronger one being towards his foreign co-religionists. The problem was to give the Punjab a new faith and a new pattern of loyalties. After spending three days and nights in the wilderness, praying for guidance, he came back, and made a simple statement: 'There is no Hindu, there is no Mussulman.'

This man was Nanak, the founder of the Sikh faith. He lived

from A.D. 1469-1539. Nanak was born of Hindu parents but was strongly influenced by the teaching of Muslim mystics called Sufis. His faith consequently was an eclectic one comprising of the teaching of the Hindu Bhaktas who had rebelled against the caste-system, ritualism and the intolerance of Brahmanical Hinduism, and of the Muslim Sufis who believed in converting infidels by persuasion not by violence and disapproved of the iconoclasm of the early Muslim conquerors. The pronouncement: 'There is no Hindu, there is no Mussulman' did not seem very startling at first sight, but as Nanak proceeded to elucidate it in his sermons and to put it into practice, its revolutionary implications became clearer. For those seeking religious guidance it meant that the God of the Hindus and the Muslim was one and the same God: what really mattered was not the form but the spirit of worship. He set an example by taking as companion a Muslim musician and by going to Hindu holy places as well as making a pilgrimage to Mecca. He joined Hindus in their temples and chanted hymns from the Vedas; he stood in line with the Muslims in their mosques and genuflected towards the Kaaba. He thus started a religious movement which ignored sectarian differences between the two communities by emphasizing what they had in common. The secular implications of the statement were more far-reaching, because he proclaimed more emphatically than anyone before him that it was not necessary to look upon one's neighbours as either Hindu or Mussulman; that the people who lived in the wide plains intersected by rivers which had given the land its name, Punjab—land of the five rivers— were one people because their interests were common.

Nanak, the Guru or the teacher, was both the founder of the Sikh faith and the father of Punjabi nationalism. He was succeeded by nine other Gurus. Although they, like the founder, were chiefly concerned with spiritual matters, they also continued to enlarge on the secular legacy left by him. When the fifth Guru, Arjun (1563-1606), decided to build the temple at Amritsar, he asked a Muslim divine, Mian Mir, to lay its foundation stone. And in the anthology of sacred writings (The Granth Sahib), he included besides the compositions of the Gurus, the works of both Muslim and Hindu saints and thus at one stroke created a non-denominational scripture and sanctified Punjabi by making it the language of prayer: hitherto the Muslims had used Arabic and the Hindus Sanskrit.

Guru Arjun was executed by order of the Mughal Emperor, Jehangir, in 1606. His son, the sixth Guru, Hargovind (1595-1644) decided to raise an army to protect the infant community. He recruited his soldiers from both communities without any distinction. The policy was continued by the last of the Sikh Gurus, Govind Singh (1666-1708). Although his father, the ninth Guru, was executed in 1675 by Emperor Aurangzeb, he did not allow the movement to become anti-Islamic. In the spring of A.D. 1699, he raised the militant fraternity—he called it the Khalsa or the pure—to fight Mughal oppression. Despite the fact that two of the Guru's sons were killed fighting the Mughals and the remaining two were executed by the order of the Muslim Governor of Sirhind, he continued to have Muslim friends and retainers. He paid the price with his life; in October 1708 he was assassinated by two Muslims.

The Sikhs who were gradually becoming a separate community with their own script, scripture, places of worship and traditions became the spearhead of a resistance movement against Mughal tyranny. Large numbers of Hindu Jats (peasants) joined the militant Khalsa and so drew the Sikhs closer to the Hindus—and estranged them from the Mussulmans. Although Nanak's mission to unite the two communities in one common faith was frustrated, the spark of nationalism that he had lit was not extinguished by the storm of religious hate that blew across the Punjab for many years after the death of Guru Govind.

The first success won by Sikh arms came in 1709, when Banda led an army of untrained peasants and after defeating the Mughal armies occupied a large portion of eastern Punjab. Banda's success was, however, short-lived and in the winter of 1715, he was compelled to surrender. He, along with over 700 of his followers, was brought to Delhi and beheaded. Despite the fact that Banda's military campaign was directed against the Muslim ruling class which he virtually succeeded in destroying his dying words were not of hatred against the Muslims but against the oppression of the Mughals. He said : 'Whenever men become so corrupt and wicked as to relinquish the path of equity and abandon themselves to all kinds of excesses, then the Divine

Avenger sends a scourge like me to chastise them; when the measure of punishment is full He grants power to people like you to punish men like me.'[1]

For a short time the Sikhs disappeared as a political force from the Punjab. The Mughal Governors of the Punjab were ruthless men who made Sikh-baiting into a pastime and 'filled the plain of the Punjab with blood as if it had been a dish'.

In 1739 came the invasion of the Persian, Nadir Shah. He went through the Punjab laying waste the countryside. He plundered Delhi and massacred over 100,000 men, women and children in cold blood. His return journey was slow because his caravan of elephants, camels, horses and mules loaded with plunder (estimated at 30 crore of rupees—£23,000,000 in addition to ornaments and diamonds, including the Peacock throne and the diamond Koh-i-Noor) could not travel faster than the thousands of men and women whom he was carrying off as slaves, who had to travel on foot. The Sikhs, whom everyone believed to have been finally suppressed, reappeared. They organized themselves into small bands, relieved Nadir Shah of some of the booty and released many of their countrymen from slavery. Their conduct during the Persian invasion brought them great credit in the eyes of the people and large numbers joined their fraternity. The Muslim peasantry of the Punjab began once again to look upon the Sikhs as brother Punjabis.

Eight years after Nadir Shah's incursion, came the first of the series of nine invasions by the Afghan, Ahmed Shah Abdali. Once more the Sikhs organized guerilla bands to harass the invading army.

It was during the Afghan invasions (1747-1769) that the Sikhs rose to power. Each time Abdali came, they retreated into the mountains and jungles. But as soon as the Afghans turned back homeward, the Sikhs closed in on them and harried them all the way up to the Indus, taking away most of their loot and freeing Indian captives. Abdali did much to pave the way for a Punjabi State. He disrupted Mughal administration in the Punjab and destroyed Maratha power in Northern India; and by his repeated incursions he forced the Punjabis to sink their

[1] *Siyar-ul-Mutakherin,* p. 403
[2] Kamwar Khan, *Tazkirat-us Salatin,* p. 178a.

religious differences and unite. Since the Sikhs had organized resistance against the Afghans, they were able to seize power. Desperadoes whose only distinction was to have harassed foreign invaders became national heroes and were welcomed as liberators wherever they went. Thus the Sikhs who numbered a little over a hundred thousand became virtual rulers of a country nearly the size of France.

During these years of struggle against the Mughals and Afghans the Sikhs evolved a constitution peculiarly their own. Since every Sikh looked upon himself as a Sardar (chief), the only organization he was willing to accept was one in which his independence and equality was guaranteed. They formed bands called *misls* (from the Persian *misal* meaning 'like' or equal) under a *misldar* chosen by virtue of his courage and daring. The misls grew larger as the area in which they operated increased. They divided most of the Punjab between them and undertook to defend the people in their zones on payment of protection tax called *rakhi*. Twelve of these military fraternities came into existence with a total fighting force of about 70,000 horsemen. In due course the misldars became petty barons and their misls private armies.

Five misls deserve notice. The most powerful were the Bhangis who were in possession of Lahore, Amritsar and most of Western Punjab. The next in importance were the Kanhayas who held the Himalayan foothills. The Phulkias spread themselves around Patiala and Sirhind. The Ahluwalias took the land between the Ravi and the Beas. The Sukerchakias were amongst the lesser important misls and owned only the town of Gujranwala (forty miles north-west of Lahore) and the neighbouring villages.

The system of misls, if it can be called a system, was obviously a makeshift arrangement suited to meet the challenge of foreign invasions. Twice a year, the Sardars used to meet at Amritsar to discuss problems of defence and when there were no such problems, to deal with frictions that had begun to take place between them. In later years these meetings of the *Sarbat Khalsa* (All Khalsa Assembly) were little more than noisy sessions where the Sardars were with difficulty restrained from coming to blows. It was obvious that if the Punjab was to be saved from being splintered into little kingdoms and to be unified and made strong, one of the misls would have to absorb the others. The contest was really between the five mentioned in the previous paragraph; of these the Sukerchakias gradually forced their way to pre-eminence.

An English traveller, Willian Forster, who witnessed the misls squabbling for power, wrote in 1783: 'Should any future cause call forth the combined efforts of the Sikhs to maintain the existence of empire and religion, we may see some ambitious chief led on by his genius and success and absorbing the power of his associates, display from the ruins of their commonwealth the standard of monarchy.'[1]

The person about whom these prophetic words were written was then only three years old. He was Ranjit Singh of the Sukerchakia misl.

[1]Forster, *Travels*, vol. I, p. 295.

CHAPTER 1

RANJIT SINGH'S ANCESTORS, BIRTH
AND THE YEARS OF TUTELAGE

RANJIT SINGH'S ancestors were humble peasant folk earning
a meagre living as farmers and raisers of cattle in villages around
Gujranwala. The first in the family to rise to prominence was
one Budh Singh, who is said to have been baptised as a Khalsa
by Guru Govind Singh himself. Budh Singh was a freebooter
whose feats of endurance and those of his piebald mare, Desan,
made them legendary. They travelled the plains of the Punjab
and swam its broad rivers in flood many times, and being
inseparable, came to be known jointly as Desan Budh Singh.
When Budh Singh died in 1718, his body was found to be riddled
with scars of sabre and musket wounds. He left his sons a few
villages they could call their own and many others in the
neighborhood which paid them protection tax—*rākhi*.

Budh Singh's son, Naudh Singh, fortified the village Sukerchak
and raised a body of men who came thereafter to be called
Sukerchakias. The Sukerchakias joined forces with other misls and
fought several engagements with Ahmed Shah Abdali. As the Afghans retreated, they took possession of parts of the land between
the Ravi and the Jhelum. Naudh Singh was killed in a skirmish
in 1752.

Charhat Singh, who was the eldest of Naudh Singh's four sons,
moved his headquarters from the village, Sukerchak, to
Gujranwala and erected battlements round the town. The Afghan
Governor of Lahore came with a small force to apprehend
Charhat Singh but was compelled by the Sardar to fly back to
the capital, leaving behind his guns and stock of grain.
Emboldened by this success, Charhat Singh extended his domains
by capturing the towns of Wazirabad, Ahmedabad and Rohtas.
But when Ahmed Shah Abdali came down from Afghanistan,

Charhat Singh fled to the jungles, and suffered the pillage of his estates. Abdali had Gujranwala's fortifications razed to the ground. Charhat Singh more than settled his account with the Afghans by chasing them on their return march and plundering their baggage train. He rebuilt the battlements round Gujranwala and reoccupied the neighbouring country. His last foray was into Jammu where most of the wealthy families of the Punjab had sought shelter when Abdali began his invasions. The Bhangis disputed his right to plunder Jammu and in one of the skirmishes, Charhat Singh fell mortally wounded by the bursting of his own matchlock.

Charhat Singh's fourteen-year-only son, Maha Singh, in- herited his father's daring and ambition. He married a daughter of Gajpat Singh, the Chief of Jind, and thereby strengthened his own position amongst the misldars. Within the walled town of Gujranwala he built a fort which he named after himself as 'Garhi Maha Singh'. He increased the number of his horsemen to 6,000 and resumed the ancestral occupation of acquiring territory. He captured Rasoolnagar from a Muslim tribe, the Chatthas; he took Alipur, Pindi Bhattian, Sahiwal, Isakhel and Sialkot. Then, like his father, he proceeded to Jammu. Its Hindu Dogra ruler fled leaving the rich city to the mercies of the ava- ricious Sukerchakia. With the loot of Jammu, Maha Singh raised the Sukerchakias from a position of comparative obscurity to that of being one of the leaders of the misl confederacy. The Kanhayas, who had replaced the Bhangis as the most powerful misl, disputed Maha Singh's right to plunder Jammu, and in one of the many skirmishes between the two misls, Gurbaksh Singh, the only son of the head of the Kanhayas, was killed. The Kanhaya Chief's pride was humbled and he agreed to betroth his grand daughter, Mehtab Kaur, to Maha Singh's son, Ranjit Singh. The Kanhaya Chief died shortly afterwards leaving his estates to his widowed daughter-in-law, Sada Kaur, the mother of Mehtab Kaur.

Maha Singh died in 1792. The legacy which Budh Singh, Naudh Singh, Charhat Singh and Maha Singh left to young Ranjit consisted of a sizeable estate in north-western Punjab, a band of intrepid horse and matchlockmen, and an ambition that knew no bounds.

Ranjit Singh was born on Tuesday, November 13, 1780[1] probably at Gujranwala! The child was named Budh Singh. When
the news of the birth of a son was brought to Maha Singh who
was returning from a victorious campaign against the Chatthas
along the river Jhelum, with prophetic insight he changed his
son's name from Budh Singh, the Wise One, to Ranjit Singh,
Victor of Battles. (Ranjit remained unlettered to the last, but won
many battles.)

Little is known of Ranjit's childhood except that he had a virulent attack of small pox which deprived him of his left eye and
deeply pitted his face.[2] Maha Singh did not have time to devote to his son's upbringing, nor did the conventions of the time
give opportunity to the mother, Raj Kaur, confined as she was
to seclusion in the zenānā (a practice which the Sikh ruling
classes had taken from the Muslims), to see much of her son
after he was old enough to be on his own. He was undoubtedly
made to attend religious services at the gurdwara (Sikh temple)

---

[1] There is difference of opinion about the place and date of Ranjit Singh's
birth. An old house in Gujranwala bears two plaques outside one of the rooms
claiming it to be Ranjit Singh's place of birth and mentioning the date as
November 2, 1780. Many historians including McGregor, Griffin, Prem Singh
and Dr Ganda Singh accept Gujranwala as the place of birth but most now
put the birth date as November 13, 1780. There is, however, a school of
historians who believe that Ranjit Singh was born in the small fortress town
of Budrukhan not far from Sind. Budrukhan was the home of Ranjit Singh's
brother, Raj Kaur, the daughter of Rajah Gajpat Singh of Jind, known in
her husband's home as Mai Malwain, the lady of Malwa. She had, as was
customary in the Punjab, come to her parental house for her first confinement.

[2] Sohan Lal Suri writes:
'The glorious prince suffered indisposition. Two hundred horsemen under
the command of Sarbuland Khan along with the master-physician Lala Hakim
Rai were sent to the Great Prince...the illness of the Glorious Prince took
a bad turn on account of the high spotted fever. There was so much fer-
mentation and pouring out of foreign matter from the body, particularly the
right eye, that it did not show signs of abating. From the excess of pain it
became a winking eye.' (The historian made a slip of the pen. He spent a
lifetime with Ranjit Singh and must have observed practically every day that
the eye which became a 'winking eye' was not the right one but the left.)
Daftar II, p. 25.

and hear the recitation of the Granth. Alongside elementary instructions in the principles of the Sikh faith, he was influenced
by the preaching of Brahmin priests who had insinuated them-
selvés in the home of the Sikh aristocracy. For the rest it was
a matter of games and hunting. In these early years, Ranjit
developed a love for horses, a love which in later life turned
into a ruling passion.

Ranjit Singh had his first experience of a military campaign
when he was ten. His father had demanded tribute from Sahib
Singh Bhangi of Gujerat, and on the latter's refusal to comply,
ejected him from his principality. Sahib Singh took refuge in the
fort of Sodhran and appealed to his kinsmen in Lahore to come
to his help. Maha Singh took Ranjit Singh with him to Sodhran
and laid siege to the fort.

The siege dragged on through the winter months. Maha Singh
was suddenly taken very ill, and fearing that he might not recover, invested Ranjit Singh as the head of the Sukerchakia misl
by daubing the boy's forehead with saffron paste, and then returned to Gujranwala. When the Bhangi Sardars of Lahore heard
of Maha Singh's illness and of the predicament of the
Sukerchakias under the command of a lad of ten, they hurried
to the relief of Sodhran. Ranjit Singh ambushed the Bhangi force
coming from Lahore many miles from Sodhran and routed it.
Maha Singh heard of his son's victory before he died. Ranjit
Singh was just able to get back in time for his father's funeral.

Ranjit Singh was too young and temperamental to bother
about the day to day management of the estate and let his
father's manager, Lakhpat Rai, continue in charge. His mother
had confidence in Lakhpat Rai's integrity but her brother, Dal
Singh, who wished to take the administration into his own hands,
found an ally in Sada Kaur, Ranjit's mother-in-law to be. The
intrigues and counter-intrigues that went on between his mother,
mother-in-law, uncle and other relations and friends made Ranjit
heartily sick of the atmosphere at home and he began to spend
most of his time out hunting and in the company of servants.
These were impressionable years; the experience made him for
ever suspicious of people who professed affection for him and
he developed an acute aversion to quarrelsome people; *dungāwālā*
(rowdy) and *takrāri* (argumentative) became words of abuse in

his vocabulary. As much of his time was spent in chase, he learnt to ride and shoot well. And since a day's hunting was followed by a drinking party, he was introduced to alcohol early in life.

A murderous assault was made on Ranjit Singh during one of his hunting expeditions. He had ridden off alone in pursuit of game when Hashmat Khan, a chief who had suffered many humiliating defeats at the hands of Maha Singh, attacked him. Ranjit's horse took fright and reared just as the Khan made a cut with his sword. Before the assailant could make a second move, Ranjit transfixed him with his lance. He cut off Hashmat Khan's head and rode back to his companions with the gory trophy impaled on his spear. He was then barely thirteen.

Ranjit Singh spent another two years hunting wild pig and deer in the woods around Gujranwala without taking any interest in his estate. His mother became anxious for his future and felt that marriage might bring him round to the responsibilities of life. She approached Sada Kaur to fix the nuptial date. Ranjit was just over fifteen years of age when he left Gujranwala for Batala, the chief town of the Kanhyas, to wed Mehtab Kaur. This alliance between the two important Sikh families was a major event for the Punjab. All the leading Sikh chiefs were present at the wedding.

The marriage was not a very happy one. It is not unlikely that Mehtab Kaur felt somewhat inhibited in giving her affections to a man whose father had slain hers: and Ranjit Singh's reaction to her reserve was to withdraw into himself. It soon became a marriage of convenience. Sada Kaur did not seem particularly disturbed at the prospect of her daughter occasionally sharing a bed with a man for whom she had little use: that sort of thing was common enough; the important thing was for her to produce sons who could be heirs to the Sukerchakia domains. Meanwhile, she could utilize the alliance to safeguard and even advance the interests of the Kanhayas. To Ranjit Singh, who was undoubtedly conscious of his own plainness, the disillusionment was great enough to change his values. Instead of trying to win affection he began to want to command loyalties—which he could only do by becoming powerful. The Kanhayas thus became a means towards this end. A curious love-hate relationship developed between Sada Kaur and Ranjit Singh. Both of them were ambitious and respected the other's ambition: they could be unscrupulous and consequently willing to overlook the other's lack of scruple; in short, being very much alike they began to understand each other perfectly.

Sada Kaur was the first to ask for help. In the summer of 1797, her possessions were threatened by the Ramgarhias and Ranjit had to besiege a Ramgarhia fortress to relieve the pressure on the Kanhayas. On his way back to Gujranwala, Ranjit Singh stayed at Lahore for three days as the guest of the Bhangi Sardars and acquired valuable information on the state of affairs in the city and its defences.

Ranjit Singh's mind was now completely obsessed with visions of power. Experience of the previous campaign had proved to him that the Kanhayas were not as strong as he had believed. His chances would be brighter if he could draw some other misl on his side. He made overtures to the chief of the Nakkais and early in 1798 took a second wife who was the sister of the Nakkai Sardar. This marriage proved to be more successful than the first. The new wife bore the same name as his mother, Raj Kaur, and had the same maternal gentleness and understanding in dealing with the wayward Ranjit. Although many other women came into his life, for no one did he have greater respect than for Raj Kaur (renamed Datar Kaur), but affectionately known as Mai Nakkain.

The second marriage gave Mehtab Kaur an excuse to return to Batala and thereafter she only made occasional appearances at her husband's home. It also soured Sada Kaur; but she reconciled herself to Ranjit's polygamous venture because she had set her heart on bigger things and was determined to see that for her own sake and the sake of her only child (and her progeny if she had any), Ranjit Singh carried out plans that she had made for him.

While Ranjit Singh was sorting out his matrimonial affairs, the management of the Sukerchakia estates reached a critical stage due to friction between Lakhpat Rai and Ranjit's uncle, Dal Singh. Lakhpat Rai was murdered while out collecting revenue. The assassins could not be found, but ugly rumours got round that Dal Singh had had a hand in the killing.[1] Ranjit Singh felt that the time had come to free himself of many advisers and take the administration of his estate into his own hands. At the age of seventeen, Ranjit Singh became the real master of his Sukerchakia inheritance.

[1]The murder of Lakhpat Rai has been subject of much speculation. Prinsep, Wade and Latif have exaggerated the support that Ranjit's mother gave to the Diwan into a liaison and conjectured that both the Diwan and Ranjit's mother were murdered by Ranjit Singh himself. Neither Sohan Lal Suri, nor Amar Nath, nor even Bute Shah (who was a newswriter in the employment of the British at the time of Ranjit Singh) make any such insinuation. The spreading of this baseless story is one of the many examples of character assassination to which Ranjit has been subjected by some historians.

CHAPTER II

THE PUNJAB AND THE
AFGHAN INVASIONS

IN THE 1790s, the Punjab looked like a jig-saw puzzle consisting of fourteen pieces with five arrows piercing it from the sides. Twelve of these fourteen pieces were the Sikh misls; the other two, the Pathan-controlled district of Kasur in the neighbourhood of Lahore, and Hansi in the south-east under the English adventurer, George Thomas. The five arrows were: the Afghans in the north-west, the Rajputs of Kangra in the north; the Gurkhas in the north-east; the British in the east; and the Marathas in the south-east.

The misl organization had ceased to be the united fraternity of the Khalsa that it had been fifty years before. When Ahmed Shah Abdali had started his incursions into India, they had fought as one under the leadership of Jassa Singh Ahluwalia. The first to default were the Phulkias of Patiala. Ala Singh had submitted to Abdali and later on the Phulkias had become collaborators. Sahib Singh of Patiala was in communication with Abdali's grandson, Shah Zaman, who was planning to re-establish Afghan dominion over Northern India. The other misls that mattered were the Kanhayas, the Nakkais, the Ahluwalias and the Bhangis. Ranjit Singh had matrimonial ties with the first two and they could be counted on to help him whenever co-operation did not hurt their own interests. The Ahluwalias were led by Fateh Singh, who was an able leader, and because he was Jassa Singh's successor, held in great esteem by the Sikhs. Ranjit Singh decided to befriend Fateh Singh. He could not, however, reconcile his interests with those of the Bhangis who held Lahore, Amritar, Gujerat and a large portion of northern Punjab. Ranjit Singh decided to break the Bhangis and make the other misldars subservient to his wishes.

A problem requiring solution almost as urgently as the disunity of the Sikhs was the presence of two alien elements in the very heart of the Punjab. Thirty miles from Lahore was Kasur, whose Pathan ruling family's loyalties were more to the land of their forefathers than to the Punjab. The rise of the Sikh misls had made them nervous. Each time Abdali had come to the Punjab, they had joined him to plunder their own neighbours. When Abdali's grandson, Shah Zaman, expressed the desire to establish an Afghan empire in India, among the first to promise him assistance was Nizamuddin Khan of Kasur.

The other alien element was the English adventurer George Thomas. Thomas deserted his ship and took employment with Indian chieftains. Later he raised a band of horsemen and set up a kingdom of his own with its headquarters at Hansi, where he built a fort named after him as 'George Garh'. His depredations extended well into the territories of the chiefs of Patiala and Jind. He saw the chaotic state to which the Sikh misls had reduced themselves. In 1800 he rode up to the Sutlej with just 5,000 men and 60 cannon. He wrote to the Governor-General offering to plant the Union Jack on the banks of the river Indus. 'This nation (the Sikhs) is not so formidable as they have been represented,' he later told his biographer, 'and in all probability never will be formidable when opposed by regular troops.' He quoted instances when Marathas had marched across the Punjab without meeting any resistance and the incapacity of the Sikh chiefs to fight the Afghans under Shah Zaman. 'I explored the country, formed alliances, and, in short, was dictator in all the countries belonging to the Seiks, South of the River Sutledge,' he boasted.

The biggest menace to a free and powerful Punjab were the Afghans who, ever since Abdali's conquests, had looked upon most of northern India as a part of their empire. Abdali's attempts to treat it as such had been frustrated largely by the Sikhs. Although his son and successor, Taimur, kept up pretensions to northern India, the best he could do was to retain his hold on Kashmir and eject the Bhangis from Multan. Taimur's son, Shah Zaman, was most ambitious and as soon as he took his father's place, he announced his intention of reestablishing the Afghan empire in India. Fortunately for the Punjab all that Abdali's progeny had inherited from him were his dreams.

Shah Zaman's first attempt in 1793 brought him as far as Hassan Abdal. Two years later, in addition to retaking Hassan Abdal, he captured Rohtas from the Sukerchakias. Ranjit Singh was thus the first Sikh chieftain to suffer at his hands. The Shah had to return home to prevent an invasion of his own country from the west. As soon as his back was turned, Ranjit expelled the Afghans from Rohtas. But the Punjab had not yet heard the last of Zaman and his Afghans.

Amongst the elements upon which Zaman counted for co-operation in the execution of his designs was the Rajput prince, Sansar Chand of Kangra. Whether Sansar Chand would ultimately have forwarded the Afghan's plans is doubtful as he too had visions of extending his kingdom from the mountainous regions to the plains. He had already taken areas adjacent to his domains from the Sikh chief's and discovered that their disunity made them an easy quarry. At about the time when Ranjit came into his own, Sansar Chand was busy planning a conquest of the Punjab.

Meanwhile a people hitherto only known as a warrior race had become a formidable power in the eastern Himalayas. These were the Gurkhas under a very able leader, Amar Singh Thapa. They had begun to move westward along the mountain ranges until they came face to face with Sansar Chand. The choice for the Gurkhas and Rajputs lay between fighting each other, or joining hands to take the Punjab and share the spoils. Disunity amongst the Punjabis made the latter alternative more feasible.

There remained the two eastern powers, the greatest of all in India at the time, the Marathas and the English. The Marathas had extended their arms right across the sub-continent. They had suffered a severe defeat at the hands of the Afghans on the field of Panipat in 1761, but it did not take them long to recover from the blow. Within a few years, they again took Agra, reduced the Mughal Emperor at Delhi to subservience and re-entered Southern Punjab. Their soldiers were better disciplined than the Sikhs and they were led by more experienced commanders. In the north they had French Generals Du Boigne, Perron and Bourquin to direct their conquests. Meerut had become the centre of the *Inde Française* where Frenchmen in the service of the Marathas congregated to drink absinthe and talk of the day when they would defeat the British and extend the Maratha Empire to all corners of India, right across the Punjab to the Khyber Pass. With the Maratha princes quarrelling amongst each other, it was not too much to hope that the whole country would fall like a ripe apple into the lap of France.

The English were less conspicuous but potentially more formidable than the Marathas. Ostensibly their only interest in the region was to protect the Nawab Wazir of Oudh whose territories extended up to the river Ganges. (They often had skirmishes with Sikh horsemen who were in the habit of crossing the river in the winter months.) The English were the most far-sighted of all the external forces threatening the Punjab. They had agents in the big cities of India, Sindh, Persia and Afghanistan, and were fully informed of what was going on. Many years earlier they had sensed the danger to themselves of a Sikh-Maratha alliance. Even now it was they, more than anyone else, who realized that Zaman's aggressive designs spelt danger to the whole of India and shrewdly guessed that the people who could be counted on to put up an effective resistance to the Afghans were not the Marathas, or the Rajputs, or the Gurkhas, but the Sikhs. They also conjectured that the one man who could organize the Sikhs was the hitherto unknown lad in his teens, Ranjit Singh. They planned strategy which showed the political genius of their race. Through their agents they urged the Sardars to unite under Ranjit Singh. The English were willing, even eager, to fight the Afghans to the last Sikh.

In the autumn of 1796, Shah Zaman 'moved from his native land and spread his owl-like shadow over the Punjab'.[1] This was the third time that he had crossed the Indus with the intention of proceeding to Delhi. Although the two earlier attempts had failed, rumours about the size of the force he had assembled caused panic in India. Shah Zaman had a well-equipped army of over 30,000 Afghans and expected large numbers of Indians to join him. There was Nizamuddin Khan of Kasur who, in return for his help, had been promised the Subehdari of Lahore. Across the Sutlej was Sahib Singh of Patiala keeping up the family tradition of loyalty to every potential conqueror. And beyond the Punjab were the Rohilla Afghans, the Wazir of Oudh

[1]Sohan Lal, *Daftar* II, p. 33.

and, strangely enough, Tipu Sultan as far south as Mysore. All of them had urged the Afghans to come to India. The Shah answered the invitation in the following words: 'We shall soon march with our conquering army to wage war with the infidels and polytheists and free those regions from the contamination of those shameless tribes.'[1] The two 'infidel' powers in India were the Marathas and the Sikhs: first in geographical order were the Sikhs.

As the news of the invasion spread, people began to flee for safety to the hills. Misldars, who had been collecting protection tax from the people and were consequently under an obligation to defend them, were amongst the first to decamp. By December the Afghans had occupied the Punjab as far as the Jhelum. Two Sikh chiefs whose territories lay across the Afghans' route to Lahore were Sahib Singh Bhangi at Gujerat and Ranjit Singh. Sahib Singh made an attempt to halt the invaders, then lost his nerve and fled eastwards.

Ranjit Singh could only raise 5,000 undisciplined horsemen armed with nothing more than musket and spear to face the Afghans who were equipped with heavy artillery and swivel guns mounted on camels. If the Afghans were to be checked, the Sikhs had to come together; otherwise they would be swallowed piecemeal. The obvious meeting place for the Sikhs was Amritsar. Ranjit Singh collected his family and his horsemen and took the road to the sacred city.

Many Sikh chieftains answered the summons of the *Sarbat Khalsa* and came to Amritsar. The majority favored abandoning the plains, allowing the Afghans to plunder their deserted cities and towns and then harassing them with their hit-and-run (*dhai phut*) tactics. The spokesman for this point of view was the elderly Sahib Singh Bhangi of Gujerat. Most of those present agreed. They had already sent their wives and children to the hills and were anxious to join them.

Sada Kaur persuaded Ranjit Singh to stay behind and fight. Ranjit Singh's bold stand turned the majority in his favour, and they agreed to back him up. He took command of the Sikh forces and advanced towards Lahore. He drove the Afghans and their Indian supporters out of the countryside and then surrounded the city. Every night his Sikhs would suddenly attack some quarter

[1]*Asiatic Annual Register,* 1799 (No. 28).

of the city and after killing a few Afghans disappear into the dark.

In January 1797, the Shah got information that his brother, Mahmud, was organizing a rebellion in Afghanistan. He left General Shahanchi Khan with 1,20,000 soldiers in Lahore and took the road back to Kabul. The Sikhs who loved preying on retreating armies followed the Shah all the way across the Jhelum and deprived him of much of his baggage. Shahanchi Khan thought this a good chance to take the returning Sikhs by surprise and intercepted them near Ram Nagar. The Sikhs turned the tables on Shahanchi Khan, and completely defeated his force. In that winter, Ranjit Singh's reputation rose from that of an obscure Sikh chieftain to the hero of the Punjab.

The humiliation of defeat rankled in the Afghan's mind. As soon as he had settled his domestic problem 'Zaman raised the dust of adversity to the sky a second time'.[1] Once more the people began to leave their homes and seek refuge in the hills. By October all the big cities of the Punjab were deserted. Zaman swore to wreak terrible vengeance on the Sikhs. In order to induce his countrymen to join him, the Shah issued a proclamation that all would be free to plunder Hindustan.[2] In command of his troops were the sons of Shahanchi Khan eager to avenge the defeat of their father.

Once more panic spread in the Punjab. At Amritsar, even the sacred shrine had only a handful of guards left to protect it. 'The timidity of the Sikhs,' wrote Collins, who was English Resident at the Court of the Mughal Emperor at Delhi, 'is undeserving of credit.'[3] Sahib Singh Bhangi evacuated Gujerat, the Afghans plundered the town and massacred the inhabitants. Hindus and Sikhs had fled earlier: the victims were Punjabi Mussulmans.[4] Gujranwala, which had been abandoned by Ranjit, met the same fate.

At the meeting of the *Sarbat Khālsā* at Amritsar, the majority were again for fleeing to the hills. And again it was Sada Kaur who reminded them that they owed a duty to the people from whom they had been taking protection tax. And if the Sardars decided to flee, she would lead those Sikhs who were

[1]Sohan Lal, *Daftar* II, p. 39
[2]PC$_{17}$ of December 24, 1798.
[3]SC$_9$ of December 14, 1798.
[4]SC$_{13}$ of December 19, 1798.

willing to follow her.[1] Ranjit supported his mother-in-law and made a passionate appeal that the holy city of Amritsar should not be left to the mercies of people who made desecration of shrines a point of honour. Ranjit's uncle, Dal Singh, who was present, told them of his success in looting an armed caravan carrying fruit for the Shah. The Afghans, he reassured the assemblage, were vastly overrated as soldiers and the Sikhs would have no difficulty in beating them. This decided the other Sardars. 'Victory is the gift of God,' they said, 'Let us make one effort to oppose Him.' Ranjit Singh was again chosen to be the leader.

The Afghans started badly. Although Zaman proclaimed publicly that he was going to extirpate the Sikhs, the people who suffered most were poor Mussulmans, who, believing that the Afghans would not touch their co-religionists, had remained in their homes. The Afghan army took all the provisions it needed from the Muslim peasantry.

Zaman wrote to his Hindu supporters, Sansar Chand of Kangra and the Raja of Jammu, not to afford shelter to Sikh families who had fled to the mountain regions under their control.[2] On November 27, 1798, the Shah entered Lahore. This time he did not allow his troops to come into the city and issued strict orders that there was to be no plundering. The war was only against the Sikhs, and if they could be isolated from the Punjabi Mussulmans and the Punjabi Hindus, half the battle would be won. If, in addition, the Sikhs could be divided into Majhails (living between the Sutlej and the Ravi) and Malwais (living east of the Sutlej) the Punjab would fall without firing a shot. On paper, the Shah's plan seemed perfect.

Nizamuddin Khan of Kasur pretended to be the leader of the Punjabi Mussulmans and was more than eager to see Afghan power established in the province with himself as Subehdar of Lahore. Sansar Chand of Kangra likewise pretended to be a spokesman of the Hindus. And there was Sahib Singh of Patiala boasting of his family's record of service to Zaman's grandfather, to speak for the Malwai Sikhs. The only thorn in Zaman's side was the eighteen-year-old Ranjit Singh, at the head of the misls of the Majha and Jullundur Doab regions.

[1]*News from Amritsar*, PC$_{18}$ of December 24, 1798.
[2]PC$_{21}$ of December 24, 1798.

The Shah sent a detachment of Afghans towards Amritsar. Ranjit Singh came five miles out of the city and after an encounter lasting over three hours forced the Afghans to retire to Lahore.[1] He followed them and encircled the capital. He cut off the Afghans' supply lines and burnt the standing crops in the neighbouring countryside. The Afghans were forced to take the offensive. Nizamuddin Khan led another detachment of Afghans against the Sikhs at Shahdara just across the river from Lahore. The Afghans were repulsed with heavy slaughter. By the time help came from Lahore, the Sikhs had vanished. The Afghans wreaked vengeance for their defeat by falling upon the unarmed local population.[2] Shahdara was almost entirely inhabited by Muslims.

Ranjit became even more daring. He rode up to the Musummum Burj (an octagonal tower of Lahore fort on the side of the river Ravi) where Shah Zaman was holding court and yelled out a challenge to the Afghan: 'O grandson of Abdali, come down and measure swords with the grandson of Charhat Singh.'[3]

Days went by and there seemed no possibility of the Afghans breaking through the Sikh barricade and proceeding towards Delhi. Zaman taunted his Afghans, but so great was the terror that they would not stir from their barracks after nightfall.

Shah Zaman gave up talk of a holy war and of exterminating the Sikhs. He sent his agent to Amritsar assuring the Sikh chiefs that their possessions would not be disturbed and asking them what they wanted. The first reply was unanimous; they wanted nothing but that the Afghans should return to their own country and leave them in peace in theirs. Zaman instructed his agents to try and sow discord among the Sikhs. The agents approached the Sardars separately and made generous offers. This manoeuvre was more successful. Many Sardars sent their agents to Lahore where they were received with flattering attention by the Shah. 'I bestow this country on you free from assessment. Continue to keep and cultivate it in confidence,' he said grandly. Ranjit Sigh also sent his representative to Zaman to negotiate for the subehdari of Lahore. Just when it seemed that Afghan

[1]PC$_{24}$ of December 24, 1798.
[2]PC$_{21}$ of December 24, 1798.
[3]Sohan Lal, *Daftar* II, p. 39.

diplomacy had succeeded in breaking up Sikh unity, a saviour appeared in the person of Sahib Singh Bedi who, by virtue of his descent from Guru Nanak and his age, enjoyed the status of father of the Sikhs. He pleaded with the Sardars to stop negotiating with the foreign invader. They agreed to abide by his decision and when the Shah's agents came again he told them on behalf of the Sikhs: 'We took the country by the sword and will preserve it by the sword.' Zaman had to give up the plan to win over the Sikhs and swore he would teach them a lesson in war. This was an empty boast as the newswriter's report of the same day states : 'the Shah's camp is always in alarm on account of the Sikhs who at night approach Lahore and keep up a fire of musketry. None go out against them.'[1]

Time was against Shah Zaman. His brother Mahmud was again stirring up trouble in Afghanistan. His soldiers had not been paid for many months and were clamouring for permission to loot the city. When the Shah refused, they told him bluntly that they would not fight any more. The Shah was compelled to give up his plans of conquest and ordered his troops back to Kabul. Before leaving, he proclaimed that as soon as he had settled matters with his brother Mahmud, he would return and conquer India.

Shah Zaman did indeed come back to the Punjab twelve years later but not as a conqueror. His brother Mahmud captured and blinded him and he turned his sightless eyes towards the Punjab, tapping his way with his cane, to beg for asylum from Ranjit Singh.

[1]PC$_{18}$ of January 25, 1799.

CHAPTER III

MAHARAJA OF THE PUNJAB

WHEN NEWS OF Zaman's departure reached the Sikh chieftains at Amritsar, they broke camp and hurried back to their estates; the only one who did not think of his private interests was Ranjit Singh. He immediately set out in pursuit and caught up with the Afghan rear not far from Gujranwala. From there to the banks of the Jhelum he kept up a running fight, taking heavy toll of the invaders' life and equipment.[1] He even tried to get ahead of Zaman to annihilate his forces before they could extricate themselves from the Punjab. But the Afghan's feet were fleeter and he escaped the intended cordon. This pursuit took Ranjit Singh to the banks of the Indus.

The people of India now heard of the new leader who had risen in the Punjab. Ranjit's popularity was well gauged by Resident Collins. He wrote: 'At present this chief is regarded throughout Hindustan as the protector of the Sikh nation; it being generally believed that were it not for the fortitudes and excellent conduct of Ranjit Singh the whole of the Punjab would ere this have become a desert waste since it is the boast of these northern savages (the Afghans) that the grass never grows where their horses have once trodden.'[2]

On the retreat of the Afghan army, Lahore was reoccupied by three Sikh chieftains: Chet Singh, Sahib Singh and Mohr Singh.[3] Like peasants who suddenly come into money, these men spent their time in drink and fornication, or in squabbling

[1] It is most likely that the Afghan cannon which have become the subject matter of an academic dispute were lost in the Jhelum in the course of this retreat. See footnote on p. 41.

[2] SC_4 of June 24, 1800.

[3] Lahore was finally liberated by the Sikhs from Afghan control in 1764, when the Bhangi Sardars Lehna Singh and Gujar Singh stole through the night and captured the governor at a nautch party. Next morning they took over the city,

amongst themselves and so disturbing the peace of the city. 'The people of Lahore,' wrote Sohan Lal, 'being extremely oppressed, raised their voices of wailing to the skies.' Nizamuddin Khan's agents had approached the leading Muslims of Lahore with the suggestion that their master be invited to take over the city. But the Muslims rejected his overtures and joined the Hindu and Sikh citizens in sending a secret invitation to Ranjit Singh.

The citizens' envoys called on Ranjit Singh. He could not determine whether the invitation was genuine or intended to embroil him with the triumvirate of the Lahore Sardars. He sent his own trusted servant, Abdur Rahman, with the envoys to study the true state of affairs in the city and advise him on a course of action. He himself went to Batala to consult with his mother-in-law. Abdur Rahman spent some days in Lahore talking to the leading citizens and then rejoined his master at Batala. He assured Ranjit Singh that the invitation expressed the genuine feelings of the people of Lahore and that very little resistance would be offered by the dissipated Sardars of whom Sahib Singh, the only one with any ability, was then away from the city.

Sada Kaur advised immediate action.

It was the worst time of the year for a military campaign. The summer's heat was scorching; the monsoons were expected to break at any moment and turn the plains into a vast marshland. It was probably just this which induced Ranjit Singh to undertake the expedition and to take the Sardar triumvirate at Lahore by surprise. He also chose an appropriate day, the last of the month of Muharram. On this day Shia Muslims commemorate the martyrdom of the two grandsons of Prophet Mohammed by going out in procession through the streets and beating their breasts to the chant of 'Hassan, Hussain: Hassan, Hussain'. In the afternoon they take out paper effigies of the tombs of their martyrs and bury them with due ceremony. Although the Muharram obsequies are observed only by the shias, the ceremonies are watched by others who frequently participate in meetings where poems recounting the heroic deeds of the martyrs are recited. As Ranjit Singh had guessed, the Sardars spent the afternoon on their balconies watching the mourners'

---

which was divided between them and Sobha Singh of the Kanhayas who had helped in the capture. In 1799, the sons of these men were in possession of the city.

processions pass though the streets and then fraternizing with their Shia friends. This had been followed by the usual carousals which went on later than on other days. By the time silence descended on Lahore, Ranjit Singh was only a few miles from the walls of the city.

From their flat roofs where they had slept, the early risers saw a silent host encircle the city. By the time the sun came up, every one of the 25,000 men was in his place and every gun was in its position. Ranjit Singh left Sada Kaur at the Delhi Gate on the eastern side, and went on to Anarkali in the south, where he was handed a secret message of welcome from the citizens. He rode round the city walls and had it mined at several places. As soon as the first breach was blown, Mehr Mohkam Din, the leader of the Lahore Muslims, had it proclaimed by beat of drum that he had taken the administration of the city in his own hands and ordered all the city gates to be thrown open. Ranjit Singh entered with his detachment through Lahore Gate in the south; Sada Kaur led in her horsemen through Delhi Gate in the east. Mohr Singh and Sahib Singh's families and retainers fled through the other gates. Chet Singh shut himself up in the fort.

A proclamation was made assuring the citizens of peace and freedom form molestation; a warning was issued to the soldiers that looting would be punished with death.

Ranjit Singh's first public act was to pay homage at the big Royal Mosque, the Badshahi Masjid, built by the Mughal emperor Aurangzeb, and then at the most frequented one in the city, the mosque of Wazir Khan. He pitched his camp alongside the Royal Mosque under the walls of the fort, and, on the advice of his mother-in-law, let Chet Singh starve himself into submission. Chet Singh's envoys came out next day and offered the fort to Ranjit if their master's life were spared. Ranjit showed the magnanimity which he was to display all his life and for which he always gained well-deserved returns. He not only agreed to spare his fallen adversary, but warmly embraced him and made him a generous grant for his lifetime. Thus did he turn a bitter enemy into a grateful friend.

On July 7, 1799, the massive gates of the fort of Lahore were thrown open to its eighteen-year-old conqueror: Ranjit Singh entered to the sound of the boom of guns firing a royal salute.

'Trumpets of happiness were blown and kettledrums of victory beaten in every direction,' wrote Sohan Lal.[1]

Lahore was one of the oldest and certainly the biggest city of the Punjab. According to legend, it had been founded by Lav, the elder son of the Hindu avatar, Rama, at the same time as Kasur was founded by his younger brother Kus. (The name Lahore being a derivation of Lavpura—the city of Lav.) It had been in the hands of the Rajputs till 1002 A.D., when the Muslims defeated and ejected them. Mahmud of Ghazni renamed it after him as Mahmudpura but the old name, Lahore, came back into circulation. The city was occupied in turn by the different tribes of Muslim conquerors of the Punjab till Babar established Mughal rule in India. The Mughals built most of the city's fortifications, palaces, mosques and gardens. While Delhi or Agra were the seats of the Mughal government, Lahore was the chief city of the Punjab and a sort of half-way house between the Indian capital and the territories beyond the North-West Frontier of India from where the Muslim rulers recruited their best fighters. For the Sikhs, Lahore was only second in importance to Amritsar. It was the birthplace of their fourth Guru, Ram Das who founded the city of Amritsar and it was the site of the martyrdom of their fifth Guru Arjun, the compiler of their sacred book, the Granth Sahib. There were temples to mark these events and the visits of the other Gurus. The capture of Lahore was consequently of the greatest significance to Ranjit Singh. The possession of the city made him the most powerful chieftain in Northern India, and since it was known to have always been the capital of the province it gave him a vague sort of title over the rest of the Punjab.

Zaman was by now back in Kabul but still toying with the idea of conquering Hindustan. He made several overtures to Ranjit Singh because Ranjit Singh was the only person who stood between him and the throne of Delhi. He sent presents of horses and an expensive dress (Khillat). Ranjit Singh took the hand of friendship profered by his erstwhile adversary and amongst the gifts he sent in return were some pieces of cannon that Zaman

---

[1]Sohan Lal, Daftar II, p. 43.

had lost in the rivers of the Punjab in his hurry to escape.[1]

As Ranjit Singh's fame increased, the attitude of the Sikh misldars turned from secret envy to open hate. The capture of Lahore caused the poison to erupt. His former colleagues turned against him and made alliances with the Bhangi chieftains who had been so ignominiously ejected from the city. Nizamuddin Khan, whose dream of being the Subehdar of Lahore had been rudely shattered, joined their ranks. The dissidents met at Amritsar, where a branch of the Bhangis was in power, and resolved to eject Ranjit Singh from Lahore. In the spring of 1800, the combined forces of the Bhangis, together with those of Nizamuddin, advanced along the road to Lahore. Ranjit Singh stopped their progress ten miles east of the capital at the village of Bhasin.

Time and circumstances were on the side of Ranjit Singh. He had the city behind him to keep him supplied with essentials. The confederacy was a loose alliance based on nothing more than a common emotion. Their leader, Gulab Singh Bhangi, seemed to be less anxious to force a decision than the others; he found the country liquor and nautch girls better suited than war to the spring atmosphere of the countryside of Bhasin. One of these drinking bouts brought on a haemorrhage which killed him. This dispirited the confederate army, which quietly melted away. Ranjit Singh returned to Lahore none the worse for the two months' outing except for the expenses of having had to keep his army

[1]There is little doubt that this gesture was made by Ranjit Singh after he had taken Lahore and not before as has been erroneously stated by most historians (Prinsep, Cunningham, Wade, Griffin, Latif and Sinha). Two letters from Resident Collins to the Earl of Mornington written in April 1800 (SC_{54} and $_{57}$) clarify the position. One states: 'My private agent at Delhi informs me that Shah Zaman is endeavouring to attach to his interest Ranjit Singh the usurper of Lahore who has lately received a rich *Khillat* from the Durrani prince. Hence it would appear that the Shah has by no means relinquished his designs on Hindustan.' The other letter states: 'Advices form Lahore mention that Ranjit Singh has lately delivered to Shah Zaman's Vakeel, 15 pieces of artillery which the Durrani prince lost in his retreat from the Punjab last year by the overflowing of the Chenab.'

The affair of the return of cannon has assumed some importance because of the view expressed by these historians that it was this gesture which led to Zaman granting the Subehdari of Lahore to Ranjit. This is inaccurate. The cannon were lost by Zaman (in which river we are not certain), recovered by Ranjit and presented to Zaman at least six months after Ranjit had become master of Lahore.

inactive in the field. Here again fortune favoured him. Just as
he was toying with the idea of raising a compulsory loan from
the city's moneylenders, a chest containing 20,000 gold mohurs
was unearthed in an old ruin, *Budhu-dā-Avā*, outside the city
walls. With the enemy scattered and the treasury replenished, the
people were finally convinced that Ranjit Singh had come to stay
as the ruler of Lahore and perhaps the rest of the Punjab.

As sunflowers turn to the rising sun, people from all over the
country began to flock to the court of the young Sukerchakia.
Sons of chiefs came to join his army; scholars and doctors came
for service; artisans and craftsmen came to obtain royal patron-
age; troops of courtesans came to seek personal favours. Ranjit
Singh installed himself in the fort and began holding regular
durbars in the octagonal tower, the Mussummum Burj, under
which, only a year ago, he had stood in his stirrups and hurled
defiance at Shah Zaman. Apart from Sada Kaur at Batala and
his ageing uncle, Dal Singh, whose advice he sought on important matters, he engaged Misr Ram Dial to look after his day-
to-day affairs, and young Fateh Singh Ahluwalia, who had
hitched his wagon to Ranjit's rising star, to guide him on
military matters. The most notable addition, however, was the
Bokhari family. Even in his youth, Ranjit Singh had developed
a sort of hypochondria and was always consulting physicians and
trying out their prescriptions for his imaginary ailments. Amongst
the first native doctors to attend on him at Lahore was Ghulam
Mohyuddin, who had been summoned to treat an eye ailment.
The doctor brought with him his elder son, Azizuddin, whom
he was training in *Yunani* (Greek) medicine. Ranjit Singh was
immediately attracted to the youth, whose refined manners and
florid speech made a pleasant contrast to the rustic uncouthness
of his Sikh courtiers. 'New blossoms are bursting on the tree of
your fortunes,' said the young man, complimenting Ranjit Singh.
When he was offered employment he accepted with more picturesque speech: 'On the tree of fidelity, the flowers of loyalty
will only give place to the fruit of perfect devotion....Precious
are the pearls of truth when strung on the bracelet of faithful
actions. Happy is the sovereign in the sunshine of whose favour
the flowers of uprightness blossom. Sweet is the fruit of righ-
teous dealing, though the husk be unpalatable'—and so on.

Azizuddin soon took his father's place as royal physician; then as chief confidant and later as Minister of Foreign Affairs. He became, as he described himself with undue modesty, 'merely a parrot of sweet sound.' He introduced two of his brothers, Nuruddin and Imamuddin, to Ranjit Singh's service.

Azizuddin was of Sufi persuasion and consequently without any prejudice against other religions. When Ranjit Singh asked him which religion he thought was greater, Hindu or Muslim, Azizuddin replied tactfully: 'I am like a man floating in the midst of a mighty river; I turn my eyes toward the land but can distinguish no difference in either bank.'

Azizuddin or Fakeer Azizuddin as he, being a Sufi, liked to be called, was an extremely able diplomat[1] possessed of a cool head— a quality very rare amongst hot-headed Punjabis. He had a philosophic detachment to his job as adviser to Ranjit Singh. 'Council is like a dice; fate like the mark upon the board. It is within your hand and yet for all that it is not within your hand.'

Ranjit Singh was still far from being the ruler of the Punjab; the capture of Lahore had won him more enemies than allies. After the experience of Bhasin, he was determined not to give them time to gang up against him. First he moved against the Jammu Raja who had collaborated with the Afghans, and in lightning marches came within four miles of the city. The Raja made his submission and paid a penalty in the form of an elephant and Rs. 20,000. In this campaign, Ranjit added the towns of Vairowal, Narowal and Sarsowal to his domains. Soon after his return from the hills, he proceeded against Sahib Singh Bhangi of Gujerat, who had plotted with the Chief of Akalgarh to attack Gujranwala.

The open rift between two leading Sardars was an invitation to foreign powers. Zaman sent envoys to negotiate with the rival factions. In the south, George Thomas prepared to march up to

---

[1]Many Europeans who met the Fakeer have written favourably of him. Lieut.-Col. Steinbach who was in Ranjit's employ and saw more of him described him as 'One of the most remarkable men at Ranjit's Court' with knowledge of Persian and Arabic poetry and an interest in collecting old manuscripts. One of the most agreeable men when not talking for a direct object (his talk is never objectless), he is full of anecdotes and of quaint pithy sayings....very able negotiator; insiduous beyond measure and a complete master of the science of humbug....a mouth piece of the stupid Sikh Sardars.
(The Punjab, pp. 97-100.)

the Sutlej and the French General, Perron, to whom the Malwa Sardars had turned for assistance, made it clear that his price would be a large slice of the Punjab. The peril produced the man. This was again Sahib Singh Bedi, who had three years earlier unified the Sikhs to fight the Afghans.

The Bedi was trying to get the Sikh Chiefs of the Cis-Sutlej (the Malwa region between the rivers Sutlej and the Jumna) to unite against George Thomas, when he heard of the conflict between the Bhangis and Ranjit Singh. He hurried north to Gujerat and in the name of the Guru ordered the parties to lay down their arms. Such was the prestige of this man that the Sardars obeyed without demur. Sohan Lal gives a graphic account of the scene. 'The Exalted One (Ranjit) untied his sword from his waist and placed it on the ground before Baba Sahib Singh. All the Sardars did the same. For one hour the swords lay on the ground and the Sardars did not do anything. Afterwards, the said Baba Sahib tied the sword round the waist of the Exalted One and said that within a short time all his opponents would be extirpated and his rule would be established throughout the country.' Ranjit Singh was persuaded by the Bedi to leave Gujerat alone. But he punished the Chief of Akalgarh who had sided with the Bhangis by capturing his fort and, on his death, annexing his estate.

When Ranjit Singh returned to Lahore, Shah Zaman's messengers were impatiently waiting for him. He learnt that some Sardars who were hostile to him had promised support to the Afghans. It was clear that their only motive was to do down Ranjit Singh even if it meant handing over the country to the foreigners. Ranjit Singh accepted the Shah's gifts and compliments and dismissed the emissaries with even richer gifts and more flattering compliments. In this way he precluded their dealing with any other Sardar. Though young in years, he knew how to match wile with wile.

The news of this not-too-secret alliance between Ranjit Singh and Shah Zaman dismayed the Sardars, who had looked forward to the Afghan invasion as a means of getting rid of Ranjit. It also caused grave concern to the British. In April 1800, the Governor-General decided to take steps to 'counteract the influence of Shah Zaman with Ranjit Singh', and issued instructions that 'a native agent appropriately qualified should be immediately dispatched to the Court of Ranjit Singh with suitable instructions for impressing the Chief with the just sense of the danger to which he would expose his interests and those of his nation by yielding to the insidious proposals of Shah Zaman'.[1]

The English sent Meer Yusuf Ali as their agent to persuade the Sikhs to have nothing to do with the Afghans. The Meer started with the Cis-Sutlej chiefs. They did not need any persuasion, but asked one of the chiefs, would the English make a defensive alliance with them and would English soldiers fight alongside the Sikhs? Yusuf Ali pleaded that he had no instructions on the subject: his brief was limited to giving advice.

The chief of Malwa treated Yusuf Ali with courteous cynicism. He had come without escort and without gifts—envoys normally had both—and had nothing to offer except good counsel. This amounted to saying that if the Sikhs beat back the Afghans, the English would applaud them.

After getting no response from the Malwa Chiefs, Meer Yusuf Ali called on Sada Kaur at Amritsar. She sent for her son-in-law. Ranjit Singh came to Amritsar at considerable personal risk, as the city was in the hands of the Bhangi family. He took the chance as he felt that he should apprise himself of the feelings of other Indian powers on the subject.

The meeting rook place on October 22, 1800, in Sada Kaur's apartments with only Ranjit's personal advisers, Fateh Singh Ahluwalia and Misr Ram Dial, present. Yusuf Ali waxed eloquent on the perfidy of the Afghans; on Abdali's massacres of the Sikhs and his blowing-up of their temple in Amritsar and of the treachery and faithlessness which were hereditary characteristics of the Durrani family. Ranjit Singh heard him in silence and remained lost in thought for some minutes after Yusuf Ali had finished. 'After weighing his answer,' reported Yusuf Ali, Ranjit observed that 'these people (the Afghans) were not to be trusted as they do not adhere to their engagements; that he himself had not the least dependence on the Durranis'. Fateh Singh sounded a different note. Zaman had presented them with robes of honour, and it would be discourteous on their part not to respond to overtures of friendship. The first meeting was inconclusive. Ranjit Singh invited Yusuf Ali to visit him in Lahore.

[1] SC$_{74}$ of April 24, 1800.

At Lahore, Meer Yusuf Ali repeated his government's fears that Ranjit Singh meant to befriend the Afghans, and in evidence mentioned the return of the guns lost by Zaman on his last invasion. Ranjit Singh thought it best to write to Collins at Delhi and, through him, inform the British Government of the circumstance of the second Afghan occupation of Lahore. He wrote[1] of his struggle against the Afghans and how he had ridden up to the walls of Lahore fort and challenged the Shah to a duel; how the Afghans had been compelled to evacuate Lahore and how Zaman had lost the cannons trying to cross the Jhelum in a hurry; and finally how Ranjit Singh, who had followed him up all the way, had salvaged them and restored them to the Shah, at the latter's request, in consideration of friendship.

The winter of 1800 passed in apprehension of yet another invasion from the North-West. In the spring came news of civil strife in Kabul and the advance of the Persians towards Afghanistan. The Punjabis heaved a sigh of relief, and Ranjit Singh's thoughts turned to giving himself a legal title over his possessions.

Although Ranjit Singh was acclaimed as the leader of the Punjab, he hesitated for some time to assume the formal title of Maharaja, because he wished to avoid doing anything which would give the other chiefs yet another reason to conspire against him: their combined strength was not inconsiderable. He was, however, conscious of the many advantages in investing himself with a legal title. The move would be welcomed by the masses, who had not had a ruler and a government of their own for many centuries. It would induce the Punjabi Muslims and Hindus to recognize the compulsions of language, political and economic interests, and way of life and throw in their lot with the Sikhs who had been fighting for an independent Punjab. The neighbouring powers would soon become accustomed to the idea that the Punjabis were a united people and Ranjit Singh was their Maharaja. What perhaps persuaded Ranjit Singh to take the final step and risk the antagonism of the Sardars was the birth of a son to the Nakkain, Rani Raj Kaur, his second and favourite wife. The desire to make his infant son, Kharak Singh, the heir-

---

[1]SC$_{95}$ of December 30, 1800. Although this letter does not indicate whether this was before or after his capture of Lahore, it is quite clear from other communications that it was after July 1799.

apparent to a kingdom proved irresistible. Although Sada Kaur was some what put out by the failure of her own daughter to produce the first son, being a far-sighted woman she reconciled herself to the idea of her daughter taking second place in a royal harem and encouraged Ranjit Singh in assuming the title of Maharaja. She no doubt felt that if her daughter did have sons, they would at least inherit the Kanhaya estates, and if possible also claim a part of their father's kingdom.

Ranjit Singh agreed to a formal investiture. Prayers were said in the mosques, temples and gurdwaras all over his domains. On the 1st of *Baisākh* (April 12, 1801), which was New Year's Day by the Hindu calendar in use in northern India, Sahib Singh Bedi daubed Ranjit's forehead with saffron paste and proclaimed him Maharaja of the Punjab. A royal salute was fired from the fort. In the afternoon the young Maharaja rode on the back of an elephant through the jubilant crowds of his subjects showering gold and silver coins. In the evening the city was illumined with oil lamps and there was a rich display of fireworks.

Neither the flattery nor the pageantry of the Court turned Ranjit's mind from the real facts. His political acumen is well illustrated in the compromise he made between becoming a Maharaja and remaining a peasant leader. Although crowned King of the Punjab, he refused to wear an emblem of royalty on his simple turban. ('My sword procures for me all the distinction I desire. I am quite indifferent to external pomp,' he said.) He refused to sit on a throne and continued as before to hold durbar seated cross-legged in his little bathtub-like chair or, more often, received visitors in the oriental fashion reclining on cushions on a carpet. He ordered new coins to be struck. These did not bear his effigy or his name but that of Guru Nanak and were named the *Nānak Shāhi* (of the Emperor Nanak) coins. The seal of government likewise bore no reference to him. The government was not to be a personal affair, but the *Sarkār Khālsāji* of the people who brought it into being; the Court for the same reason came to be known as the *Durbār Khālsāji*. And with all the flatterers about him, the title by which he preferred to be addressed was the plain and simple *Singh Sāhib*. These conventions were a complete departure from the accepted traditions of oriental courts, where protocol was rigidly observed to keep the monarch as far away from the masses as possible. Ranjit Singh did not want to, nor ever did, lose the common touch.

The most important consequence of taking on the title of 'Maharaja of the Punjab' was that thereby Ranjit Singh assumed rights of sovereignty not only over all Sikhs (the government itself being *Sarkār Khālsāji*), but also over the people who lived within the ill-defined geographical limits of the Punjab. The title gave Ranjit Singh a legal right to demand that territories which had at any time paid revenue to Lahore—territories such as Jammu, Kashmir, the Rajput hill States, Multan, Bahawalpur, Dera Ismail Khan, Dera Ghazi Khan, Mankera and others—should pay tribute to him and owe allegiance to the Lahore Durbar.

Ranjit Singh did not derive his title from either the Mughals or the Afghans: it was given to him by that mystic entity the *Panth Khālsāji*. He acknowledged no earthly superior. He was impelled by the weight of tradition that has grown up over the years, that it was the destiny of the Sikhs to rule (*Rāj Karey -gā Khālsā*) and that perhaps he had been chosen by the gurus to be the instrument of their inscrutable design. With this assurance Ranjit Singh was able to harness the dynamic energies of his people and with a clear conscience launched himself on a career of conquest and annexation.

Immediately after his coronation, Ranjit Singh reorganized the administration of Lahore. He had the city walls and gates, which had suffered many sieges, repaired, and posted pickets at all strategic points to check crime, which had increased enormously under the Bhangi misrule. The city was divided into different wards under a *Chaudhri* (headman), who was responsible for the peace of his locality and could call out the police when order was disturbed.[1] He also reorganized the administration of justice in the city; since the majority of the population subscribed to the Muslim faith and wished affairs to be regulated by the law of the Shariat, he set up separate courts for Mussulmans. Nizam Din was appointed Chief Kazi (Judge) with Mohammed Shah Puri and Saidullah Chishti as the two Muftis. For those Muslims who, like the Hindus and the Sikhs, preferred to be governed by the customary law of their caste or district, the

[1] The first Head of Police of Lahore was one Imam Baksh who always rode a donkey and was therefore known as *Khar Sawār*.

RAJA SANSAR CHAND
(Photo: Private collection)

2. RANJIT SINGH AND HIRA SINGH
(Photo: Victoria & Albert Museum)

3. Maharaja Kharak Singh conferring with his Chief Minister,
Dhian Singh. Nau Nihal (his son) and Hira Singh (son
of Dhian Singh) seated on his right.
(Photo: Collection of T.W.F. Scott, Esq.)

Maharaja set up separate courts under judicial officers appointed by the durbar. A chain of dispensaries were opened in different parts of the city where *Yunāni* medicine was dispensed free of charge. Hakim Nurudddin, the younger brother of Fakeer Azizuddin, was appointed Chief Medical Officer.

Ranjit Singh did not make any changes in the agricultural system or land revenue that had prevailed since Mughal rule. Every village had a revenue collector (*muqaddam*) and a circle of villages (*tāppāh or tāluqāh*) was in the charge of a *chaudhri*. In addition to these two, there was the keeper of fiscal records, the *qānungo*. The officials were themselves proprietors of land in their respective villages or circle and were compensated by reduction in revenue.

Revenue was collected directly from the cultivator of the land. The amount and manner of payment varied but care was taken that all the regular and irregular charges (e.g. supply of grass, timber, fruit, eggs, chicken, etc.) to touring officials which went under the title *mulba* (literally 'rubbish', or feudal dues in the forms of gifts on marriages or festivals to members of the royal family or the Rajas) never amounted to more than half of the gross produce calculated on the standing crop or after harvest: if the revenue was paid in cash, the sum was calculated on the value of half the produce. The rate was not considered extortionate and allowed the agricultural community to thrive.

As important as the right over land which was guaranteed to the actual cultivator was the ownership of wells. As a matter of fact, the most reliable evidence of the ownership of land was the inscription on a well (sometimes placed on the inside to save it from mutilation). The right to dig a well was exclusively that of the cultivator. The proprietor who did not till the land himself or through hired servants had to be content with a nominal title. The same applied to a jagirdar whose right to the revenue did not in any way invest him with a title to the land from which it was collected.[1]

The system had worked well for many centuries and Ranjit Singh saw no reason to change it.

---

[1] From a Report prepared by Sir A. Temple on the Jullundur Doab, PC$_{143}$ of December 29, 1852. Also 'Land Revenue Administration under the Sikhs', by S.R. Kohli, in the *Journal of the Punjab Historical Society*, 1918.

At the end of Ranjit Singh's forty years of rule, the income of the State was as follows:

1. Revenue from the provinces of Lahore
   Multan, Kashmir and Peshawar   1,75,57,741
2. Nazaranas   6,03,657
3. Customs and Excise   15,31,634
4. Jagirs   91,96,000

                   2,88,89,032

The figure of three crore rupees sounds extremely modest today. It should, however, be borne in mind that at the time the price of the staple food, wheat, was fourteen annas per maund. In 1961 it fluctuated between Rs. 18 and 20 per maund, i.e. more than twenty times as much.

Within a short time Ranit Singh convinced the people of Lahore and the neighboring districts that he did not intend to set up a Sikh Kingdom but a Punjabi State in which the Muslims, Hindus and Sikhs would be equal before the law and enjoy the same privileges and duties. He invited talented Muslims and Hindus to join his service and paid assiduous respect to their religious institutions by participating in their festivities. At Dussehra he went through the ritual of the worship of arms like the Rajput warriors of old and arranged mock battles between his troops to commemorate the battle of Rama against Ravana. At *Diwali* all public buildings, including the palace, were illuminated. During *Holi*, he went out among the throngs and made merry, often in a manner quite unbecoming to a monarch. On *Basant* he paid homage at the tomb of the Muslim divines, Madho Lal and Hussain.[1] On *Amāvās* and *Bāisākh* he joined his co-religionists in bathing at Amritsar or Taran Taran.

With the affairs of Lahore settled, Ranjit Singh turned his attention to the Pathan colony in Kasur. He ordered one of his officers, Fateh Singh Kalianwala, to bring Nizamuddin to book.

[1]Hussain and Madho Lal were two Sufi poets of Lahore whose attachment to each other was the cause of much scandal. They composed verses under a corporate pseudonym Madho Lal-Hussain. They are buried alongside in a tomb close to the Shalamar Gardens where their death anniversaries are celebrated with singing of their compositions. Muslims, Hindus and Sikhs pay homage at this shrine.

The Pathans met the advancing Lahore troops half way. After a sharp engagement they withdrew behind the walls of their town. In Sohan Lal's picturesque language: 'Like a moth, Nizamuddin fell upon the lamp of the glory of the armies, burnt his wings and having failed to carry on the open battle, became besieged.'[1] It was a short siege, as the Lahore troops succeeded in blowing up one of the gates and charging in. The Pathans laid down arms, paid a heavy indemnity and agreed to recognize Ranjit Singh as their sovereign. Fateh Singh Kalianwal took three of Nizamuddin's brothers as hostages to Lahore.

Next came the turn of Sansar Chand of Kangra. The Rajput had anticipated trouble and took the offensive by coming down from the hills and occupying many villages in the estates of Sada Kaur. When Ranjit Singh turned up at Batala, Sansar Chand lost courage and withdrew his forces from the plains. Ranjit Singh reoccupied the villages taken by the Rajputs and in addition annexed some of Sansar Chand's territory, including two prosperous towns, Nurpur and Naushera, which he gave to Sada Kaur. He also give her territory round Sujanpur which he captured during this campaign.

On his way back to Lahore, Ranjit Singh stopped at Taran Taran to bathe in the sacred waters of the tank surrounding the temple. Fateh Singh Ahluwalia, who had been invited earlier, joined him and in full view of the hundreds of thousands of peasants and Sardars who had congregated, Ranjit Singh and the Ahluwalia exchanged turbans as a symbolic gesture of having become brothers in the faith (Dharam Bhai). They signed a solemn pledge that thereafter their friends and enemies would be common; that they would visit each other as frequently as possible and in every conquest made by their joint efforts, Ranjit Singh would give at least one district to Fateh Singh.

Fateh Singh Ahluwalia made his first formal call on Ranjit Singh a few days later. He was received in full durbar like a prince of royal blood with gun salutes. After the ceremonial reception the two proceeded to the western regions and induced Muslim landowners of Pindi Bhattain to ally themselves with the new Punjab State. They submitted and paid tribute in the form Ranjit liked best: by giving him four hundred of their best breed

[1]*Daftar* II, p. 53.

of horses. The allies crossed the River Jhelum, incorporated Dhanni-Pothohar (Rawalpindi and Campbellpur districts) within the Punjab. Both these regions were given over to Fateh Singh. The next to be subdued was Jassa Singh Doloo of Chiniot, who had been an ally of the Bhangis and, in the words of Sohan Lal, 'had raised his head to the sky with pride and strayed from the path of obedience'.[1] Doloo kept the besiegers at bay for two months and only submitted when he was reduced to dire straits. Ranjit Singh admired his tenacity and took him into his service.

While Ranjit Singh and Ahluwalia were occupied in the north, Nizamuddin Khan took advantage of their absence and plundered some villages near Lahore. Ranjit Singh hurried back and made straight for Kasur. Nizamuddin withdrew his troops into the town, which he had prepared for a long siege. Heavy guns had to be brought from Lahore to pound the walls of the fort. Nizamuddin surrendered and was again pardoned and allowed to hold his fief.

Ranjit Singh was far more considerate in dealing with his Muslim adversaries than he was with the Sikh or the Hindu. His treatment of the family of the Nawab of Multan was yet another example of his generosity in dealing with Punjabi Muslims.

Since the Afghan incursions, Multan, a district of the Punjab, had begun to have closer administrative affiliations with Kabul than with Lahore. It had been taken by the Bhangi Sardars more than once, but their indifference towards the welfare of the people had created a certain amount of animosity towards the Sikhs and an aloofness from the sense of Punjabi nationalism that was gathering force in the rest of the province. This was particularly marked in the case of the ruling class which, being Muslim, found the alliance with the Afghans more convenient than with the Sikhs, and had successfully ejected the Bhangis. Ranjit Singh was determined to reclaim Multan and early in 1803 announced his intention of bringing the city within the country to which it belonged. Almost to a man his Sardars advised him against undertaking the expedition. They felt that they were not equipped to invest so powerful a fort, nor face a combination of hostile tribes that the Nawab of Multan would inevitably bring into the

[1]*Daftar* II, p. 54.

field against them. Nothing, however, restrained the impetuous Ranjit and he marched out of Lahore at the head of his troops.

Nawab Muzaffar Khan had, as was anticipated, roused the Muslim peasantry of the neighboring district to come to his aid. They were, however, unable to withstand the Lahore troops, which entered the suburbs of Multan without difficulty and trained their artillery on the mud fort which stood in the heart of the city. Muzuffar Khan thought it discreet to make his submission. He paid an indemnity and agreed to send his quota of revenues to Lahore instead of to Kabul.

Ranjit Singh returned home in triumph. The victory celebrations were followed by festivities to mark the engagement of his three-year-old son and heir, Kharak Singh, to Chand Kaur, the infant daughter of Jaimal Singh of the Kanhaya misl. For Ranjit Singh the event had personal significance. At one of the nautch parties his eye fell upon a young and attractive Muslim courtesan, Mohran, and he fell violently in love with her. A few days later the girl left the sordid atmosphere of a brothel to go to live in the royal harem. Mohran enjoyed Ranjit Singh's confidence for many years, and the Maharaja had a coin minted in her honour.[1] Since she did not veil herself and was often seen in the Maharaja's company, many stories began to be circulated of her influence on him.

---

[1] The *Ārsiwālā Sikkā* (currency of the mirrored ring) is said to have been issued in imitation of the currency of the East India company, which bore the profile of Queen Victoria. These coins have the figure of a peacock; the Punjabi plural for the bird being *Moran*.

CHAPTER IV

THE TAKING OF AMRITSAR AND THE REORGANIZATION OF THE ARMY

THE PUNJAB'S second largest city, Amritsar, was commercially more important than Lahore. It was the chief trading centre to Northern India, where caravans brought goods from Central Asia and exchanged them for the products of India. In its narrow, winding streets were business houses trading in all conceivable kinds of goods: silks, muslins, spices, tea, hides, matchlocks and other kinds of armaments. Because of the rich merchants, subsidiary trades such as those of gold and silver smiths had grown up. Besides its riches, Amritsar had sanctity in the eyes of the Sikhs. It was founded by the fourth Guru, Ram Das, and it was here that the fifth Guru, Arjun, had compiled their scripture, the 'Adi Granth', and built the temple in the centre of the sacred pool. Twice a year at least, all Sikhs who could, came to Amritsar to bathe in the pool and make their offerings at the shrine. As far as the Sikhs were concerned, Amritsar was the most important city in the world. Anyone who aspired to be the leader of the Sikhs and the Maharaja of the Punjab had to take Amritsar to make good his title.

Amritsar was divided between nearly a dozen families owning different parts of the city. In each of the localities these families had built themselves tiny fortresses and they maintained retinues of armed tax collectors who mulcted the traders and shopkeepers as often as they could. There was constant friction between the tax collectors of the different Sardars which often broke out into fighting in the streets. The citizens were thoroughly weary of this state of affairs and secretly approached Ranjit Singh to take over the city. Ranjit Singh's agents had already reported that there was little likelihood of unity between the Amritsar Sardars. The only family of any real importance was that of the widow of the Bhangi chief, who had drunk himself to death at Bhasin four years earlier, and her son Gurdit Singh. This woman, Mai Sukhan, was in occupation of the fort of Govindgarh and was supported by the Ramgarhia misl.

In the autumn of 1802 widow Sukhan's rent collectors fell out amongst themselves in squeezing the city's wealthiest banker, Aroor Mal, who was compelled to move his business from her zone to another. Aroor Mal appealed to Ranjit Singh to restore order in the city.

The combined forces of Ranjit Singh, Sada Kaur and Fateh Singh Ahluwalia encircled Amritsar. The Sadars mounted cannon on their city fortresses and decided to fight it out. The Bhangi widow also prepared to resist, hoping that the Ramgarhias would come to her rescue. Ranjit Singh took the city piecemeal, overwhelming the Sardars one after another. The Ramgarhias did not appear; Mai Sukhan was persuaded to surrender and to accept a pension for herself and her son.

The fort of Govindgarh was a valuable acquisition. With it Ranjit acquired five big cannon, including Abdali's massive Zam Zama, made of copper and brass, which had caused havoc amongst the ranks of the Marathas in the battle of Panipat. The Bhangis had taken it from the Afghans and since then it had come to be known as the *Bhangion ki tope*.[1]

More important than the acquisition of the fort and the cannon was the acquisition of the services of a remarkable soldier, Akali Phula Singh. This man belonged to the militant order of the Nihangs (also called Akalis), who had since the days of Guru Govind Singh formed the suicide squads of the Khalsa armies.[2]

[1] It saw service in many of Ranjit's campaigns, and after his death, faced the English in the Anglo-Sikh wars. Thereafter it was 'pensioned' and put on a pedestal in Lahore's main street. It has been immortalized by Kipling as Kim's gun.

[2] The word Nihang is Persian meaning crocodile. The order became very popular among the Sikhs. The Nihangs, also known as Akalis, wear blue and dedicate their lives to the service of the community. The order has degenerated into a set of beggars notorious for the quantities of hashish they can consume. Nevertheless, they are an extremely picturesque lot — the Sikh version of Cervantes' Don Quixote with speech full of braggadocio. A Nihang describes himself as *sava lakh* (the equal of 1,25,000) or as an army (*fauj*). When he goes to urinate he says he is going to 'conquer the fort of Chittor' or 'give rations to a Kazi'. Death is simply an order to march. Coarse food like gram is 'almonds'; onions, 'pieces of silver'; a chillie, 'a quarrelsome dame'. A

Phula Singh had dedicated his life to the care of Sikh shrines and was an ardent protagonist of a Khalsa kingdom. He was largely responsible for Ranjit Singh's success at Amritsar. He brought with him between two to three thousand Nihangs to join the State army.

Ranjit Singh disliked fanaticism of any kind and never really took to Phula Singh or the Nihangs; *Kul faham wā Kotāh andesh*—of crooked mind and short sight—he pronounced them. Nevertheless, he found them an extremely useful counter-weapon against the Muslim crusaders (Ghazis) and was full of praise of their daring in battle. He owed many of his most celebrated victories to the desperate valour of the Nihangs.

Ranjit Singh was given a tumultous reception in the holy city. He rode through the narrow streets on his elephant to the temple, bathed in the sacred pool and made a large grant for it to be rebuilt in marble and gold leaf.

The capture of Amritsar brought additional lustre to Ranjit Singh's name and Indians from the British territories began to flock to his standard. Amongst them were deserters from the forces of the East India Company, mainly Hindustani Muslims and a few Eurasians. The Maharaja had already been impressed with British prowess in the field of battle and was most anxious to know why they had triumphed, often with inferior equipment, over the armies of the princes of India. A platoon of deserters paraded before him and he saw for the first time soldiers march in step and make battle formations on simple words of command. He offered the deserters employment as drill sergeants and also sent a batch of young Punjabis across the border to enlist in the Company's forces and learn whatever the English had to teach. Sikh soldiers were reluctant to learn from Hindustani sepoys.

---

one-eyed man was, and often is, called Lakh-netra Singh—the lion with a hundred thousand eyes—and so on.

Phula Singh was born in a village Shinh (Amritsar District) in A.D. 1761 and joined the Nihang order early in life. He was allowed many liberties by the Maharaja. An anecdote mentions an incident when Ranjit Singh, who was riding on his biggest elephant, passed by the balcony from which Phula Singh was watching the procession. 'O, you one-eyed man, where did you get that he-buffalo?' yelled Phula Singh.

The Maharaja humbly joined his hands and replied: 'It is the gift your honour gave me.'

The Sikhs were horsemen and considered fighting on foot beneath their dignity. The business of marching in step seemed to them singularly silly: *ruqsi-i-lulooān*, the bloody fool's ballet, sneered the Sardars. They claimed with some justification that it was the Khalsa cavalier with his matchlock and spear, fighting as a one-man army on his own, who had won all the battles and justified the sobriquet *savā lakh* (equal to a hundred and twenty-five thousand men). What could the contemptible little Hindustanis drilled like automatons teach the Khalsa? Ranjit Singh was not impressed by the boasting. He promised better terms to young Punjabis who joined his new infantry battalions and who agreed to be trained by Hindustani and Eurasian drill masters. He watched them being put through their paces every morning and evening and gave them and their mentors handsome rewards. At the end of nine months' rigorous training Ranjit's new army was born. It was the most prominent part of the parades and mock battles which took place during the Dussehra celebrations in the autumn of 1803.

After Dussehra began the campaigning season.

Ranjit Singh sent emissaries to the independent principalities of the province to invite them to declare their allegiance to the government of the Punjab. (Some of them had continued to attach themselves to Afghanistan, or pretended to do so in order to avoid paying revenue to the Lahore Durbar.) Amongst those who contemptuously turned down Ranjit's invitation was Ahmed Khan Sial, who owned the territories around Jhang. He was also the Punjab's best breeder of horses.

Ranjit Singh led his new troops against Jhang. Ahmed Khan, who had enlisted large numbers of mercenaries from the neighbouring tribes, appeared in the field at the head of a formidable host. The battle commenced with a cannonade from either side. When their gunpowder was exhausted, the Sial horsemen charged. Ranjit's infantry battalions withstood the fierce onslaughts and once the enemy cavalry had spent itself moved to the counter-attack. The Sials broke their ranks and galloped to safety behind the walls of their fortress town. Ranjit's elephants crashed through the gates and compelled the citadel to lay down arms. Ahmed Khan slipped through the cordon and fled to Multan. It took him some time to appreciate that Ranjit Singh was not wanting to appropriate the Sial territory for personal gain but to induce them and the other tribesmen of the region to throw in their lot with their Punjabi kinsmen. Some months later Ahmed Khan made his submission and was reinstated at Jhang as a vassal of Lahore. The Zemindars of Ucch, near Jhang, cast their lot with Ranjit.

The short campaign proved that the decision to adopt the British method of training and warfare had been correct. Ranjit Singh decided to intensify the training and organize his army. In the spring of 1804 he could see the different units on parade and finally settle the divisions and commands. After extensive manoeuvres and inspections he called a grand durbar of the chiefs and military commanders in the fort of Govindgarh and announced that the army was to be divided into three sections. One was to be directly under the Maharaja's command and ready for action at short notice. This section consisted of cavalry, infantry and artillery and the pick of his generals, such as Hari Singh Nalwa, Hukma Singh Chimini and Desa Singh Majithia. Heavy artillery was under the command of Chaudhry Ghause Khan; infantry, trained in European methods, under Sheikh Abdullah and Roshan Khan. There were over 13,000 men in these units. The second section consisted of the forces of the Sardars who were liable for military service in lieu of the *jāgirs*. These were largely the Sardars of the Bhangi family who had been reinstated in their possessions after joining the Punjab State. They were obliged to furnish fully-equipped soldiers in times of war. This section could account for another 10,000 men in the field. The third section consisted of the militias of the misls which, like the Kanhayas, the Nakkais and some others, were allies of Ranjit Singh. The total fighting force which Ranjit Singh could put into the field was 31,000 men.

The reorganization carried out at Amritsar gave a clearer picture of the forces available and fixed the responsibility for putting them into the field. Once the responsibility had been fixed Ranjit Singh set most exacting standards of efficiency in march, manoeuvre and marksmanship. If the troops were slovenly in dress or ill-trained, he did not hesitate to punish the officer responsible by reducing his rank and levying heavy fines. But his usual method was to encourage men by reward rather than to threaten them with penalties. He made it a point to spend three to four hours of his day watching his troops at parade and never did a day go by when he did not reward a gunner or a cavalier for good performance. And since he invariably accompanied his armies to battle, he was always on the lookout for acts of bravery which he rewarded with handsome grants of land and pensions.

CHAPTER V

THE ENGLISH AND THE MARATHAS

IN THE FIVE years following Ranjit Singh's capture of Lahore and his assumption of the title of Maharaja of the Punjab, the situation on his eastern frontier changed completely. In 1800, the powers to be reckoned with were George Thomas at Hansi, the Scindia who held Delhi with its puppet Mughal Emperor, and beyond Delhi, the English. In 1801, Thomas was eliminated by Scindia's French General, Perron, who then became the most powerful man in Eastern Punjab. He exploited the gratitude of the Cis-Sutlej Sardars for ridding them of Thomas and had many exchange turbans with him. He forestalled the English in their designs in this direction by warning the Sikhs about them. In a letter to Bhag Singh of Jind (Ranjit's uncle) he wrote: 'It is an invariable custom with the English first to gain a footing by the excitement of avarice, by the promise of assistance or other flattering terms, and then by gradual steps to assume the government of the country, viz. Cheyt Singh, Tipu Sultan, Nawab Kasim Ali Khan, Nawab Asafuddowlah, Nizam Ali Khan and others.'[1] Through Bhag Singh, Perron made overtures to Ranjit Singh. Bhag Singh did his best to persuade his nephew not to make any commitments to the English when their agent, Meer Yusuf Ali, called on him at Lahore. Ranjit Singh was shrewd enough to know that the overtures, whether made by the Afghans, the French or the English, had for their object the extension of suzerainty over the Punjab. But he also knew that if he refused to deal with foreign agents, his enemies within the State would certainly make contacts with them with the object of breaking his insecure hold on the country. Ranjit Singh dealt with Perron and the English as he had earlier dealt with Shah Zaman. In a letter[2] to Collins, he explained his position with unusual

[1] SC$_{51}$ of March 19, 1801.
[2] SC$_{49}$ of August 16, 1802.

candour. 'Bhag Singh accompanied by Vakeels on the part of Perron, Sahib Singh (of Patiala) and Louis (a subordinate of Perron—of whom more later), are arrived here with presents for me. They have proposed to me to enter into terms of amity and friendship with Perron....As Bhag Singh is under many obligations to Perron, he is set to gain me by every mode of persuasion, urging at the same time the great desire of the general to have a meeting with me. In fine, although my friendship for the Governor-General and you is great beyond the possibility of what I can feel towards anybody else, yet I must preserve appearances on this occasion in consideration of what is due by me to the will of my uncle.'

The Frenchman's dreams of creating a Perronistan in the Punjab had a rude awakening. At first his subordinate, M. Louis, mulcted the chief of Malwa and behaved with discourtesy toward them. Perron had Louis arrested and reprimanded. He had scarcely rehabilitated himself with the Malwais when his master, the Scindia, recalled him from the Punjab to help fight the British. Luck was against the Marathas and they suffered a series of defeats. With the setting of the Scindian sun, set the hopes of Perron and he faded out of the Indian scene. The English became masters of Delhi and Agra, as well as of the person of the Mughal Emperor. They also came a step closer to Ranjit: all that separated them was the remaining Maratha chief, Jaswant Rao Holkar, and the Sikh chiefs of Malwa.

Within two years of the defeat of Scindia, Holkar clashed with the English. Holkar failed to follow up his early success and let the initiative pass to the British commander, Lord Lake, who inflicted a crushing defeat on him at Deeg. Holkar and his Rohilla confederate, Amir Khan, fled for help to the Sikhs and spent several months at Patiala trying to get the chiefs of Malwa to join them. Holkar also invited the Afghans to reinvade India. When Lord Lake resumed his pursuit, Holkar and Amir Khan crossed the Sutlej and arrived at Amritsar. Lake came up to the Beas. Both Holkar and Lake sent emissaries to Ranjit Singh, who was then at Multan.

Ranjit Singh realized the gravity of the situation and sent word to all his principal Sardars to join him at Amritsar to give him counsel.

A meeting of the *Sarbat Khālsā* consisting of the leading Sikh chiefs and dignitaries was called. Both sides of the case were presented. On the one side there were the refugees, Holkar and Amir Khan, who had sought shelter and it was a matter of honour for the Punjabis to protect them. Holkar had, in addition, ingratiated himself with the Sikhs by paying homage at the Sikh temple and making a handsome donation. He flattered Ranjit Singh as brother and the only hope of the Hindus of India. (Fortunately, Ranjit knew of Holkar's negotiations with the Afghans.) On the other side were the English demanding that Ranjit Singh expel Holkar from the Punjab or suffer the consequence of the Anglo-Maratha conflict being extended to his domains. The position that Lord Lake took up left no doubt in anyone's mind that the English demand was no idle threat.[1] To urge his point of view, Lake had sent Bhag Singh of Jind to Amritsar.

Ranjit Singh inspected Holkar's Europeanized troops and saw for himself how much better they were than the bulk of his own army. He could not, however, understand why they had fled before Lake: instead of embarrassing Holkar with awkward questions, he decided to see things for himself. He disguised himself as a common soldier and with a band of trusted retainers visited Lake's encampment and spent the day watching his Indian sepoys and English soldiers on parade. In the evening he went to the English commander's tent and asked to see Lord Lake. His one eye betrayed him and he was recognized. What passed between the Sikh and the Englishman at this meeting[2] is not known, but Ranjit Singh returned to Amritsar convinced that the British were too strong for Holkar, and perhaps even stronger than Holkar and his own forces combined.

Ranjit Singh's last resort was to his Guru. He went to the temple and prayed for guidance. He took two slips of paper and had the name of Lake written on one, of Holkar on the other,

[1]SC$_{19}$ of Decemeber 14, 1805. In a dispatch Lake wrote: 'I resolved to occupy a position on the bank of the Beas at a distance of about thirty-five miles from Amritsar, and forty-five miles from Ludhiana, which, while it secured my supplies, would be likely to give Ranjit Singh confidence to oppose Jaswant Rao Holkar or at all events to deter him from embracing the cause of that chief.'

[2]Ranjit mentioned this escapade to many friends without saying what the two had discussed. Lord Lake makes no mention of this incident.

folded them and placed them before the Holy Granth. After a short prayer, he picked up one of the slips and opened it. It bore the name of Lake.

Ranjit Singh firmly refused to be drawn into the Anglo-Maratha conflict and began to mediate for a settlement. Fortunately for him Lord Wellesley, the British Governor-General, who had pursued an aggressive policy against the Marathas, was replaced by Cornwallis, who was given specific instructions not to engage in more wars or make any further annexations. The orders from London were to allow Holkar to resume his possessions. Ranjit's mediation was consequently successful. The Marathas and Rohillas recrossed the Sutlej and disappeared from the Punjab's horizon for ever. The British now became the sole power of substance in the east and only the loose conglomeration of the Malwa chiefs remained between them and Ranjit Singh.

Holkar and Ranjit sized up each other's character in the short period of their association. When Holkar discovered that despite his sermons on patriotism and Hindu-Sikh unity, Ranjit Singh had sent his uncle, and Fateh Singh Ahluwalia, to treat with the English, he said tauntingly: 'From the boundaries of the Deccan to the outskirts of the Punjab I have searched for a man of courage and valour to join me in my battles... but the more I searched, the more I found he was elusive. There is nothing in the world except man, but the real one is wanting.' Ranjit Singh's comment on the double dealing of Holkar was as brief and blunt as one might expect of a Punjabi peasant. Holkar, he said, was a *puccā harāmzādā*, an absolute bastard.

The Treaty of Lahore was signed on January 1, 1806, by Ranjit Singh and Fateh Singh Ahluwalia with the British. The Sikh signatories agreed to 'cause Jaswant Rao Holkar to remove with his army to the distance of 30 kos from Amritsar immediately, and will never hereafter hold any further connection with him or aid or assist him with troops, or in any other manner whatever'. In return, the English promised that their armies would not enter the aforesaid chiefs' territories nor form any plans for seizing their possessions or property.

The strain of the preceding months affected Ranjit Singh's health. While bathing at the temple of Sri Katasji in the salt range at

Khewra, where he had gone for rest, he caught a chill which developed into a fever. It was several weeks before he could even stand on his feet. He was brought back to Lahore in a palanquin and on the doctor's advice stayed in the Mughal garden at Shalamar, a few miles beyond the city walls to the east. During this convalescence, he had the canal which supplied water to the garden reopened and the fountains and water-channels cleansed. New fruit trees and flower beds were laid out. Ranjit Singh spent many days amongst flowers and the playing fountains till his health was fully restored.

'Why do they call this beautiful garden Shalamar?' he asked one of his courtiers.

'Because, O Noble One, the Persian word Shalamar means "pleasing to the heart".'

'But this is the Punjab, not Persia,' exclaimed Ranjit. 'In Punjab, the word *Shālāmār* means the "killer-of-love" and in this garden love is kindled, not killed. Let it hereafter be called Shalabagh, the garden of the beloved.'

Shalamar, or Shalabagh as he liked to call it, became Ranjit's favourite resort outside the city. It was the scene of many pleasant meetings and a place of entertainment for distinguished visitors. He often repaired to it to escape the hot and malodorous vapours of Lahore. Here wine flowed like the water of the fountains and the tinkle of dancers' bells was heard till the late hours of the night.

CHAPTER VI

THE PROFESSION OF A SOLDIER

'I FOLLOW the profession of a soldier and do not indulge in any pleasure or amusement but that of endeavouring to extend my conquest,' wrote Ranjit Singh in a letter in July 1805[1] introducing himself to Mr. Seton, the new British Resident at Delhi. The next three years fully proved his contention for rarely were his feet out of the stirrup.

Immediately after the danger of the Maratha-British conflict in the Punjab was over, the chiefs of Malwa resumed their favourite pastime of bickering and intriguing. All at once a petty squabble developed into a major crisis which threatened to convulse the whole of the South-Eastern Punjab. The bone of contention was an insignificant hamlet called Daladi on the border separating Nabha's territories from those of Patiala. In the squabble for possession of this hamlet an agent of Patiala was murdered. Rioting flared up all over Malwa. Jind supported Nabha; Thanesar and Kythal lined up behind Patiala. In one of the skirmishes the Chief of Thanesar was killed: Patiala avenged the death of his supporter by inflicting a bloody defeat on Nabha. Then both parties approached Ranjit Singh to arbitrate between them. Ranjit decided that this was a good opportunity to extend his suzerainty over Malwa and consolidate his hold on the estate-holders that lay on the route. He crossed the Sutlej with an army of 20,000 men. On the way to Patiala he passed through the territories of the Fyzullapuria misl, the Sodhis of Kartarpur, the Dallewalia misl and through the prosperous towns of Ludhiana and Jagraon. Everywhere the chiefs paid him tribute in cash, cannon, horses and elephants.

At Patiala the chiefs of Malwa awaited Ranjit Singh. But Sahib Singh of Patiala had second thoughts about the wisdom

[1]No. 266 Srl. 51a of September 29, 1805.

of having invited Ranjit and, not knowing what to do in the situation, simply locked himself up in his fort. A couple of rounds of cannon fire reminded him of his duty as a host and he came out to welcome his guest. Thereafter Ranjit was lavishly entertained and assured by the Malwa chiefs that they looked upon him as the Maharaja of all the Punjab.[1]

Ranjit Singh's verdict on the incident in the village of Daladi was to exonerate Jaswant Singh of Nabha from responsibility for the murder of the Patiala agent. He compensated Patiala by giving him three large-sized towns—Bassi, Talwandi and Jagraon with their neighbouring villages. The Raja of Jind was given Ludhiana and Fateh Singh Ahluwalia got many villages. The meeting broke up with further protestations of loyalty to Ranjit Singh.

On his way back to Lahore, Ranjit spent some days in the jungles near Jullundur hunting tiger and wild boar. While he was engaged in the chase Fateh Chand, brother of his one-time enemy, Sansar Chand, approached him for help against the Gurkhas who had occupied the hill tract between Jammu and the Sutlej and had besieged the fort of Kangra. Ranjit Singh had no love for Sansar Chand, who had once allied himself with the Afghans and twice invaded the plains of the Punjab. Nevertheless he realized that if the Gurkhas succeeded in taking Kangra, their power in the north would become formidable. Ranjit Singh agreed to help the Rajputs and marched his army towards the Himalayas. The Gurkha Commander, Amar Singh Thapa, heard of his approach and sent messages of goodwill with offers of money if Ranjit

[1] A newsletter from Patiala dated November 4, 1806 (SC$_7$ of November 27, 1806) describes the scene: 'The meeting of the chiefs took place on a bank with precautions on both sides. Great respect was paid to Ranjit Singh. Sahib Singh (Patiala) said to him: "Jaswant Singh (Nabha) has acted towards me in a very extraordinary manner." Ranjit Singh replied: "He is your brother; all of you are alike to me. I have only come to settle your disputes." Raja Sahib Singh observed: "If you had considered me in the same light as Bhag Singh (Jind) and Jaswant Singh you would not have fired at me so furiously." Ranjit replied: "This took place at the request of your brother and uncle, otherwise I consider you greater than myself." Sahib Singh said: "I am yours." Bhai Lal Singh (Kythal) said to Ranjit Singh: "You are the chief and the light of our tribe. Now that you are come into this country you will act according to your goodness and excellence."' Sahib Singh did not get rid of his suspicions. The newsletter goes on to say: 'After this Sahib Singh in conversation with the Ranee said Ranjit Singh is a great villain'.

Singh would stay neutral. Ranjit Singh was anxious to see that the powerful fort of Kangra did not fall into the hands of the Gurkhas and spurned their overtures.

Ranjit Singh pitched his camp at Jwalamukhi—the town celebrated for its volcanic mountain whose flame was an object of veneration to millions of Hindus. His troops moved on to the relief of Kangra.

The Gurkhas had been tired out by months of siege. With the onset of summer, an epidemic of cholera had broken out in their ranks. Fatigue and disease left them with no stomach to fight a fresh adversary. Amar Singh Thapa abandoned the siege and retired to Mandi Suket, swearing vengeance on Ranjit Singh.

Sansar Chand came to Jwalamukhi to thank and pay tribute to Ranjit Singh.

Ranjit Singh was still in the hills when he received news of the birth of twin sons to his first wife, Mehtab Kaur. There was rejoicing in the royal camp. When Ranjit Singh returned to Lahore he gave away large sums in charity and the city was illuminated for several nights. The young princes were given the names of Sher Singh and Tara Singh.[1]

Ranjit Singh had not been a long time in his capital when he was called upon to take action against the Pathans of Kasur. Nizamuddin, who had been defeated twice by the Durbar troops,

[1]Most English and Muslim historians have stated that these children were not borne by Mehtab Kaur but were taken from women of menial classes and at the instance of her mother passed off as hers by Ranjit. They also state that Ranjit Singh did not believe the sons to be his and had very little to do with them. Both these statements are inaccurate. What gave rise to the suggestion of illegitimacy was Ranjit's strained relations with Mehtab Kaur and her mother, Sada Kaur. Mehtab Kaur spent a lot of her time at her mother's home. Ranjit saw little of the two princes for some years and the first born Kharak Singh remained the favourite. When Sada Kaur fell from power and the princes came to stay with their father, Kharak Singh and his mother gave currency to the gossip in order to counteract any possibility of Ranjit preferring Sher Singh, who was fast becoming the father's favourite. (Kharak Singh wrote as much in a personal letter he sent to the British Governor-General.)

Bastardy is more easily insinuated than proved—or disproved. But if the father's attitude can be taken as any indication of the facts, it is quite clear that Ranjit Singh believed the children were his and Mehtab Kaur's. Court historians have a lot to say of Ranjit's joy at the birth of his sons and the jubilations in the camp.

was dead. His brother, Kutubuddin Khan, had taken his place and was apparently eager to aim another blow at Ranjit. He enlisted a large number of Ghazis, fortified Kasur and stocked the fort with provisions to outlast a prolonged siege. He persuaded Muzaffar Khan of Multan to supply him with trained soldiers and material. Ranjit Singh sent his trusted adviser, Fakeer Azizuddin, to tell the Pathan that the days of religious crusades were over and he should continue faithful to the Punjab Government. Kutubuddin dismissed Azizuddin with the taunt that, since the Fakeer ate the salt of the infidel, he was unworthy of attention.

Ranjit Singh led his army himself. To give the Ghazis a taste of their own kind of religious fanaticism, he had Akali Phula Singh bring along his band of desperado Nihangs.

The battle commenced on the morning of February 10, 1807, with a clash between the Ghazis and the Nihangs—the Muslim crusaders versus the Sikhs. The Nihangs drove the Ghazis behind their stockades. The artillery took over. For one month Sikh guns fired on the walls of the Kasur fort without making any impression. One night Sikh miners tunnelled their way to the base of the western bastion and placed a heavy charge of gunpowder under it. It was fired in the early hours of the morning and tore a large gap in the walls. Phula Singh's Nihangs charged through the breach and captured the citadel. Kutubuddin was arrested while trying to escape and brought before Ranjit Singh.

Ranjit Singh showed the magnanimity which so much contributed to his success as a leader of men. He forgot Kutubuddin's tirades against the Sikh infidels, his household's treacherous conduct over the years and their repeated attempts to overthrow the Lahore Durbar. Kutubuddin was not only forgiven but given a handsome jagir across the Sutlej at Mamdot.

Ranjit Singh did not want to leave Muzaffar Khan unpunished for his share in the Kasurians' defiance of authority; from Kasur the army was ordered to proceed southwards to Multan. Muzaffar Khan tried to interest his Muslim neighbours in his plight but no one was willing to give anything more than good advice. When the Durbar troops entered the city, he submitted and paid Rs. 20,000 as penalty for his indiscreet assistance to Kutubuddin.

Ranjit Singh returned from Multan to find an invitation to visit Patiala awaiting him. This was from Sahib Singh's wife, Aas Kaur, asking for his good offices to settle her dispute with her husband. She wanted her son, Karam Singh, to take over the administration of the State in the lifetime of the father—which Sahib Singh had naturally resented. Ranjit Singh proceeded to Patiala at the head of a large army. The Chiefs of Malwa once more acknowledged his suzerainty by paying him tribute in cash and by giving expensive presents. Ranjit Singh's verdict was a careful compromise: Sahib Singh was to continue as Maharaja as long as he lived; his son, Karam Singh, was to receive a jagir of Rs. 50,000 a year. Both parties accepted the judgement and paid the 'arbitration fee': the Raja gave Rs. 70,000 in precious stones; the Maharani, a brass cannon. Amongst the others who waited on Ranjit Singh and paid tribute were the chiefs of Kythal, Shahabad, Shahpur and Ambala.

On his way back to Lahore, Ranjit Singh ordered the siege of Naraingarh, a town in the domain of the Raja of Sirmoor, who had refused to acknowledge the Government of Lahore. The Raja put up a surprisingly stout resistance. Ranjit Singh's favourite officer, Fateh Singh Kalianwalia, who led a rash frontal attack, and two other senior officers were killed. Naraingarh was taken after heavy loss but without the Raja of Sirmoor, who was able to get away to the hills.

Ranjit Singh continued on his homeward march through Naushera, Morinda and Bahlolpur. On the way he heard of the death of another of his companions, Tara Singh Gheba, head of the Dallewalia misl, who had accompanied him to Patiala. Ranjit retraced his footsteps to offer his condolences. He fixed a pension for the widow and the deceased's family and incorporated the Dallewalia's forces in the State Army. The estates, which were worth over 7 lakhs a year in revenue, extending over the towns of Rahon, Nakodar and Naushera, were merged with the Durbar.

The administration of the Dallewalia estates was entrusted to Diwan Mohkam Chand, who had joined Ranjit's service earlier that year. The Diwan had served with the Bhanghis, twice fought against the Durbar troops and had impressed Ranjit Singh with his knowledge of military strategy. Ranjit Singh offered him the

rank of Commander of Cavalry and Infantry and sent him
against the Rajput chieftains of the north-eastern Himalayas.
Within a few months the Diwan reduced Pathankote, Jasrota,
Chamba and Basohli. He advised the Maharaja to hold a durbar
and formally invest the chieftains with robes of honour. This was
a clever move, as refusal to attend would indicate rejection of
the Durbar's sovereignty.

Invitations were sent to princes and estate holders, and those
who responded were invested with robes of honour and confirmed
in their possessions. After the ceremonial durbar was over, Ranjit
Singh and Fateh Singh Ahluwalia set out against the few chiefs
who had ignored the invitations. Sialkot was captured after a
three-day siege; Akhnur submitted without a fight; the Bhangi
of Gujerat had to get Sahib Singh Bedi to intercede on his behalf
before he was forgiven; the Kanhayas, whose daughter was
engaged to marry the heir-apparent, were let off with a light
tribute and the attachment of a part of their estate. The last
conquest of the year was the fort of Sheikhupura, the only one
of the three major forts of the Punjab which was in hostile hands;
its reduction was of the utmost importance as it was only twenty
miles from the capital.

Two years of ceaseless campaigning added many new territories to the Durbar. Their administration had to be organized
and the finances of the State put in order. Till then, Ranjit's
finances had been managed by the banking house owned by
Rama Nand of Amritsar. Ranjit Singh took into his employment
Diwan Bhawani Das, who had been an accountant in the service of Shah Zaman. Bhawani Das opened a chain of government treasuries in the big cities and introduced a proper system
of accounting. He was, however, more able than honest, and had
on several occasions to be reprimanded. 'His hunchback was full
of mischief,' wrote Sohan Lal.

The size of the Maharaja's household and visitors to the Court
had also increased enormously and necessitated the appointment
of a Royal Chamberlain. The Maharaja's choice fell on a
handsome Brahmin youth from Meerut called Khushal Chand,
who had enlisted as a common soldier. Khushal Chand was
promoted to the rank of *Jemādār* in the palace bodyguard, and
then appointed *deorhidār*—keeper of the royal palace. This post

was of considerable importance, since anyone who wanted a personal interview with the Maharaja had first to approach the keeper of the *deorhi*. It gave the incumbent political power as well as a handsome income from presents. Khushal Chand accepted the Sikh faith and came thereafter to be known as Jemadar Khushal Singh. He introduced two relations of his to the Court; a nephew, Tej Singh (who, after Ranjit Singh's death, played a treacherous role as Commander of the Sikh armies in the first Anglo-Sikh war), and a younger brother, Ram Chand, renamed Ram Singh after conversion to Sikhism. This family of Brahmins exerted a baleful influence on the Court. It was one of the rare instances of Ranjit Singh misjudging the quality of the men he employed.

CHAPTER VII

FRIENDS AND RIVERS

IN THE DECADE that Ranjit Singh had been Maharaja of the Punjab the situation on the frontier had changed considerably and some of the dangers that had threatened his kingdom had been resolved. The Afghans were busy quarrelling among themselves. The Rajputs of the north and the Gurkhas had cancelled each other out and were no longer in a position to challenge Ranjit's supremacy in the Punjab hills. The Marathas, who had accounted for George Thomas, had in their turn been accounted for by the English. The only external power of consequence that remained were the English, who were now masters of the whole of India except Sindh and the Punjab.

Ranjit Singh had consolidated his hold over much of the Punjab north of the river Sutlej. He had eliminated the Pathans of Kasur, taken tribute from the chiefs of Multan and North-Western Punjab, and had merged the six misls occupying territories in this region in the State of Lahore. All that remained to make an independent and unified State of the Punjab a reality was to incorporate the remaining six misls holding lands between the Sutlej and the Jumna. The two major problems at the end of the first ten years of his rule were the need to define the frontiers with the British and to integrate the Cis-Sutlej chiefs in the Punjabi State.

Ranjit Singh had already crossed the Sutlej on two occasions and been acclaimed as the sovereign of the Punjab; with spontaneous enthusiasm by the populace, with some reluctance by the rajas. Even the latter had submitted to his orders and paid him tributes as they would to an overlord. His suzerainty over Malwa was an accomplished fact in all but title. The only thing that remained was for the English on the eastern side of the Cis-Sutlej States to give legal recognition to a state of affairs that in fact existed.

The only weak point in Ranjit's claim to sovereignty over Malwa was that in 1805, when Lord Lake had chased Holkar across the plains of Eastern Punjab, Ranjit, fearing that the English Commander would not only destroy the Marathas but might also invade his territory, had suggested the river Sutlej as the boundary between the two kingdoms. But neither Lake nor the Governor-General had taken any notice of this suggestion. Their sole object was the annihilation of the Marathas. Once that was achieved the Board of Directors of the East India Company, which had been brought to the verge of bankruptcy by the Maratha campaigns, gave strict instructions to their officers not is involve themselves in any more wars and to consider the river Jumna as the western extremity of English possessions in India.

In the three years between 1805 (when the Maratha campaign ended) and 1808 much water had flowed down the Sutlej and the Jumna. Ranjit Singh had resumed his claim to be sovereign of the Sikhs and the Punjab and twice substantiated his title as far as the Malwa States were concerned without a word of protest from the English. But in the three years the East India Company had refilled its coffers and was ready for more adventures.

Ranjit Singh's action in taking over the territories of Tara Singh Gheba, who had died in 1807, had caused alarm amongst the Malwa chiefs. It was taken as concrete proof, if proof were needed, that he meant to reduce the chiefs to the position of pensioners. Soon after the expropriation of Gheba's estate, Mohkam Chand crossed the Sutlej and, with more zeal than discretion, proceeded to take Anandpur-Makhowal and Whadni (near Ferozepore), along with fifteen neighbouring villages. Apprehension turned to panic and the Malwa Sardars turned to the only power which could preserve them and their families in their palaces and privileges—the English. The situation took a sudden and unexpected turn in their favour. The events that brought this about occurred neither on the banks of the Sutlej nor the Jumna, but on those of the Thames and the Seine. Napoleon Bonaparte had risen to supreme power. One after another the European powers fell before him: Austria at Austerlitz, Prussia at Jena, Russia at Friedland. Tsar Alexander and Bonaparte signed the Treaty of Tilsit with a not-too-secret understanding that if England continued hostilities against France,

Russia would join the French in combating her. Although the British Navy commanded the seas, the land route to India through Persia, Afghanistan, Sindh and the Punjab was open to the Franco-Russian armies. The British Government decided to revise its policy of regarding the Jumna as its western frontier. Lord Minto, who had taken over as Governor-General in June 1807, ordered troops to be moved up to Karnal to protect Delhi from the north. Skinner's Horse were sent to patrol Hariana. Then the grand strategy of erecting a series of dams against the possible tide of Franco-Russian invasion was taken in hand. The dams were to be in Persia, Afghanistan, Sindh and the Punjab. Four missions were consequently sent out: Malcolm to Persia, Elphinstone to Kabul, Pottinger to Sindh, and Metcalfe was chosen to negotiate with Ranjit Singh.

The idea of sending a British delegation to Lahore was mooted early in 1808. When intelligence was received that Ranjit Singh might come to Hardwar to bathe in the Ganges, the British Government decided to exploit the situation 'by acts of kindness and attention to render the circumstances of Ranjit Singh's visit to the Company's dominions subservient to the plan of pleasing and conciliating him, thereby rendering it the basis of future intercourse and friendly connection'.[1] Metcalfe was chosen to receive the Maharaja. His instructions on this occasion show clearly what the British regarded as their northern frontier. Metcalfe was ordered 'to proceed to the banks of the Jumna and wait for the arrival of Ranjit Singh'. On the return journey he was to escort the ruler 'up to the British frontier'—which was against the banks of the Jumna.

Ranjit Singh cancelled his Hardwar visit at the last moment. Metcalfe had therefore to proceed to the Punjab.

Meanwhile the Malwais got together in Samana to discuss their future. The feeling which prevailed was that the British, who had already come up to the Jumna, would inevitably proceed further north in due course; that they were stronger than Ranjit Singh; that whereas the British would at least guarantee their personal privileges and status and that of their descendants, Ranjit Singh would most certainly take away their power and merge their territories into the Durbar. A venerable patriarch expressed

[1]Seton to Governor-General, February 18, 1808. Also SC_8 of April 4, 1808.

their views in the following words: 'We do not have a long time to go since both the British and Ranjit Singh mean to swallow us. But whereas protection will be like consumption which takes a long time to kill, Ranjit Singh's advent will be like a stroke of paralysis which will destroy us within a few hours.' The meeting decided to send a delegation to the British Resident in Delhi.

The delegation consisted of the chiefs of Jind, Kythal, Jagadhari, and the agents of Patiala and Nabha. Ranjit Singh got to know the plans of the Malwais and sent his agent to accompany their delegation. The delegates met the English Resident three or four times but since Ranjit Singh's agent was present, not a word was said about the frontiers. Then Ranjit's agent, believing that his master's suspicions had been unfounded, left Delhi to proceed on pilgrimage towards Gaya. The delegates at once went to Seton and presented a lengthy memorandum asking for protection from Ranjit Singh. Seton forwarded the memorandum to the Governor-General. The Company's policy still being no-farther-than-the-Jumna, the Governor-General decided that the delegation should be officially ignored. The delegates waited in Delhi for two months, then turned back to the Punjab without the guarantee they had sought. They awaited Ranjit Singh's reactions with understandable trepidation. Ranjit Singh invited the Malwa chiefs to Amritsar and gave them a solemn assurance that he would not annex their States and would treat them as equals. The chiefs agreed to come into Ranjit's camp. 'Between the lion and the wolf they had to come to terms with the deadlier of the beasts.'[1]

Metcalfe set out for the Punjab in the last week of July, 1808.[2] The instructions of the Governor-General to Metcalfe admitted clearly that he did not think his government had any rights over

[1] E. Thompson. *Lord Metcalfe*, p. 75.
[2] A month before Metcalfe's visit, a Captain Matthews had visited the Chiefs of Malwa and had secret talks with Sada Kaur whom he reported to be hostile to Ranjit Singh. Matthews sent detailed reports of Ranjit Singh's character, administration and armed strength to his government. According to him Ranjit Singh had fourteen battalions of matchlockmen of 1,000 each; 6,000 cavalry and 11 brass pieces of small calibre. The soldiers were well paid: between Rs. 8-10 p.m. and there were 900 deserters from the Company's service in the Maharaja's army.

Of the administration of Lahore, Matthews wrote: 'This part of the Punjab, as well as other parts where the Raja's authority exists, is under a good police

the Malwa States. He stated that they were not to interfere in Ranjit's ambition in that direction 'because it would involve the protection of States unconnected with us by the obligation of defensive alliance'. At the same time, the British Government wanted 'to avoid a declared concurrence in Ranjit's hostile designs against the States in question and until it is known in what degree the security of the British Government may require a cordial union of its interests with those of Ranjit Singh, it is not easy to determine what sacrifices it may be expedient to make for the attainment of that object'...[1] In short, Malwa was to be used as a pawn in the game.

Ranjit Singh did not believe that the object of the British Government was only to safeguard itself against a French invasion because there was only real evidence of a French plan to invade India and in any case France was a long way off. The French Government had made no attempt to establish contact with him, nor to his knowledge, with the Sindhians or the Afghans. The British on the other hand were sending an envoy to Kabul with the object of making an alliance with the Afghans who were the traditional enemy of the Punjabis, particularly of the Sikhs, and with whom Ranjit Singh had been in constant conflict. They were also sending an envoy to the Amirs of Sindh and Ranjit Singh was toying with the idea of expanding his kingdom in that direction to the sea. Besides that, Ranjit Singh had information that British agents were active in Malwa encouraging the chiefs to renew their request for British did not

---

and safe for travellers, it seldom happening that capital crimes or robberies are committed.'

Matthews was received by the Maharaja on June 23, 1808. He describes Ranjit Singh as 'a man of excellent understanding possessed of a most liberal, generous, friendly mind, untinctured with prejudices of any kind...'

'The Raja is not only a most unaffected and pleasing man in his manners but of a very good understanding, brave and liberal and seems to be quite the soldier and very fond of military exercises, but regrets that he can get no Europeans into his service... He is both feared and believed by his men and frequently leads them on to the assault of forts; being a fatalist he says it is in vain for a man to screen himself and that what is to be his end must inevitably be so. He is a most capital horseman and rides every morning till 7 o'clock with only few attendants on the fine level plain between the walls of the town and the river, has beautiful horses some of which are from Iran and Kandahar, but the finest are bred in this country.'

[1]SC₃ of June 20, 1808.

mean to extend such protection. It was obvious that even if the British did not mean to extend such protection, they were not averse to fostering the demand and then using it as a bargaining point with Ranjit.

Ranjit Singh sent Hakim Imamuddin, the brother of Fakeer Azizuddin, to greet Metcalfe on the latter's arrival at Patiala; this was to make the Englishman realize that he was thereafter to consider himself in Ranjit's domains. Ranjit also summoned some of the Malwa chiefs including his uncle, Bhag Singh of Jind, and Lal Singh of Kythal, to Lahore. Metcalfe found their absence from their States and their paying court to Ranjit an unpleasant prelude to his mission and threatened to 'warn them of the natural consequences of incurring the displeasure of the British Government'.[1] He received other chiefs who came to call on him and heard all they wanted to say against Ranjit Singh. Sahib Singh of Patiala made a dramatic gesture by presenting the keys of his citadel to the Englishman and begging him to return them to him to symbolize British protection over Patiala. 'The ceremony was quite unnecessary,' reported Metcalfe. Nevertheless he 'endeavoured to assure him that the British Government entertained the most friendly sentiments towards him'.[2]

The Malwais resumed their efforts of playing the British against Ranjit Singh. They told Ranjit Singh that the British meant to annex his kingdom. They told Metcalfe that Ranjit was massing troops to fight the British. Even Imamuddin's assurance that the troops had been called up long before and were on their way to Bahawalpur and Multan did not calm Metcalfe's fears. The atmosphere was thoroughly vitiated with suspicion on either side.

Ranjit Singh called a meeting of his ministers. It was suggested to him that the man who had most knowledge of treating with the English was one Prabh Dial, an employee of Fateh Singh Ahluwalia. Prabh Dial was asked to assist Fakeer Azizuddin and Mith Singh in the negotiations on behalf of the Lahore Durbar.[3]

---

[1]Metcalfe, No. 7 of August 18, 1808.
[2]Metcalfe, No. 8 of August 24, 1808.
[3] The negotiations throw some light on the character of Ranjit's mother-in-law, Sada Kaur. She alternated between fierce loyalty and hatred for her son-in-law. She was amongst the first to send word to the English that if they decided to invade the Punjab they could count on her support. Her daughter, Mehtab Kaur, personally called on Captain Matthews to convey this message.

The first meeting between the youthful Sikh monarch (twenty-seven) and the even more youthful English ambassador (twenty-four) took place at Khemkaran near Kasur on September 12, 1808. Metcalfe was aggressive from the very start. He had been put off by Imamuddin's appearance at Patiala; he did not like being received by Diwan Mohkam Chand and Fateh Singh Ahluwalia before meeting Ranjit; he did not like the fact that the meeting should have been arranged to take place without pomp and ceremony at Kasur instead of in the capital; he did not like the dry bed of the river for the location of his tents; an unseasonal thunderstorm did not improve his temper. He insisted on form and protocol and looked upon any assumption of informality as a slight to his status as a representative of His Britannic Majesty.

Ranjit Singh assuaged Metcalfe's temper by receiving him most cordially. He came out of his private tent and embraced the Englishman and members of his party. He conducted them to the royal enclosure and made them sit on chairs alongside his own, and presented Metcalfe with an elephant, a thoroughbred horse, strings of pearls and expensive shawls from Kashmir; other members of the party were also given presents. No business was conducted at this meeting, but Ranjit Singh did ask his visitor what matters of moment had brought him to the Punjab during the rainy season when the rivers were flooded and the sun hot. Metcalfe evaded a direct reply. When one of the courtiers said that the British were celebrated for good faith, Ranjit made a cryptic remark: 'We will now know whether the word of the British Government includes everything.'

Even at Kasur, Metcalfe was tactless enough to receive a delegation of the Malwa Sardars. This irritated Ranjit Singh and he sent a note to Metcalfe stating that he expected the Englishman to take his leave in three or four days. 'Although it is difficult to feel the satiety from interviews of friends whose hearts are united,' ran Ranjit's letter, 'yet affairs of State must be attended to. Consequently, I am about to march immediately for the settlement of certain districts. In my nation it is considered very auspicious to march on the first day of the moon...therefore

But when it almost to war she was the one to restrain Ranjit. Amongst the others who hunted with the hounds and ran with the hares was Ranjit's uncle, Bhag Singh of Jind.

be pleased to make friendly communication on the part of the Governor-General....my anxiety cannot admit of longer expectation.'

Metcalfe ascribed Ranjit's note to unwarrantable jealousy. He reiterated the friendship between their States and came to call on the Sikh ruler three days later. This meeting went well and was full 'of the greatest good humour' and 'much friendly conversation on various subjects'. Three days later, Metcalfe came down to the real business. To a full durbar he read out a statement to the effect that his Government had information that the French, who were trying to establish themselves in Persia, had designs on Kabul and the Punjab and 'the interests of all the States in this quarter required that they should unite in defence of their dominions and the destruction of the enemy's armies'.[1]

The Maharaja and his courtiers gave Metcalfe's oration an enthusiastic applause. Then Ranjit began to question him on the details.

'How far does the British army propose to advance to meet the French invasion?' he asked.

'Beyond Kabul, if necessary.'

'Is the British army ready for action?'

'The British army is always ready for action.'

'When are the French expected to invade these parts?'

'The moment in which the enemy might be expected can not be at present ascertained.'

'In that case,' concluded Ranjit Singh, 'there is time for us to think things over.'

He thanked the Englishman for this illuminating address, expressed his willingness to co-operate and said how much he was looking forward to an alliance with the British 'which has long been the wish of my heart'. Ranjit Singh told his advisers to ask any questions they wished.

'What if Shah Shuja joined the French?' asked one.

'He will not be so blind to his interest as the French invariably subjugate and oppress those who join them; they overthrow the governments of their allies, plunder and lay waste their countries,' replied Metcalfe.

'What is Holkar's attitude to these proposals?'

[1]'The information which the Company had collected as to French designs amounted to a handful of mist.' Thompson, p. 77.

'He is at peace with the British.'

At this stage, Prabh Dial came, whispered some words in the Maharaja's ears and then told Metcalfe that they would like time to deliberate and would give him their reply next day.

The day following, Ranjit's advisers called on Metcalfe and while agreeing to the British proposal for joint defence against a French invasion, suggested that they go further and 'establish the strictest union between the two States and put an end to the reports that were constantly circulating throughout the country, of an approaching dispute with the British Government and the Raja'. To make their point clear they referred to a letter written by Ranjit Singh to the Governor-General asking for a clear statement of the British attitude to his status as sovereign of all the Sikhs. Metcalfe was unwilling to discuss the question as it dealt with 'a one-sided interest', whereas his mandate was to discuss only questions of mutual interest. Fakeer Azizuddin corrected him. The settlement of a common frontier was as much a question of mutual interest as that of making an alliance. Metcalfe tried to evade the issue by stating: 'The boundary of the government's territories is fixed; there is no design whatsoever to exceed it.'

'Where has the government fixed its immutable boundary?' asked the Fakeer.

Metcalfe was in a tight fix. The British had established their military camp at Karnal, sixty-seven miles north-west of Delhi, to defend Delhi. Perhaps it would be safe to mention the farthest point he could: 'Karnal,' replied Metcalfe.

Prabh Dial informed Metcalfe that Karnal belonged to Gurdit Singh, an old friend of the Maharaja. Metcalfe sidetracked the issue by launching on another harangue on the villainy of Napoleon Bonaparte. When he finished his oration, Diwan Mohkam Chand made a suggestion that really put Metcalfe out of countenance. 'The British,' he suggested, 'should sign an agreement with the Maharaja before sending a mission to Kabul.'

Metcalfe had no answer to these questions and sought shelter behind diatribes against the French and accusations of suspicion on the part of Ranjit Singh and his consellors. Nevertheless, Ranjit Singh sought out Metcalfe next day and asked him bluntly about his government's policy regarding the Malwa States. Metcalfe avoided giving a direct reply and only lauded British

rule in Delhi and British moderation in not having extended their
dominions up to the Sutlej. But, warned Metcalfe, if Ranjit Singh
insisted on getting a formal declaration of policy instead of
leaving it as vague as it was, he would run the risk of the
Governor-General declaring for the Sutlej. To soften the blow
Metcalfe threw a bait to Ranjit—which is a fair sample of the
envoy's method. He told him that the alliance he was propos-
ing was a purely defensive one; but if Ranjit wanted to pros-
ecute his territorial designs on Afghanistan, the British Government would not interfere. This double-faced dealing did not
impress Ranjit because he knew of the impending negotiations
between the British and the Afghans. He returned to his counsellors and in sheer disgust ordered breaking up of the camp.

Metcalfe rose one morning to see the Maharaja's entourage
on the move. He sent his munshi to ask Ranjit, who was su-
perintending his army across the river, where he was bound for.

'Faridkot,' came the reply.

The choice of Faridkot was significant. The Raja had revolted
against the authority of Patiala. Ranjit Singh as an overlord of
Patiala, was taking on the duty of bringing Faridkot back to obedience.

Metcalfe arrived on the scene the day after Faridkot had been
taken. He congratulated the Maharaja's emissaries who came to
receive him and asked when they could resume negotiations.
There was another exchange of sarcasm. Ranjit Singh said that
he would be in Faridkot for eight days and was at the envoy's
disposal: he hoped eight days would be long enough. Metcalfe
replied that if the Raja was willing, one day would be enough;
if not, a hundred would not do. Ranjit Singh added that he was
glad to hear that only one day was needed for the business.
Would the Englishman send him precise proposals?

The draft proposal which Metcalfe presented had three clauses.
It provided for joint action against the French invasion, passage
for British troops through the Punjab to the frontier to meet the
invaders, and the establishment of a military depot and an intelligence post in the Punjab if the action took place beyond the
Indus.

Three days later, the Durbar presented Metcalfe with a draft
of counter proposals. This also had three clauses; the British

should extend most favoured nation treatment to the Durbar as it would to them (the Afghans were not to be given preference; nor should the British enter into any alliance with the rulers of Bahawalpur and Multan); Ranjit Singh's suzerainty over the whole of the Sikh nation was to be recognized; the British were not to entertain any disaffected Sikh chiefs or meddle with the traditions of the Khalsaji; and the alliance should be in perpetuity.

Metcalfe was willing to make the alliance perpetual but not willing to commit himself about the other two clauses. And he expressed surprise that the Durbar had said nothing about the alliance against the French invasion.

After a fortnight, Ranjit Singh proceeded to Malerkotla, where Metcalfe followed him. The Pathan ruler of Malerkotla submitted to the Durbar and Metcalfe had to ignore his plea to intercede on his behalf and have the levy imposed to him reduced.

At Malerkotla, Metcalfe was received by Ranjit Singh at another meeting where all the courtiers were present. They pressed Metcalfe to concede their master's sovereignty over the Sikh nation at once. Metcalfe replied that this would have been done if there had been full confidence on both sides. Then Ranjit Singh took up the discussion himself: 'I take it that your despatches have satisfied your government that the necessary state of confidence exists.'

'No, they have not,' replied Metcalfe frankly. 'I have described the attitude of the Lahore Durbar as one of jealousy and suspicion.'

Ranjit Singh treated the envoy's bold assertion with equal candour. 'It has been reported to me that the British Government entertains the design of taking the Punjab,' he stated.

'There have been rumours of designs on the part of the Maharaja of advancing to Delhi but the British have ignored them,' replied Metcalfe.

'The British are strong enough to be able to ignore them,' remarked one of the counsellors.

'I have no doubt of British sincerity,' continued Ranjit Singh, 'except for their reluctance to recognize my suzerainty over the Sikh nation. I do not ask for much because all Sikhs acknowledge the supremacy of the Khalsa State.'

'Then, why agitate about it?' asked Metcalfe. 'In any case, the matter has been referred to the Governor-General.'

'My people must wonder what we have gained in these six weeks of negotiations,' stated the Maharaja.

Metcalfe replied angrily that he might well ask that question himself. The discussions went on desultorily without any result. Ranjit Singh informed Metcalfe that he was moving to Ambala. If the Englishman cared to continue negotiations, he should follow.

Metcalfe was indignant and at first refused to go. Then he was persuaded to follow Ranjit Singh up to his next halt, Fatehgarh-Gongrana. There were more meetings, exchanges of notes and orations by Metcalfe on the benefits that the Durbar would derive from its alliance with Britain. Just when he felt that his oratory had hit its mark, the shrewd Bhawani Das asked the Englishman's permission to speak his mind, and on being given it, said: 'All the advantages accrue to the British for the real object of a French invasion would be the British and not the Sikhs.'

'No,' answered Metcalfe emphatically, 'you do not know the French as I do. The French will destroy your independence.' When that happens, observed one of the others, there would be no question of the Durbar not aligning itself with the British. For the benefit of the Englishman, the counsellors came out with the choicest Punjabi abuse for the French. The Maharaja and his courtiers proceeded to Ambala.

Metcalfe remained at Gongrana where he committed many of his thoughts to paper. It is clear from what he wrote that he had come round to the view that Ranjit's suzerainty over the Malwa States was an accomplished fact, and if his government really desired his friendship, they should recognize that sovereignty; the only thing that bothered him was the position of the few chiefs who had not yet submitted to Ranjit's overlordship. If his government gave unconditional recognition, it would be forcing some unwilling people into Ranjit's arms. If it made recognition conditional on Ranjit's ability to bring them within his fold, it would be encouraging Ranjit to commit aggression. Metcalfe's chief concern was with the exact wording of the recognition—not with its substance.

Meanwhile Ranjit proceeded on his triumphant march through the region, welcomed by the people wherever he went. From

Ambala he went to Shahabad, from Shahabad to Patiala. There he met the petrified Sahib Singh who had betrayed him more than once. Ranjit Singh embraced him and in the presence of the venerable Sahib Singh Bedi, who was always wont to appear when the Sikhs were threatened with disruption, exchanged turbans with the Patiala Raja. Ranjit Singh had given clear proof that the land between the Jumna and the Sutlej was under his control and almost all the chieftains of the area acknowledged his suzerainty.

The British government now performed a complete *volte face*. After what had passed between Metcalfe and Ranjit, the British could no longer rely on Ranjit for help against anyone. Why not at least prevent Malwa from falling into the lap of a potential enemy? Lord Minto decided to take the Malwa State under British protection. He ordered the Commander-in-Chief to mobilize forces available near Delhi and march them northwards to the Punjab frontier. At the same time Metcalfe was instructed to continue negotiations and play for time till Colonel Ochterlony was ready for battle.

Was the French invasion a complete bogey?[1] Were the professions of friendship for Ranjit Singh only an excuse to visit his territory, make contacts with subversive elements and then overthrow him? Lord Minto belonged to the Imperialist school; so did Metcalfe and most young Englishmen in India. The liquidation of all native States and the establishment of Pax Britannica was an article of faith with them.

Ranjit Singh was blissfully unaware of the stab in the back that Minto had planned for him. He returned from the tour of Malwa to Amritsar where the populace gave him a hero's welcome, singing songs of joy and showering him with flowers. For several nights the house and the temple were illuminated and fireworks lit the skies. The monarch and his people gave themselves up to the merry-making and carousals which go with Diwali, the festival of lamps. Metcalfe was now like a hunter

[1]Sohan Lal Suri does not even mention France in his report on Metcalfe's mission.

The opinion of V.G. Kiernan, *Metcalfe's Mission to Lahore*, p. 5, is illuminating: 'The negotiations with Ranjit Singh were in fact to turn so little on French affairs, that it might be permissible to suspect Napoleon of being in this case a mere red herring, and the mission of being sent to initiate a penetration of the Punjab.'

on a *machān* with his bead drawn on the lion and seemed to relish his quarry's carefree approach to its doom. He reported the Maharaja's return to Amritsar to the Governor-General in the following words: 'Ranjit Singh in everything he undertakes is impatient; but the cause of this extraordinary impatience on this occasion was a desire to see his favourite mistress, Mohran, from whom he has been separated for nearly three months. In her arms he has been resting after the fatigues of his march.'[1]

Metcalfe arrived in Amritasar on November 10, 1809, with the Governor-General's ultimatum. He had, however, to 'spin things out'. Ochterlony needed time to march up to the frontier, British agents had to make sure of the collaboration of the Malwa Sardars, and Metcalfe's colleague, Elphinstone, had yet to finish his mission in Kabul. Occasionally, Metcalfe had a twinge of conscience. 'I could not forget that I had been sent to establish an alliance and not bring on a war,' he wrote in his diary. But this did not last long. He was sure that his government could find something in the behaviour of Ranjit Singh which wold give it the excuse to go to war against the Sikh. 'His conduct would soon have given an opportunity to get rid of any embarrassment which our engagement with him might have caused,' he wrote. He confessed to some confusion which his government's new policy had produced in his mind. 'There was certainly an impression in my mind that the government was not prepared immediately to oppose Ranjit's Singh's pretensions by arms, which was founded on the policy pursued in the last three years during which he had been allowed to make much progress in effecting his purposes, and from your joint instructions I conceived that the government wished to have the ques-

[1]The Englishman did not fare too badly himself. Once the tension of having to negotiate had given place to the easier position of being able to dictate, Metcalfe also relaxed in the arms of a native mistress. But unlike the Sikh who flaunted his passion for Mohran in the face of everyone, Metcalfe kept his liaison a secret till the end of his life. (Only in his will did he acknowledge the progeny of his indiscretions at Amritsar; no native blood could sully the proud name of the Metcalfes.) His peerage lapsed with him. It is curious that his official biographer, Kaye, makes no reference to Metcalfe's Indian mistress—although he does, obliquely, to the children she bore him. Kaye has a lot to say about Ranjit's drinking and carousals but carefully avoids saying anything about Metcalfe's mode of relaxation. According to Edward Thompson, Metcalfe actually married a Sikh lady by 'Indian rites'. A marriage by Sikh rites involves conversion to Sikh religion.

tion left without decision or discussion; although I thought it possible that the government might be induced by his abominable behavior to oppose him, I was not confident of that.'

How far war with the English was from Ranjit's mind at the time the English were preparing to take the field against him is shown by the fact that by Diwali almost all his troops were back across the Sutlej (only a few small detachments remained at Ambala and in its neighbourhood).

Metcalfe handed over the Governor-General's letter personally 'with the intention of observing its effect'. He was robbed of the pleasure, because Ranjit Singh calmly put it aside without opening it and invited the envoy to join him in the festivity. 'I entered into the spirit of the scene as I thought proper. I took an early opportunity of retiring; but the Raja and his friends were even then evidently incapacitated for business.'[1]

Metcalfe waited eagerly all next day for the blast of his time bomb. Ranjit Singh had forgotten all about the missive in his pocket. Metcalfe's nerves became frayed waiting for the agonizing moment. He sent a reminder through his clerk. Ranjit had the clerk read out the note and discovered that 'the Governor-General had learned with surprise and concern that the Maharaja aims at the subjection of chiefs who have long been considered under the protection of the power ruling in the north of Hindustan'.[2] This contention was followed by a reference to Ranjit's note to Lake, suggesting the Sutlej as the boundary between the two States.

The Maharaja heard the contents of the letter with complete calm. A man who had come to sign a pledge of friendship had handed him an ultimatum with the sanction of war. He said he would let the envoy have his reply soon.

According to one account, he sent for his horse and rode away without informing anyone. He spent the morning riding hard and having got anger out of his system summoned his counsellors. Before they arrived, Metcalfe handed him another note that all the territory east of the Sutlej that the Durbar had taken under its control since the arrival of the mission should be reassured

[1]Metcalfe, No. 42 of December 11, 1808.
[2]Metcalfe, No. 43 of December 12, 1808.

forthwith. Ranjit Singh decided to return to his capital.[1]

Metcalfe stayed on in Amritsar to make direct contacts with the people.[2] He paid a visit to the temple, placed a generous offering before the Granth Sahib and gave expensive presents to the priests.[3]

Metcalfe arrived in Lahore on December 17, and was received in court. He described Ranjit as trying to 'maintain a lively conversation on general topics. He frequently, however, sunk into a reverie, and displayed in his countenance much care and thoughtfulness.'[4]

Negotiations were again taken up. Metcalfe was more than willing to wait since he had not yet heard that Ochterlony had completed his military preparations. 'I continue to suspend the communication of the proposed measures until I may have information that the state of preparation of the intended detachment render it expedient,' he wrote to his government.[5]

On the 21st Ranjit Singh again received Metcalfe; all the ministers were present. The Durbar's case was presented by Fakeer Azizuddin and Prabh Dial. The Maharaja, they said, had twice before gone across the Sutlej, both times at the invitation of a local chief, and Diwan Mohkam Chand had made many annexations in that region for the Durbar; the British had said absolutely nothing about them. On the contrary, ever since they took possession of Delhi they had made it clear that they would

[1]Metcalfe gave another reason for Ranjit's hurried departure from Amritsar. In a letter of December 14, 1808, he wrote: 'His favourite mistress, Mohran, who is of the Moosulman faith, lately converted a Hindu of the Khatree caste to the Moosulman religion, whether by force or persuasion I do not know. The town of Umritsar has been in a state of ferment in consequence for many days.... The population on one occasion outrageously plundered the houses of all the Moosulman dancing girls of whom Mohran was formerly one and forced the Raja to agree that they should be removed from the town.'

[2]Metcalfe was able to gauge the loyalties of Ranjit's Sardars in the event of a conflict and he reported on them to his government. Amongst those whom Metcalfe reported as would-be collaborators was Ranjit's mother-in-law, Sada Kaur.

[3]He spent a total of Rs. 2,605/- at the shrine 'having reason to believe that a compliment from him to the temple would be acceptable to the whole tribe of Sikhs'. (Metcalfe, No. 46 of December 15, 1808.) It was not. News of British design against the Punjab had got round. Soon after Metcalfe left Amritsar, the offering and the money were thrown away. (Kiernan, p. 31.).

[4]Metcalfe, No. 48 of December 18, 1808.

[5]Metcalfe, No. 50 of December 20, 1808.

have nothing to do with the affairs of the country north of the Jumna.

After defeating the Marathas, Lord Lake had withdrawn every one of his soldiers from this region. At that time the quarrel between the Raja and Rani of Patiala was at its height and one word from Lake would have settled it. But he had refused to interfere. The British Resident at Delhi had refused to meddle in the affairs of Malwa when he had received their delegation and those very chiefs had acknowledged Ranjit's overlordship without a word of protest from the British.

It must have occurred to Metcalfe that these arguments were precisely the ones he had used a month earlier in trying to persuade his government to acknowledge Ranjit's rights over the Malwa States. But times had changed and now Metcalfe's brief was different. 'No,' he maintained with more vigour than truth, his government was not aware that Ranjit's incursions in the Malwa States amounted to 'settled conquest'; that Seton had not assured the Malwa chiefs of protection because at the time it was not considered necessary. And as to the Malwa chiefs acknowledging Ranjit's overlordship, Metcalfe asserted that 'he had not heard of it; that the British Government had not heard of it; that if it had, it could not have agreed to it, and could not now pay any attention to it'.[1]

The Maharaja continued to keep calm but it was obvious that his disappointment was acute. According to Metcalfe, he re-marked that 'as I (Metcalfe) had been sent expressly to confirm and increase the friendship subsisting between the two States, he had expected the complete accomplishment of all his views, that his disappointment was now very great: and that he could not refrain from observing that it was an extraordinary kind of friendship that I had established.' The last sentence Ranjit spoke before closing the conference was: 'Do not let the same injury arise in friendship, which would be the result of enmity.'

That was not an end of British 'friendship'. Next day Metcalfe broke the news that a British force was moving up to the Sutlej. And when later in the day he heard that the Maharaja had sent for Mohkam Chand and was getting ready to go to Amritsar, Metcalfe became very angry. He accused Ranjit Singh of wanting

[1]Metcalfe, No. 51 of December 22, 1808.

to resist the British by force. '*C'est animal est tres mechant; quand on l'attaque, il se defend.*'

The Durbar was of two minds. Some counsellors were for resisting, others for peace at any price. The leader of the fight of the British-group was Mohkam Chand. It was more honourable to die fighting than to capitulate without firing a shot, he said with some passion. At his instance orders were sent to all the Sardars to bring their forces to face the British on the Sutlej. The forts of Govindgarh, Phillaur and Lahore were strengthened and stocked with provisions for long sieges. Within a few days nearly 100,000 Punjabis answered the call to arms. But even with this vast fighting force, Mohkam Chand could not assure the Durbar of victory against the Company's better trained and potentially more numerous army. Fakeer Azizuddin was for appeasement and avoiding hostilities as far as possible. The Fakeer was strongly backed behind the scenes by Sada Kaur.[1] Ranjit realized full well that if he lost now, all would be lost. If he could ward off the danger for the moment, he would live to fight another day. He decided to swallow his pride and to accept the Sutlej as his eastern boundary. But if Ochterlony crossed the river, he would fight the British to the finish.

On January 2, 1809, Ochterlony left Delhi for Karnal at the head of three infantry battalions, a regiment of cavalry and some artillery. His instructions were to compel the Durbar to give up its recent conquests; on the way he was to call upon the Malwa chiefs for assistance. If any of them showed sympathy with Ranjit Singh they were to be told plainly what was in store for them. He was also instructed not to lose the opportunity of making contacts with disaffected elements in the Lahore Durbar.

On February 9, 1809, Ochterlony made an official proclamation on behalf of his government that the Chiefs of Malwa were under British protection; the Durbar's forts including those at Kharar and Khanpur were to be raised and the Durbar was to

---

[1] This intelligence was conveyed to Ochterlony by his informer in Ranjit's court. According to him Sada Kaur had 'urged (Ranjit) in the most earnest manner to avoid hostilities with the British power, which as coming from one who has so much cause of complaint and dissatisfaction will probably have greater weight at this moment than he has been accustomed to pay to her representations'. (Ochterlony on February 2, 1809 in SC$_{102}$ of March 13, 1809.)

withdraw all its forces to the western banks of the Sutlej.

Ranjit Singh informed Metcalfe that he had ordered the Durbar troops to evacuate Ambala. Metcalfe demanded the evacuation of Farikdot and Saniwal and once more accused Ranjit Singh of preparing for war. The Englishman's great bugbear was Diwan Mohkam Chand whose presence at Ludhiana was to him a clear proof of the Durbar's hostile intentions. Metcalfe warned the British Commander-in-Chief that war was inevitable. In that case, wrote back the Commander-in-Chief, keep the Punjabis talking for some days so as to give him time to plan his strategy. But he must not prolong the negotiations too long, bearing in mind that too much of the cool campaigning weather must not be wasted.[1]

The Malwa Sardars were back to their old game of backing the winner. They greeted Ochterlony with professions of loyalty. Sada Kaur was with them; so also was Ranjit's uncle, Bhag Singh of Jind. (He did his best to convince the British Commander that Ranjit did not want war.) The agents of these Sardars at Lahore continued to profess support for Ranjit Singh.

The negotiations were resumed at Amritsar. Ranjit Singh agreed to all the conditions imposed by the British except giving up Faridkot. Metcalfe agreed to refer the question of Faridkot to Calcutta chiefly because it gave him the excuse of postponing the signing of a treaty of friendship, for which the Durbar had become more insistent than ever.

Metcalfe kept up the injured tone of an aggrieved party and used it to put off the signing of a treaty. Ranjit Singh flattered him. 'You are the Aristotle of the age; be pleased to say if a treaty is delayed, and the establishment of the military post takes place, how can I be at ease?' He had already given in all along the line, were not the British willing to make even a gesture of compromise? 'Even the oyster returns a pearl when it receives a drop of rain,' he pleaded.

Metcalfe would not budge. For now he had decided that Ranjit Singh's kingdom across the Sutlej should also be subverted and his rule put to an end. He recommended a full-scale invasion of the Punjab and tried hard to find an excuse for doing so. He objected to Ranjit's counsellors; Mohkam Chand was 'a fire-eating

[1]Metcalfe, No. 58 of January 12, 1809.

war-monger'.[1] He incited Ranjit Singh against the Diwan by telling him that the Diwan was insubordinate, that the real ruler of the Punjab was not Ranjit but Mohkam Chand. He also referred to Mith Singh sarcastically as Ranjit's 'favourite friend'.

Ranjit Singh refused to be provoked into giving Metcalfe the excuse he wanted. Then Metcalfe lost patience and refused to wait for an excuse. On January 22, 1809, he advised the Commander-in-Chief that 'the Raja has nominally taken the field'. He also took 'the responsibility of recommending to His Excellency's (the Commander-in-Chief's) attention the invasion of the Punjab, as a measure urgently desirable with reference to the state in this country in the event of inevitable hostilities...'[2]

Metcalfe's exhortation to war took both the Commander-in-Chief and Resident Seton by surprise. Nevertheless other British units were alerted and a force under Major St Leger was asked to be prepared to join at short notice. However, the necessity for invading the Punjab suddenly vanished. Napoleon attacked Spain and with his armies bogged down in Europe it was unlikely that he would now advance towards India for some years to come. British policy towards Ranjit Singh underwent a corresponding change. On January 30, 1809, Ochterlony received fresh instructions. 'The reduction or subversion of the power of the chieftain (Ranjit Singh) which under other circumstances was considered an event highly desirable and expected to be a probable consequence, though not settled purpose, of the approximation of our troops to the frontier of the Punjab is no longer of the same importance to our interest.' Ranjit Singh could be left alone. His friendship was no longer necessary and his chagrin could perhaps be lessened if he was allowed to retain his 'old conquests' in Malwa and the military post was withdrawn further back from his frontier.

Ochterlony continued his march.[3] At Patiala, the dim-witted Sahib Singh received him in a state of 'childish joy'. Nabha was

[1]At one of their meetings Mohkam Chand had darkly hinted: 'You haven't seen the Sikh soldiers in battle.' Metcalfe retorted: 'You haven't seen the British.'
[2]Metcalfe, No. 63 of January 26, 1809.
[3]An incident in Ochterlony's march shows the attitude of the British at the time. Two of Ranjit's agents met Ochterlonoly at village Nathi and represented the difficulties of the Lahore Durbar in dealing with the impetuous and haughty Metcalfe who had refused to clarify the British attitude to Ranjit

little less jubilant: he had received many favours from Ranjit Singh. So also had Bhag Singh of Jind who wanted to exchange the city of Ludhiana (given to him by his nephew but taken over by the British) for Hariana, Karnal and Panipat. The Malerkotla Nawab was reinstated in his possessions.

Ranjit Singh's reputation amongst his own people was at its lowest. The enemy was massing his armies on the frontiers; an enemy outpost had been set up on the Sutlej. And Ranjit Singh, who was the chief of a race known for its pugnacity, was giving in without a fight. The cold war that had gone on during the preceeding six months had produced such a state of tension that a small incident almost set light to the powder magazine. February 25, 1809, was Muharram and the Shia Muslims in Metcalfe's escort took out a procession in the streets of Amritsar. It also happened to be the day of Holi and a large number of Sikhs, chiefly Nihangs with their celebrated leader Akali Phula Singh, had foregathered in the city for the celebration. The Shia processionists wended their way through the streets till they came to the opening in front of the Golden Temple where the Sikhs were at prayer. The Nihangs remonstrated with the processionists to take another route. Arguments led to a scuffle and the Shia sepoys came to a head-on collision with the Nihangs. It is not known who were the aggressors. Even Metcalfe was doubtful and conceded that the first shot had probably been fired by one of his escort.[1] There were more casualties on the side of the Nihangs than on that of the Shias. This fact, in view of

Singh's old possessions. Ochterlony agreed to convey the gist of these representations to his government and halt for two days to enable the agents to report to Ranjit. He did not think the short delay would make much difference, particularly as the government had said it no longer wanted war. Metcalfe took umbrage at this interference with his functions. The Governor-General reprimanded Ochterlony and ordered him to continue his march. Ochterlony resigned his command and had to be persuaded later to withdraw his resignation.

Ochterlony found Metcalfe's impression that Ranjit Singh had no following in Malwa to be far from the truth. As he went through the region he discovered to his surprise that Ranjit's influence beyond the Sutlej was 'far more considerable than he had supposed, and likely to be productive of further mischief'. Some Sardars, notably Jodh Singh Kalsia, decided to abandon their estates and crossed over to Ranjit Singh to help him fight the British.
[1]Metcalfe, No. 72, of March 7, 1809.

Metcalfe's own admission that 'matchlocks of our assailants carried further and with surer aim than our musquets', does not lend support to the theory of Nihang aggression.[1]

Metcalfe could not utilize this incident as an excuse for war. His report blamed Akali Phula Singh, but not the Maharaja, who turned up on the scene immediately and personally helped to quell the riot. He also sent envoys to Metcalfe to apologize for the lack of courtesy shown to his guests and promised compensation. Seton in Delhi received a garbled version of the incident and was sure that war was inevitable, being, as he confessed, 'in some measure influenced by the reflection that the Sikhs are a wild and ferocious people'. Ochterlony also admitted that if any more incidents had taken place (the Nihangs were threatening vengeance) he had made up his mind to cross the Sutlej.

Fortunately, before the news of the incident could reach Calcutta, the Governor-General had dispatched two drafts of 'treaties' to be offered to the Durbar with orders to Ochterlony and Metcalfe regarding the details. The catastrophe of war was thus averted in the nick of time.

The two drafts consisted of three articles each and were almost identical. They provided for perpetual friendship and most-favoured nation treatment for the Lahore Durbar; recognition of the Maharaja's sovereignty over territories north of the Sutlej; and permission to keep troops south of the Sutlej to police his estates south of the river. One of the drafts had a clause appended to the second article to the effect that Ranjit Singh renounced all claim to sovereignty over Sikh chiefs to the south of the Sutlej and all right of interference in their concerns. It was made clear that this was not to force Ranjit Singh to cede his 'ancient conquests' and if he did not like it, it was not to be pressed.

The wrangling over Faridkot went on for some weeks more. Metcalfe again lost his patience and advised St. Leger to take the town by assault, assuring him that by the time the Sikhs assembled their forces the monsoons would make the Sutlej

[1]Nor the legend created by British historian that although outnumbered the sepoys worsted the Akalis and so impressed Ranjit Singh with their superior discipline that he promptly decided to Europeanize his army. His army had begun to be 'Europeanized' in 1803.

unfordable. On April 3 Faridkot was also evacuated. On the 25th
the treaty was formally signed at Amritsar—without the additional clause of the second draft. There was a week of farewell
parties. Metcalfe left the Punjab on May 2 well pleased with
himself.

Despite the treaty and the festivities that followed, ill-will
continued on both sides for quite some time. On the Durbar's
side there were people like Diwan Mohkam Chand and Akali
Phula Singh of the do-or-die school who felt that the Maharaja
should tear up the treaty and fight. Contacts were made with
the Marathas, Rohillas and Begum Samru and the air in northern India was thick with rumours of a Sikh-Maratha alliance to
expel the English from India. The English were perturbed by these
rumours and moved a detachment of troops to Hansi to prevent
Scindia or Holkar from joining up with the Punjabis.

The Maharaja kept a cool head. He listened to Mohkam
Chand, for whom he had great respect and admiration, but
refused to take his assurance of Maratha collaboration seriously.
'Let the Marathas make the first move and I will join them,'
he said. As months went by these rumours died down, the clouds
of suspicion cleared and relations between him and the English
became cordial. By the end of that year the Governor-General
was able to write to the Maharaja expressing satisfaction at the
relations existing between them. Replied Ranjit Singh with enthusiasm: 'Judge by the state of your own heart, what is the state
of mine.'

The Treaty of Amritsar was a grievous blow to Ranjit Singh's
dream of a unified Punjab. Although for the rest of his life he
professed friendship for the English nation, this friendship was
strongly tinged with fear of their might. It is strange that despite the experience of dealing with Metcalfe, Ranjit Singh seldom
distrusted the word of an Englishman.[1]

There was some heart-searching in London and Calcutta about
the ethics of the occupation of the Malwa State so soon after
the passing of the resolution that the Jumna would be the final

[1]Ranjit Singh's critics frequently became his warmest supporters, viz. Metcalfe,
Ochterlony, Wade, Jacquemont, Sir Alexander Burnes.

boundary—and without provocation from any quarter. The Secret Committee of the Board of Directors in London when reviewing the Treaty of Amritsar, was constrained to remark that there had been a departure from the principles laid down on October 19, 1801, and February 27, 1806, fixing the western limits to the possessions in India. Perhaps it was this sense of guilt which made the English effusive in their protestations of friendship for Ranjit Singh and helped him to overcome the animosity that Metcalfe's visit had aroused in him.

It is true that with the passing of the British menace, Ranjit Singh was free to turn his attention to other areas of the Punjab not within his jurisdiction. But even this freedom was circumscribed by the Treaty of Amritsar, as the English interpreted it later. Although they had agreed to have nothing to do with the affairs of the country west of the Sutlej, to them the Sutlej did not mean the river down to the sea but only as far as it joined the Indus; nor apparently were the lands beyond the Indus construed as being lands west of the Sutlej.

CHAPTER VIII

THE CAPTURE OF KANGRA AND THE INTEGRATION OF WESTERN PUNJAB

AFTER THE loss of face which followed the debacle in Malwa, Ranjit Singh had to achieve something spectacular to restore his prestige amongst his people. As soon as the Treaty of Amritsar was signed, troops were withdrawn from the Sutlej and ordered towards Kangra.

The Gurkhas under Amar Singh Thapa had once more advanced westward along the Himalayan range, sweeping the forces of the hill chieftains before them and were trying hard to capture the fort of Kangra. Sansar Chand appealed both to the English and Ranjit Singh for help. To counteract Sansar Chand's move, the Gurkhas also asked the British to help them conquer Kangra and offered tribute to Ranjit if he would stay away. The British turned down the Gurkha request and the Rajput plea on the grounds that by the Treaty of Amritsar they could not interfere in the affairs of people living to the west of the Sutlej. The Durbar rejected the overtures of the Gurkhas because it considered Kangra to be a part of the Punjab and would feel obliged to defend it against all outsiders. Sansar Chand's request was favourably received, but it was considered necessary that Kangra should first declare itself a part of the Punjab and surrender the fort to the Durbar's troops. Sansar Chand, who had been fighting a losing battle against the Gurkhas, agreed to the Durbar's terms.

The Durbar ordered the hill chiefs of the Kangra region to stop selling provisions to the Gurkhas, and its troops cut the Gurkhas' supply lines with Nepal. Ranjit Singh arrived in Kangra and demanded admission to the fort. Sansar Chand began to prevaricate. The fort, he promised, would be handed over as soon as the Gurkhas withdrew. Ranjit was not one to be taken in by this ruse, particularly by Sansar Chand, who was known not to be a man of his word. Since there was no time to argue, Ranjit promptly put Sansar Chand's son, Anirudha Chand, whom he held as hostage, under arrest. Sansar Chand yielded and on August 24, 1809, a detachment of the Durbar's troops took possession of the fort.

The Gurkhas held on stubbornly despite their limited rations. Ranjit Singh let them run out of provisions and when they started to retreat, attacked them in full force a couple of miles beyond the fort. Amar Singh Thapa turned back to face the Punjabis and placed his troops in battle formation along a hillside known as Ganesh Ghati. The hill Rajputs who had suffered at the hands of the Gurkhas opened the attack. The Gurkhas disposed of the Rajputs without much difficulty. Punjabi artillery also made little impression on the Gurkhas, who had entrenched themselves behind an escarpment. Knowing that Thapa's men had been short of food for many days and would be unable to stand the strain of hand-to-hand combat, Ranjit Singh ordered the infantry to charge. The Sikhs with their long curving *kirpāns,* closed in on the Gurkhas with their short *khukris.* Ranjit Singh, who was watching the action from a mound, mounted his horse and plunged into the fray. The battle-worn and famished Gurkhas retreated from Ganesh Ghati in disorder.

The stubborn fight put up by the Gurkhas impressed Ranjit Singh. When the action was over, he not only allowed Amar Singh Thapa time to retire without further molestation, but also ordered his Sardars to help the Gurkhas in collecting their equipment. Some of the hill Rajas, who utilized the opportunity to plunder their vanquished foe, were severely reprimanded and made to restore the loot. The remnants of the Gurkha army rested at Mandi for a short time and, being pressed by Durbar troops, resumed their weary homeward march. The Gurkha menace to the Punjab was ended for ever.

On December 24, 1809, the Maharaja entered the fort of Kangra. Amongst the chiefs who paid him homage were the rulers of Kangra, Chamba, Noorpur, Kulu and Datarpur.

Ranjit Singh could face his people once more. The towns and villages through which he passed on his way homewards were decorated to welcome him. When he reached Amritsar early in January, the guns of Govindgarh fort barked their greetings and at night all the houses in the city and the Golden Temple were illuminated in his honour. The Maharaja rode through the brightly lit streets on the back of his biggest elephant and showered silver coins on the populace. The scenes of jubilation were repeated at Lahore. Patiala and Jind sent their agents to felicitate Ranjit Singh. The short eclipse of the sun on his fortunes was over.

The victory at Kangra was an important milestone in Ranjit Singh's life. Ten years earlier, when he had become Maharaja of the Punjab, there was a cordon of hostile powers girdling his kingdom. Now he had only one powerful neighbour (the English), and they were friendly.

Ranjit Singh turned his attention once more to mopping up the little principalities which pock-marked the whole of the Punjab. Since the Mughals had ceased to be effective and the invasions from the north had destroyed administrative control, every town and village had to fend for itself. Anyone who had the means built himself a small fort, enlisted as many ruffians as he could to form his private army and levied tribute on the neighbouring village. The Sikhs had themselves risen to power in this way. But no government worth the name could tolerate private armies, private forts and arsenals which could be used to defy the central authority.

The method adopted was simple. If a misldar died, the government would allow his heir succession only on condition that he handed over his fortresses, disbanded his army and became a jagirdar of the State. Similar consequences followed when the members of a misldar's family fell out amongst themselves. In this way the estate of the Fyzullapuria misl and those of the Bhangi Sardar of Gujerat, who had fallen out with his son, were resumed.

Ranjit Singh personally conducted the operations against the Baloch tribes. In a short campaign he took Khushab and Sahiwal. While Ranjit was busy taming the Baloch tribes, his generals were fanning out in all directions, bringing scattered principalities under the authority of the Lahore Durbar. Diwan Mohkam Chand annexed the possessions of the Fyzullapuria misl with their chief town, Jullundur; Mian Ghausa took Patti and other villages near Taran Taran; Hukma Singh Chimini took Jammu and then joined the Maharaja on the Salt Range to assist him in the capture of the fort of Kusk which gave the Durbar control of the salt mines of Khewra; Desa Singh Majithia annexed the hill State of Mandi and Suket. Amongst the important places seized in these whirlwind operations were Daska, Hallowal and Mangla on the Jhelum, which opened up the northern Himalayan regions.

The Nakkais were virtually wiped out. The Durbar was not influenced by the Maharaja's or the heir-apparent's relationship with the misl, nor by the fact that the Nakkai Chief, Kahan Singh, was in the employ of the Durbar. Kahan Singh was given a jagir of Rs. 20,000 and the entire area which included Chunian, Dipalpur, Sharakpur and Kamalia was attached to the State. When the Nakkai agent protested, Ranjit Singh told him naively that he would give the territories to be readministered by Kharak Singh for was not the prince a grandson of the Nakkais? Sada Kaur's misl, the Kanhayas, also suffered partial eclipse. Her territories were spared, but those of her brother-in-law in the hill regions along the Beas were seized. These successive victories put the Maharaja in buoyant spirits. On July 2, 1810, when he saw the new moon, he ordered a salute of guns in its honour.

While the Maharaja was in the region of Khushab he received news of the arrival of Shah Shuja, brother of Shah Zaman in the Punjab. A little digression on affairs in Afghanistan may be permitted.

After the death of Ahmed Shah Abdali and his son Taimur, the real power in Afghanistan passed from the royal family, who were of the Saddozai clan, into the hands of the Barakzais led by Wazir Fateh Khan. Taimur's sons, Zaman, Shuja and Mahmud, mounted the throne and were unseated as if it were a game of musical chairs. Zaman, who had made four attempts to conquer India, was overthrown and in his place the Barakzais installed Mahmud. Mahmud put out his brother Zaman's eyes, hoping thereby to put him permanently out of the picture. But Zaman's place was taken by Shuja, who ousted Mahmud from Kabul. When Lord Minto sent out his envoys to make alliances against a possible French invasion, Shuja seemed firmly installed. But hardly had Elphinstone turned his back on Kabul when the Barakzais expelled Shuja and put back their nominee, Mahmud, in power. At the time we are speaking of Shuja had come to the Punjab to explore the possibility of enlisting Ranjit Singh's help in getting back his throne.

The Maharaja received Shuja with great courtesy, but what transpired at this meeting is not really known and can only be guessed at by Ranjit Singh's subsequent actions. Apparently Shah Shuja mentioned his title to some territories, particularly Multan and Kashmir, and wondered if he could get Ranjit Singh's help in reconquering them. The Maharaja's reply was not reassuring and the Shah left hurriedly for Peshawar.

Ranjit Singh did not form a very favourable impression of Shuja but he felt that the Afghan might very well try to reestablish himself at Multan and use it as a base of operations. Ranjit Singh decided to forestall this possibility and ordered his scattered forces to head for Multan.

Muzaffar Khan appealed to the English for help and even offered to hand over the city and the fort to them. The English would not violate the terms of the Amritsar treaty and pleaded helplessness. Then Muzaffar Khan prepared himself to fight Ranjit Singh single-handed.

Durbar troops occupied the city without much trouble. The massive fort, however, defied the Lahore artillery. The short Punjab winter gave way to the heat and the dust storms for which Multan is famous. The Maharaja become short-tempered and in his impatience he took many risks, for which officers and men paid with their lives. When Muzaffar Khan discovered that the besiegers were in trouble, he came out of the fort and attacked them. Durbar troops were put on the defensive and had to dig themselves in. The intense heat, however, settled the issue for both parties. Muzaffar Khan paid a nominal tribute to the Durbar, but the fort of Multan remained unconquered in his hands.

1811 had been a stormy year. Hardly a week went by without the citizens of Lahore being awakened at midnight or disturbed in their siestas by the clatter of the hooves of dispatch riders bringing news from distant fronts, followed by the deafening report of cannon to announce a victory. The Maharaja was back home by the autumn. He moved out of the palace in the fort to the garden of Shalamar for a well-deserved rest from the heat and fatigue of many months of fighting.

On Diwali, the Maharaja called a gathering of the States' Sardars, Generals and Counsellors at Amritsar; the venerable Sahib Singh Bedi presiding, they discussed the campaigns of the past year and the opinion was that although they had done well, their army was still not as efficient as that of the English. (Ranjit's uncle, Bhag Singh of Jind, who was present, assured them of it.) More deserters from the Company's forces had arrived in the Punjab. Fakeer Azizuddin and Bhawani Das were instructed to select well-built and good-looking young men and enlist as many as possible. The question of Multan was raised and it was unanimously agreed that it was not good enough to receive tribute from Muzaffar Khan; Multan was an integral part of the Punjab. Thereafter the Maharaja and his Ministers rode through the gaily decorated bazaars and received the ovations of the citizens.

Before the end of the year the Afghan royal family was on the Maharaja's doorstep again. Shuja, who had bidden farewell to Ranjit Singh at Khushab, had been able to regain the Afghan throne—but only for four short months; Wazir Fateh Khan Barakzai had again put Mahmud back on the seat. Shuja found his way to Attock where the Governor, Jahan Dad Khan, gave him asylum. Then, suspecting Shuja of trying to win over Wazir Fateh Khan, Jahan Dad (who was bitterly opposed to the Wazir) had Shuja put in chains and sent for safe custody to his brother, Ata Mohammed, the Governor of Kashmir.[1]

The harems of Shuja and the blinded Zaman had been given asylum and were living in Rawalpindi on a pension granted by the Durbar. While the Maharaja was busy with his military operations, it was reported to him that Zaman had been sending out envoys to foreign powers to negotiate for the restoration of his family to the throne of Kabul. Ranjit Singh found this émigré government in his territories somewhat embarrassing. To put an end to the intercourse with foreign powers, he gently suggested that the families might live in greater comfort and security in the capital. In the month of November the one-time conqueror

---

[1]Sohan Lal's version is slightly different. According to him, Ata Mohammed inveigled Shuja from the home of his brother, Jahan Dad, with an invitation and then imprisoned him. The invitation according to Sohan Lal ran: 'If you decided to come our way at present, all the objects and ends will be gained and the bride of purpose will come to take the seat in the parlour of happy desire.'

of Lahore and his concourse of wives and relations came back
to the city as beggars. The Shah was treated with·great honour.
State troops escorted him to the house set apart for him in the
city, where the Maharaja, dressed in ceremonial saffron, welcomed him with an embrace and presented to him a sum of
Rs. 1,000.

Thereafter, the one thing that disturbed the peace of the Afghan
refugees was the arrival of the agent of Wazir Fateh Khan to
solicit the help of the Maharaja for the conquest of Kashmir
where Shuja was imprisoned.

The year ended on a happy note. Towards Christmas time,
a British agent, Evaz Ali Khan, arrived at Lahore with an
English stagecoach and other gifts from the Governor-General.
The gesture marked the end of the period of Anglo-Sikh tension
and suspicion. Early in 1812 Metcalfe, who was now Resident
in Delhi, reported to his government that:

'Ranjit Singh's flourishing and vigorous power forms a contrast
with the distracted, weak and troubled state of the rival kingdoms of his neighbours.... He is irresistibly supreme in the
Punjab. Feared at home and respected abroad, he manages his
government with ability and free from all cares and apprehensions.'

It is true that in the first month of 1812, Ranjit Singh was able
to put aside cares and apprehensions and indulge himself in
arranging a spectacular wedding for his son, Kharak Singh.
Metcalfe was not far wrong when he surmised that: 'Kharak
Singh's marriage promises to be one of the most splendid
exhibitions that have occurred in India for many years.'[1]

---

[1]PC$_{18}$ of February 21, 1812.

CHAPTER IX

A PUNJAB WEDDING

IN JANUARY 1812, invitations were sent to the Governor-General and the princes and nobles of Hindustan to attend the wedding of Prince Kharak Singh. The Governor-General nominated Colonel Ochterlony to represent him. The Colonel accompanied the Rajas of Patiala, Nabha, Jind and Kythal across the Sutlej. Friend and foe were equally welcome. Sansar Chand of Kangra came himself; the Nawabs of Multan and Bhawalpur sent members of their families to represent them.

The concourse of princes, courtiers and commoners which formed the bridegroom's party left Lahore on elephants, camels and horses. They passed through Amritsar and arrived at the bride's home at the village of Fatehgarh in the district of Gurdaspur. The wedding took place amid scenes of lavish splendour,[1] the like of which had not been seen in India since the days of the Mughal emperors at the height of their power. Jaimal Singh Kanhaya loaded his daughter and the guests with presents of brocades, jewelry, elephants, cows, etc. Even Ranjit Singh felt that he had been too extravagant, and on the way back when the party stopped at Amritsar, he tried as politely as he could to ask his guests to leave. But his nature being what it was, he also invited them to come to Lahore with him. Ochterlony, Bhag Singh of Jind, Sansar Chand and the Raja of Kythal accepted the invitation.

At Amritsar, Ranjit Singh took Colonel Ochterlony inside the Govindgarh fort where the State's treasuries were kept and to which none but the most trusted officials were allowed entry. Ranjit Singh brushed aside Diwan Mohkam Chand's protest that

---

[1]The bride's father, Jaimal Singh Kanhaya, had to spend Rs. 15,000 a day just to feed his guests from the time they left Lahore. In addition, he gave Ranjit another Rs. 50,000 towards the expenses of the bridegroom's party.

this was an unwise thing to do because he wished to convince
the Englishman that the Treaty of Amritsar was a treaty of
friendship and friendship could only grow out of complete confidence. At Lahore again, despite the protests of some of the
courtiers, he took Ochterlony by the hand and showed him every
portion of the fort; its gun emplacements, its secret passages, even
its most vulnerable points. Ochterlony paid a glowing tribute to
the Maharaja's generosity and utter candour. Ranjit Singh told
Ochterlony that he intended taking Kashmir from the Afghans
and admitted his failure at Multan without making any excuses.
He spoke of English armed strength with respect. 'If Ranjit's
opinions are decisively formed on any one subject, they are on
his utter inability to contend with the British arms,' noted
Ochterlony.

Ranjit Singh and Ochterlony let their imaginations run riot.
They decided that an Anglo-Punjabi military alliance would be
a good thing; together the two could conquer countries like Afghanistan and Persia and forever end the danger of a French
invasion. Before going that far, they could jointly conquer
Multan and Kashmir. Ochterlony was so taken up by the whole
idea that he even wrote an offical note to his Governor-General
and, being a man with a practical bent of mind, examined places
in Lahore which could be converted to a storehouse to assure
a regular supply to British troops of their tot of hooch.

'It could not escape me that for mere temporary purposes the
tomb of Jehangir and its enclosure would contain grain and
liquors sufficient for a month's expenditure of a large army.'

The Governor-General was impressed with the Colonel's effusive
praise of Ranjit's hospitality and agreed to consider the
Maharaja's request for a supply of muskets as a gift. The
muskets were sent along with an English horse and a basket of
spices of the sort which were sent regularly to the Mughal
Emperor. But the Governor-General positively declined the proposal of joining Ranjit Singh in an expedition against Multan
or Kashmir. This was exactly what Ranjit Singh desired. He was
now sure that the English would not interfere if he undertook
the campaigns himself.

CHAPTER X

KASHMIR AND THE KOH-I-NOOR

AS SOON AS the wedding guests had departed, the Afghan problem came to the fore. Wazir Fateh Khan's agent had been waiting patiently to find out whether Ranjit Singh would join the Barakzais in invading Kashmir. There was also Zaman, and, even more anxious that he, Shuja's senior wife, Wafa Begum, and her sons, who were terrified at the prospect of the Barakzais and Mahmud capturing Shuja, who was in detention in Kashmir. They exhorted Ranjit Singh to invade Kashmir on his own and keep Mahmud and the Barakzias out. The Afghan agent offered an equal division of the loot and 9 lakh rupees every year to the Durbar on behalf of the Barakzais. The refugee family made a counter-offer with the only thing they had of any value— the precious gem, the Koh-i-noor diamond.[1]

Early in the spring, the pick of the Durbar's troops were ordered to the Kashmir frontier under the command of Diwan Mohkam Chand; Prince Kharak Singh accompanied him as the titular chief. Jammu and Akhnoor, which were already a part of the Durbar's domains, were garrisoned; Bhimbar and Rajauri were taken by sudden assault and their chiefs, Sultan Khan and Agar Khan, were captured and brought to Lahore. By the summer, the eastern approaches to the valley of Kashmir were in the hands of the Punjabis. Wazir Fateh Khan understood the tactics of Diwan Mohkam Chand and hastily crossed the Attock into the Punjab. As soon as the Maharaja heard of the Afghan intrusion in his territory he set out from Lahore and in quick marches arrived at Rohtas. The Wazir could no longer bypass

---

[1]Sohan Lal states this clearly enough: Wafa Begum was stricken with grief and anxiety.' She sent a message that: 'If the Maharaja puts forth good effort and brings about the occasion when the honourable Shah may come to Lahore, an invaluable piece of diamond would be offered in compensation for this service.'

him and enter Kashmir. Ranjit Singh sent a note to the Wazir asking him to explain his presence in the Punjab.

The Wazir asked for a personal meeting. It seems that the report his agent had made of the negotiations had left the Afghan uncertain whether or not the Durbar would collaborate in the invasion of Kashmir and on what terms; Wazir Fateh Khan wanted to know for himself. He was so determined on the conquest of the valley that in the event of Ranjit Singh's refusal to let him go ahead, he had arranged to have the Maharaja assassinated.[1] If, however, the Maharaja agreed, he would repeat the offer of the equal division of the loot and 9 lakhs per year.[2] The Wazir turned up for the interview with eighteen of his brothers fully armed and prepared to commit the foul murder at a signal given by him. The need to assassinate Ranjit Singh did not arise as he readily agreed to join in the venture. There is little doubt that Ranjit Singh meant to stick by his word and that the Afghans had no intention of honouring theirs. Ranjit Singh proved his good faith by suggesting that the two armies should take the Rajauri route which lay through territory already under this control rather than the one through Muzaffarabad, which might be under snow that time of the year. He provided an army of 12,000 men under his ablest generals, Diwan Mohkam Chand and Dal Singh, to accompany the Afghans. The two armies left Jhelum in the first week of December 1812.

On his return to Lahore the Maharaja was once more approached by Wafa Begum through her agents with an offer of the Koh-i-noor if her husband was delivered safely to her. Ranjit Singh again reassured her that it would be done and informed her that he had given special instructions to Diwan Mohkam Chand that his first concern was to be the rescue of the Shah.

It did not take long for the shrewd Mohkam Chand to realize that Wazir Fateh Khan meant to trick him. He warned the Maharaja and told him that the Wazir had taken two big forts with their treasuries without giving anything to the Durbar. Nevertheless, Ranjit Singh instructed Mohkam Chand 'not to be-

---

[1]Burnes, *Travels*, vol. III. p. 237.
[2]The exact terms of the agreement are not known. According to British sources Ranjit was to get 11 lacs per year or half of Kashmir. (Metcalfe to Governor-General, PC_5 of January 8, 1813.)

tray the least dissatisfaction or doubt, and to conform with the wishes of Fateh Khan with whom he would settle accounts, should he violate the engagements ratified by oaths'[1]. The Afghans pressed on through the Durbar's territory at frantic speed and were soon two marches ahead of Mohkam Chand's troops. The Diwan had no doubt that if the Afghans reached Shergarh first, they would do violence to Shah Shuja who was imprisoned there. He took a short cut and, having arrived at the fort before the Afghans, immediately assaulted it. Wazir Fateh Khan reached in time to join in the assault and force Shergarh to capitulate. While the Afghans were busy looking for the treasury, Mohkam Chand's soldiers searched the dungeons and brought away Shah Shuja to their camp. Wazir Fateh Khan demanded custody of the Shah. On Mohkam Chand's refusal to comply, he tried to take Shuja by force. When this failed, he accused the Diwan of breaking his word and refused to share the booty.[2]

Ranjit Singh was now convinced of Wazir Fateh Khan's dishonesty and opened negotiations with Jahan Dad Khan, the Governor of Attock (whose brother, Ata Mohammed had been ejected from Kashmir and who was inimical to the Wazir). Jahan Dad Khan realized that he could not withstand Wazir Fateh Khan himself; he also knew the fate that awaited him if he were defeated and fell into the Wazir's hands. He accepted Ranjit's offer of a jagir and handed over the fort of Attock to Fakeer Azizuddin.

The messenger bringing the news of the surrender of Attock arrived in Lahore well after midnight. The Maharaja was awakened and told the good tidings. He roused the entire palace staff and ordered guns to be fired. The city rocked with the crash of cannon and no one could get any sleep. In the early hours of the morning, the Maharaja rode out on his elephant showering gifts on his bleary-eyed but happy subjects.

[1]PC$_{31}$ of March 26, 1813.

[2]It is maintained by some accounts that the Governor of Shergarh had formally submitted to Shuja and asked his forgiveness before the fort capitulated and that Wazir Fateh Khan paid homage to Shuja. The Shah himself suggested that once Shergarh capitulated, he was free to go where he liked. He chose to go to Lahore because his family was living there. Sohan Lal supports the former version.

Wazir Fateh Khan discovered to his great chagrin that a fort that was considered the gateway to India was in the hands of the Punjabis.[1] He was loud in his protestations of a breach of faith. He left his brother, Azim Khan, in charge of Kashmir and returned to Peshawar. From there he wrote asking Ranjit Singh to evacuate Attock or take the consequences.

Shah Shuja was received with the same pomp and ceremonial as was his brother a year earlier and was delivered safely to Wafa Begum at Mubarak Haveli—a mansion placed at the disposal of the Afghan refugees. The very next day a message was sent asking for the delivery of the Koh-i-noor. Neither Shuja nor his wife bothered to reply to the note. Reluctance to part with so precious an object[2] was not surprising, but the Durbar had paid heavily for the Kashmir venture: over 1,000 lives had been lost and the treasury was depleted. In addition, Wazir Fateh Khan had taken possession of Kashmir without sharing the loot, and had certainly no intention of giving him 9 lakhs of rupees a year as stipulated.

A reminder was sent to Wafa Begum. She denied having the diamond with her and said that it had been pawned with a moneylender in Kandahar. Ranjit knew this to be a lie and offered to make a token payment of 3 lakhs of rupees and assign a jagir

[1]The British welcomed the passing of the fort from Afghan to Punjabi hands because it made an Afghan, or any other foreign invasion of India, more difficult. According to Sohan Lal, Metcalfe sent a letter of congratulations to Ranjit Singh and advised him never to give up the fort-and even obliquely hinted at the possibility of British help if necessary for the purpose. (*Daftar* II, p. 142.)
[2]The Koh-i-noor or the 'Mountain of Light.' Perhaps the most brilliant of all the diamonds of the world, was taken from the famous mines of Golconda and came into the hands of the Mughal Emperors. The Persian, Nadir Shah, took it along with the Peacock Throne from the Mughal Mohammed Shah in 1739 when he sacked Delhi and massacred its inhabitants. On Nadir's assassination in 1747, it came into the hands of Ahmed Shah Abdali and after his death into those of his son and successor, Taimur.

Taimur had a large number of sons, who, immediately on their father's death in 1793, began to fight amongst themselves. Shah Zaman, the fifth son, happened to be in the capital at the time and was able to take over the government and all the royal treasures—including the Koh-i-noor. His seven years' rule which included four attempts to conquer India came to an end when he was dispossessed and blinded by another brother, Mahmud. But the diamond did not fall into Mahmud's hands. From Zaman it came into the possession of yet another brother, Shah Shuja, and his wife, Wafa Begum. It was from Shah Shuja that the Koh-i-noor came to Ranjit in the manner narrated.

of Rs. 50,000 a year to the family in lieu of the Koh-i-noor. Even this offer did not bring round the Begum or her husband. Ranjit Singh's patience was exhausted; he made a peremptory demand and placed a heavy guard round Mubarak Haveli. Shuja, who had till then been treated as a royal guest, became a prisoner.

Many days went by without any move from the Shah. The rations supplied to his household were reduced and the Kotwal was instructed to treat the Shah's family as being under arrest. Shuja realized that there was no way out and at last agreed to honour his wife's word. A date was fixed for the delivery of the diamond.

On June 1, 1813, Ranjit Singh rode up to Mubarak Haveli with 600 horsemen to take over the Koh-i-noor. Shuja embraced Ranjit Singh and conducted him to the royal suite. They inquired about each other's health, and then fell silent. The prolonged silence got on Ranjit Singh's nerves and he whispered to one of his courtiers to remind the Shah of the object of his visit. The Shah beckoned to a servant and ordered him to bring the diamond from the Zenana. The servant came back with a bundle which he presented to the Maharaja. Ranjit Singh unwrapped the bundle and out came the diamond. He turned the stone round under his single eye and let Bhawani Das, who was with him and had seen the diamond with Shuja's family before, satisfy himself that it was the Koh-i-noor. Then he rewrapped it in the same cloth and without a word of thanks or farewell, hurried out of the room.[1]

[1] The Koh-i-noor episode has been deliberately distorted by historians inimical to Ranjit Singh. Fortunately Shah Shuja mentions the incident himself in some detail. The narrative after his release from Shergarh runs as follows: 'Mohkam Chand on the part of Runjit Singh informed us that his master was anxious that we should proceed to Lahore as soon as at liberty and visit the residence of our seraglio in that city; he also mentioned that his master's fame would increase by our going.' The Shah arrived in Lahore escorted by Mohkam Chand. He continues: 'On the morning of the second day, Ram Singh waited on us and demanded the Koh-i-noor for his master. We confessed that it was not in our possession, but after experiencing hospitality and assistance from Ranjit Singh, we should take his wish into consideration. Ram Singh attended the next day and received the same reply. We then experienced privation of the necessaries of life and sentinels were occasionally placed over our dwelling.' Shuja mentions Ranjit's offer to pay Rs. 40-50,000 and help to recover territory in the north which the Shah expressed willingness to accept. 'He then proposed an exchange of turbans, which is among the Sikhs a pledge of eternal friendship and we then gave him the Koh-i-noor. Two days after, the interdiction was

Ranjit Singh was delighted with the possession of the famous diamond. A week after he had acquired it he brought it out for examination. The Maratha newsletter of a week later says:

'Yesterday the noble Sarkar kept showing the Koh-i-noor, which had been very kindly given to him by Hazrat Shah Shuja-ul-Mulk, to the jewellers from whom he asked the price. It was found in weight equal to three hundred and a few more "Sarakhs" and in value it was declared priceless as no other similar jewel existed anywhere else.'

Shah Shuja was by no means reduced to penury by the loss of the Koh-i-noor. He continued to receive an allowance from the Durbar and still owned, as was proved subsequently, considerable wealth in gold and jewels.

Relations between Ranjit Singh and Shuja had been poisoned for ever. A few days later Ranjit Singh had concrete evidence of the ingratitude of the Afghan refugees. The newsletter of June 23, 1813, narrates the incident:

'Pir Batish, in charge of the police station, came in and stated that Mulla Hassan and Qazi Sher Mohammed Khan, the companions of Huzrat Shuja-ul-Mulk, had written some letters of their own accord and under their own seal to Sardar Fateh Khan Wazir; that as the messenger carrying those letters had been brought to him as a captive, therefore, he submitted those letters to the Noble Sarkar. It was written in them that the Noble Sarkar was all alone at that time in Lahore, that he had no troops with him, that if he (the Wazir) would send his troops it would not be difficult to capture Lahore.....'

Ranjit Singh was not a man of quick temper, but once his wrath was aroused, his moods could be very black indeed. He sent for

removed from our visits to the dwelling containing our family.' (*Calcutta Monthly Journal*, 1839. Autobiographical sketch by Shah Shuja written by himself in Ludhiana 1826-7 and translated by Lieut. Bennett of the Artillery.)

The facts do not do any discredit to Ranjit Singh. If he had wanted to rob the refugees, there was nothing to stop him from doing so. He knew that the diamond was with them from February 1810 when Wafa Begum came to his kingdom right up to June 1813 when he received it. Seeing the way the Koh-i-noor had been taken away from India, even a forcible repossession would not have been inexcusable. But the course Ranjit followed was an honourable one.

Shahzada Haider, the son of the blind Shah Zaman and nephew of Shah Shuja, as well as Qazi Sher Mohammed Khan, and questioned them. They had nothing to say. Ranjit Singh sent them back to Shah Shuja demanding an explanation of their conduct. The Shah wrote back that these persons had written without his knowledge and that the Maharaja was at liberty to treat them as he desired. It was obvious that Shuja was lying.[1]

[1]Shuja himself wrote to Ochterlony admitting his complicity in the plan to betray his host in inviting his erstwhile enemy, Wazir Fateh Khan, to send his brother to invade the Punjab. The letter (PC_{12} of November 12, 1813) ran as follows: 'Two months ago Mahmud Hussain Khan arrived here from my brother Mahmud with the intention of proceeding to you. When he arrived at Lahore, you will have heard the secrets were discovered by the interception of letters and Mahmud Hussain Khan in consequence put in confinement where he remained about two months.' Shuja sent his own emissary Mohammed Amir, to Ochterlony saying that he would personally explain what the Shah had to say. The letter went on : 'As we worship the same God, it is our duty jointly to extirpate the tribe of infidels who are so many in the garden of Ranjit. As soon as the flame of war shall have been lit and troops under Wazir Fateh Khan put in motion against that quarter, God willing, we shall soon put them in confusion and disorder and then divide the Punjab between us.' The plan apparently was that while the Lahore troops were busy against Wazir Fateh Khan his brother, Azim Khan the Governor of Kashmir, should invade the Punjab and 'settle the business of infidels in this city'.

On her arrival at Ludhiana, Wafa Begum wrote several letters to the Governor-General detailing the circumstances in which she came to Lahore and pleading for intercession for her husband's release. In the first (vol. 58a *Persian Letters*, December 20, 1814) he wrote: 'We had no treaty subsisting with Ranjit Singh, but when we took refuge in his domains, he procured the delivery of the King from the sons of Mukhtar-ul-Dowlah' (i.e Wazir Fateh Khan). Neither in this nor on the second where she complained of the seizure of her agent Balak Ram and her maidservants did she make any reference to Ranjit having wrongly taken the Koh-i-noor. And in the third she openly admitted the fact that her husband had been plotting Ranjit's downfall while his guest in Lahore. 'His Majesty wished to meet you and discuss with you what was for the interest of both States.... It was the pleasure of the most High Power that this scheme should be discovered by Ranjit Singh who accordingly placed his Majesty under a guard.'

It is clear that Shuja had opened negotiations both with Wazir Fateh Khan (who had decided to throw over Mahmud and back Shuja instead) and the English. The Wazir had proposed an invasion of the Punjab from either end. In his letter he has waxed poetically eloquent.

'I am prepared to dive to the bottom of the deep
Determined to seize the pearl of desire, or perish in the attempt.
My resolution is fixed and I will execute my design
The crimson tide shall mantle my cheek with joy
Or freeze in my lifeless veins.'

Ranjit Singh did not want to do more than was necessary. The two men were taken in custody and handed over to the Kotwal. Shuja was summoned to court. The newsletter of August 21, 1813, records the Maharaja's instruction to Kharak Singh, to bring Shuja 'well guarded and in perfect safety' and a letter to Shuja asking him to accompany the prince without delay as 'the Noble Sarkar had to consult him regarding certain matters'. What passed between the two is not stated, but it is reasonably certain that Ranjit Singh asked him to part with some more of his wealth and the Shah denied having any left. Ranjit Singh knew Shuja was lying again; a fortnight later Ranjit said in open court that Shuja had with him 'one saddle beset with jewels worth 25 lakhs of rupees and one big bedstead of turquoise fixed upon four legs, each of which was studded with a big diamond, and said that he proposed demanding these articles from him for himself'. The courtiers advised him to be cautious as the Koh-i-noor episode had already brought him a bad name. Ranjit ignored the advice and sent a search party of women to the Afghan harem. The newsletter of March 4, 1814, narrates the sordid episode:

'Ram Singh, the man in charge of the affairs of the Noble Sarkar, came in and stated that he had gone to the *dera* of Shuja-ul-Mulk, had demanded the jewellery, had sent five maidservants to the ladies' side of the palace, that they had brought every-thing that could be found in the interior such as jewellery, turquoise, pearls, small boxes, carpets and the like, and the Huzrat Shah Shuja-ul-Mulk had wept and cried aloud that he did not resist the will of God.'

The Afghan household was plunged in melancholy and for some days the Shah refused to eat any food. The guard on Mubarak Haveli was reduced and the royal entourage given some free-dom of movement. This relaxation of surveillance gave the Begum, and then the Shah himself, the opportunity to escape from Lahore.

Wafa Begum disappeared in November 1814. 'Can it be possible that those caught in the trap of dejection and trouble should not step outside?' she said. Ranjit Singh was eager to know how the escape had been effected and persuaded Wafa Begum's young son, Shahzada Saghir, to tell him. He did not take any additional measures to prevent others of the party leaving because about five months later (on April 13, 1815) Shuja, his two sons, and others of the party also escaped.[1]

[1]The escape was quite dramatic. The Shah and his staff dug a subterranean tunnel for Mubarak Haveli to the main drain of the city. Then one night one of his servants dressed like a king took his place, while Shuja himself made his way through the tunnel out of the city, where transport was already awaiting him. Before his disappearance could be noticed he was well away from Ranjit's clutches. Travelling by night, he went through Sialkot to Kashmir and across the mountains to the Kulu Valley and on to Simla. From there he went down to the plains and joined Wafa Begum and 600 of his other wives at Ludhiana.

CHAPTER XI

VICTORY AT ATTOCK. FAILURE
IN KASHMIR

RANJIT SINGH'S pleasure at having become master of Attock was tinged with apprehension because Wazir Fateh Khan threatened to rouse the tribes of the North-West Frontier against the Punjabis and the garrison in the Attock fort was too small to withstand a determined assault. Consequently, he thought it politic to keep up correspondence and exchange of gifts with the Wazir, who had promised to help in the capture of Multan if Ranjit gave him Attock. A relief force was in the meantime hurriedly sent forward to Attock. Then the tone of Ranjit's letters changed: he told the Afghans that he would not discuss Attock until after they had captured Multan for him. To make Attock more secure, Durbar troops occupied a forward post at Haripur.

Wazir Fateh Khan addressed several rude notes to Ranjit Singh and then roused the tribes in the vicinity of Attock to expel the infidels from their midst. Afghan troops surrounded that fort and cut off the supply route to Lahore.

The Maharaja asked Diwan Mohkam Chand to take charge of the operations. The Diwan sent Hari Singh Nalwa, and the battery commander, Mian Ghausa, ahead and followed with the main Punjabi force. The Punjabis crossed the river Attock and came face to face with Fateh Khan and his Afghan army. For three months the two armies faced each other without either offering battle. The winter gave way to spring and the short spring to the intense heat of summer. Then Diwan Mohkam Chand manoeuvred to place his force between the Afghans and the river and wrote to the Maharaja for permission to take the offensive. He did not have to wait for the order, as the Afghans, who had been cut off from their supply of drinking water, were forced to take the initiative. They made repeated charges on the

Punjabis in order to break through to the river. The doughty Diwan had the legs of his elephant chained so that it could not run back and kept his lines intact. Afghan assaults were repulsed by steady fire from the Punjabi infantry. The Punjabis could slake their thirst and return to battle; the Afghans had to fight in the sweltering heat of July without a drop of water to drink. The battle for the fort of Attock changed into a running battle for the banks of the river Attock. The Punjabis held off the Afghans until the Afghans were exhausted with thirst. Then Mohkam Chand ordered his cavalry to charge. The Afghans broke their ranks and fled, leaving their heavy guns and equipment to the victors and over 2,000 of their comrades dead on the field.[1]

This was the first victory of the Punjabis against the Pathans. That it should have been on the field of Attock was of even greater significance. The fort had been traditionally regarded as the sentinel of India. It was wrested from the Hindu Raja Jaipal in 1000 A.D. by Mahmud Ghazni and since then had remained in the hands of the invaders. Its recapture meant the liberation of Northern India from the Afghan menace.

When the news of the victory at Attock was received in Lahore, the city went wild with joy. All business was stopped and the people came out in the streets to sing and dance and yell themselves hoarse. The cannon of the fort began to roar. The Maharaja rode out of the palace to join them and scattered the usual largesse among the cheering crowds.

The success at Attock did indeed go to Ranjit Singh's head. In a full Durbar held in July to receive the felicitations of his courtiers, the newswriter records same people having stated that 'the extirpation of the English who wear the mask of friendship but hold us in deadly hate should be attempted'. Ranjit Singh replied: 'After the conquest of Kashmir and Peshawar it should be a subject of consideration.'[2]

Hardly a month had passed after the victory at Attock when Ranjit's mind turned to the vale of Kashmir. And once an idea entered his head, it could not be dislodged. He announced his plan at the annual muster of forces at Dussehra. Diwan Moh-

---

[1] A different version of the battle is given by Sir Olaf Caroe in *The Pathans*, p. 289.

[2] PC$_{17}$ of August 6, 1813.

kam Chand advised him against it as it was not the campaigning season for the mountains. But the impetuous Ranjit would not listen to the ageing Mohkam Chand and ordered the Diwan's grandson, Ram Dyal, a strapping youth of twenty, to lead the campaign against Kashmir.

The Maharaja passed through Amritsar, Pathankot, Adinanagar and halted at Sialkot in the foothills, which was to be the base camp. By the time all the troops had assembled and the details of the attack were finalized, autumn had given way to winter. Ranjit Singh moved on to Rohtas. He got word from his advance columns that the pass of Pir Panjal was blocked by a premature fall of snow. At the same time, information was received that Wazir Fateh Khan was keeping a watch on the progress of the Durbar troops in the mountains with a view to attacking the Punjab from Multan in the south. Ranjit Singh left a part of the forces with Ram Dyal with instructions to prepare the ground for a campaign in the spring, and hurried back to his capital.

Ram Dyal spent the winter months setting up a chain of food depots and collecting information on the strength of the forts, the loyalty of the inhabitants and the possibility of supplies between his advance post at Rajauri and the valley of Kashmir.

The troops were on the move as soon as they received news of the spring thaw in the mountains. By June the entire campaign force of nearly 50,000 men were encamped at Wazirabad. Diwan Mohkam Chand was lying ill in Phillaur and his place was again taken by his brave but inexperienced grandson, Ram Dyal. All the Punjab's famous generals were with the army—Hari Singh Nalwa, Meeth Singh Bharania, Jodh Singh Kalsia and the master gunner, Mian Ghausa. Ram Dyal with 30,000 men proceeded towards Baramgulla and Shupaiyan. The remainder of the force, under Ranjit Singh's personal command, headed for Poonch. The pincer movement began in the last week of July. Just then the monsoons broke in the hills.

The Maharaja was held up at Rajauri by the torrential rains. The force under Ram Dyal struggled on bravely until it reached the narrow pass of Baramgulla. There the guns of a small fortress commanding the valley brought it to an unexpected halt. There seemed no way of getting at the fort, which was on the other side of the valley, divided by a fast-moving hill torrent, or silencing its guns which were several hundred feet above them.

Agar Khan, chief of Rajauri, who only a couple of years earlier had been taken captive of Lahore, came to the rescue. He led Ram Dyal to a spot in the ravine where the stream coursed over large slabs of rock and was fordable. Ram Dyal chained the feet of his biggest elephants and stood them side by side in the bed of the stream. The troops crossed over this pachydermous bridge and in the surprise attack which followed carried the mountain fortress of Baramgulla. This was on July 20, 1814.

The column pressed forward through Adampur and Haripur till it reached Shupaiyan. Azim Khan, brother of Wazir Fateh Khan and the Governor of Kashmir, had stopped further progress with his army of Afghans. The heavy downpour added to the difficulties of the Punjabis; the Afghans were in well-covered entrenched positions. Ram Dyal decided to fight a delaying action until additional forces should arrive. Ranjit Singh sent Bhaia Ram Singh with 5,000 men towards Shupaiyan. Azim Khan's irregulars harassed Ram Singh's column all along the valley and forced it to a standstill. Ranjit Singh fared no better at Poonch. As he began his march forward, the entire population decamped after burning the standing crops and removing their livestock and chattels. The problem of food supplies became acute and Poonchi snipers would not allow the Durbar's reconnaissance parties to venture very far. Then cholera broke out amongst the Punjabi troops. (Amongst the victims was the gunner, Mian Ghausa, who died on the way to Lahore.) The Afghans and the Poonchis took the offensive and pushed Ranjit Singh out of the hills.

Ram Dyal doggedly stood his ground not far from the capital, Srinagar. Azim Khan did not want to have the Punjabis in the valley for longer than he could help. Having failed to dislodge Ram Dyal, he opened negotiations with him. There was an exchange of presents. Azim Khan professed friendship for Ranjit Singh and promised not to side with his enemies. Ram Dyal extricated himself from an awkward position and returned to Lahore.[1]

[1] There seems no evidence for Prinsep's statement that Azim Khan let the Lahore troops go unmolested because of his personal regard for Ram Dyal's grandfather,

This was Ranjit Singh's second failure in Kashmir and a sad blow to his pride. A bigger blow awaited him. After the Dussehra celebrations, when he had gone for a short rest to the Shalamar Garden, he received the news of the death (at Phillaur on October 29,1814) of his comrade-in-arms, Diwan Mohkam Chand. The Maharaja was stricken with grief. He had come to rely on the Diwan for advice on military matters and also to respect him as if he were his own father. The General was cremated with full military honours and statewide mourning was ordered. His son, Moti Ram, was recognized as successor to the Diwan's estate; the grandson, Ram Dyal, was confirmed in his military post.

Ranjit Singh had to suspend military operations as his presence was required in the capital because of the hostilities that had broken out between his eastern neighbours, the Gurkhas and the English. An envoy from Nepal, Prithi Bilas, came to Lahore to ask for Ranjit's help in expelling the English from India. In addition to the usual flattery about Ranjit Singh being the defender of the Hindus and the hope of Hindustan, the Nepalese made tempting offers of money. Prithi Bilas told Ranjit Singh of the first few engagements in the hills where the Gurkhas had had the English on the run. The Gurkha tried to convince the Sikh that the English were not as invincible as they were made out to be.

The Durbar had not forgotten that six years earlier Amar Singh Thapa had proposed to Ochterlony a joint Gurkha British invasion of the Punjab,[1] and that it was Ochterlony who had rejected the Gurkha suggestion. It was felt that it was the turn of the Punjabis to show their good faith by offering to help the British in their hour of trial. Fakeer Azizuddin was sent to Colonel Ochterlony in Ludhiana to convey the offer of assistance. The tide of battle had already turned in favour of the English. The Governor-General sent the Maharaja a letter full of expressions of gratitude, but he declined to accept any help. It was

---

Diwan Mohkam Chand. Apart from there being no record to support it, it is hardly likely that consideration of this sort would weigh with those who looked upon the Sikhs who formed the bulk of Ranjit Singh's army as 'infidels' and did not spare them even when they laid down arms.

[1]The Lahore Durbar, p. 13.

well known that Ranjit Singh was not the sort of person who gave something for nothing.

Ranjit Singh watched the Anglo-Gurkha war with close interest from Lahore. At the same time he analysed the causes of his own failure in Kashmir. His men were obviously not suited for mountain warfare. He recalled the agility of the Gurkhas in the battle of Ganesh Ghati in 1809; and a number of Gurkha deserters were now available for service. He absorbed large numbers into his army and raised some battalions composed purely of Gurkhas. He also felt that his army was not properly administered; there was confusion in the purchase of stores and equipment and in the payment of salaries. A couple of years earlier Ganga Ram, a Kashmiri Brahmin from Delhi, had joined his service as an accountant. Ganga Ram was asked to take charge of all military accounts and, at his recommendation, another Kashmiri, Pandit Dina Nath,[1] was engaged to help him. More important than either the men or the money was the hostility of the country through which the Lahore troops had to pass that had ultimately caused the failure in Kashmir. Even the chiefs of Bhimbar and Rajauri, who were with the Punjabis, had wavered when they saw the Lahore forces in trouble; they were now openly defying the Durbar's authority. After Dussehra the Maharaja himself accompanied a unit of his army to Wazirabad and sent it forward on a short campaign in which Bhimbar, Rajauri and Kotli were taken. Early in January 1816, troops were moved into Nurpur and Jaswan and the Kangra Valley. These troop movements indicated another attempt to invade Kashmir. But when the snows thawed and everyone was keyed up for a campaign in the mountains, the unpredictable Ranjit ordered the army southwards, where the six months following March are like a blazing inferno.

The object of the southern campaign was to forestall Wazir Fateh Khan's moves in that direction. Besides this, almost all the southern Nawabs had been tardy in paying the revenues due to Lahore.

The bulk of the Durbar's troops were placed under the command of Misr Diwan Chand, a new officer who had rapidly risen

[1]Dina Nath distinguished himself as one of Ranjit's ablest and most loyal administrators. He was made Diwan and later invested with the title of Raja.

in the Maharaja's estimation; the remainder were led by Ranjit Singh himself. Since the Muslim chiefs were prone to declare any skirmish with the Sikhs a 'Jihad' and enlist large numbers of fanatical Ghazis, Ranjit Singh asked Akali Phula Singh to bring along his band of Nihangs.

Diwan Chand's first objective was Bahawalpur. The Nawab made his submission, paid Rs. 80,000 in cash and promised to pay a further Rs. 70,000 annually. Muzaffar Khan of Multan was, as usual, obstructive. Some of his forts were occupied and parts of Multan plundered by the Nihangs before he paid up his arrears. Similar tactics had to be adopted against the new Nawab of Mankera.

The heat of the desert became too much for Ranjit Singh and he returned to Lahore. His army, however, continued its operations. The entire estate of Ahmed Khan Sial of Jhang, who had been in arrears for three years, was attached and the Nawab pensioned with a jagir; Fateh Singh Ahluwalia incorporated Ucch within the Durbar's territories.

Later that summer, Abdul Samad Khan of Din Panah, an important tributary of Muzaffar Khan of Multan, turned up at Lahore loudly protesting against the harsh treatment meted out to him by his overlord. The Maharaja received him with marked courtesy and invited him to be a guest of the State. Mubarak Haveli, vacated by Shah Shuja's family, was put at his disposal. It was obvious that the Nawab of Din Panah was treated with exaggerated attention in order to be used in the campaign against Multan.

Decks had now been cleared for action both against Kashmir and Multan. But before Ranjit Singh could make up his mind between going to the mountains or the desert, a domestic problem demanded his attention.

The upbringing and training of the heir-apparent, Kharak Singh, had been causing the Maharaja some concern. The boy was good-natured and well-meaning but of no great intelligence. Ranjit Singh had entrusted responsible work to him so that he could gain experience for his future duties as the head of the State. He had been given lands to administer and was put in command of many important campaigns. An able officer, Bhaia Ram Singh, was assigned to be his companion-tutor as well as manager of his estates.

Bhaia Ram Singh had disgraced himself in the Kashmir campaign and had been severely reprimanded. The public reprimand encouraged many courtiers who did not like Ram Singh to spread rumours that he was corrupt and had made a fortune for himself out of the Prince's estate. The Maharaja sent for his son and Ram Singh and asked them to show him their account books. Kharak Singh pleaded ignorance. Ram Singh was put out of countenance and was unable to explain many of the figures. Ranjit Singh lost his temper and in full Durbar ordered his son to get out of his sight. Ram Singh was placed under arrest.

Investigation into Ram Singh's affairs proved embezzlement of large sums of money. Five lacs in cash and jewellery was recovered from his banker in Amritsar and confiscated to the State. Kharak avoided coming to the Durbar for many days.

The Maharaja's counsellors advised him that he had been too severe and that, if he really intended Kharak Singh to succeed him, it was important that he should build up his son and not disgrace him in the eyes of the people. Ranjit Singh saw the wisdom of this advice and decided to reinstate Kharak Singh. In order to quash all rumours of differences with his son, he called a grand Durbar on September 27, 1816, and, in the presence of all the nobles, put the saffron mark of succession on Kharak Singh's forehead.

A month after the investiture of Kharak Singh, the Maharaja went to Amritsar to celebrate Diwali. On the evening of the festival the city was rocked by a severe earthquake followed by a violent gale which made it impossible for anyone to light their oil lamps. Then the palace chamberlain, Jemadar Khushal Singh, had a nervous breakdown and it was feared that he might lose his mind altogether. All these were interpreted as portents of evil caused by the Maharaja's harsh treatment towards someone. Ranjit Singh was a superstitious man and betook himself to Jwalamukhi to invoke the aid of the goddess to ward off further calamity. Amongst the people who cashed in on the Maharaja's penitent mood was his son Kharak Singh, who obtained pardon for his manager, Bhaia Ram Singh. Ram Singh was brought out of prison and loaded with gifts. He was given charge of the Durbar's new acquisitions—the estates of the Ramgarhias which had been attached and included important towns like Qadian and Govindpur.

The prayers and the pardons did not, however, rid the mind of the superstitious Ranjit of his fears, and he almost willed himself to sickness. He was out hunting when he was caught in a squall. He was hot and let himself be drenched in the rain to get cool. When he got back to he camp he drank copious draughts of ice-cool water. He caught a chill, which was followed by a high fever, and had to be brought back to Lahore in a palanquin. At Lahore his condition took a turn for the worse and it was feared that he would die.[1] Gradually the fever subsided but he had to remain in bed for one month before he was strong enough to stand on his feet. When the doctors pronounced him fit, he was allowed to wash his long hair. The news was received with jubilation in the city and, as on other happy occasions, the people illuminated their rooftops with oil lamps.

---

[1]There is a tradition current in the Attariwala family that when the doctors had pronounced the Maharaja's case as hopeless, Nihal Singh went round his bed three time praying to God that Ranjit's life be spared and his taken instead. The Maharaja recovered and Nihal Singh died soon after.

There is no reference to this incident by Sohan Lal, who stated that the Sardar's death was caused by excessive intake of a drug called *Chob Chini*. The story is obviously based on a similar one—of Babar's prayer and his circumambulating around the bed of his sick son Humayun.

CHAPTER XII

THE FALL OF MULTAN

'With four things rare Multan abounds
Heat, beggars, dust and burial grounds.'

THESE FOUR 'gifts', as the original Persian saying goes, explain some of the historical importance of the city of Multan. It is situated in the centre of a hot, dusty plain in the fork of two of the Punjab's important rivers, the Sutlej and the Ravi, which supply it with water for irrigation and carry merchandise between the Punjab and the sea. Since it is a prosperous agricultural and trading centre, beggars from poorer areas flock to it. It is one of the oldest cities in the Punjab: many generations of citizens lie buried in its sprawling graveyards.

Ranjit Singh had made four attempts to take this 'city of the four gifts', but had only succeeded in capturing the town: the enormous mud and brick fort which rose in the middle like a mountain had defeated him every time. Without the fort, possession of the city did not amount to very much: the guns from its walls could reach any part of Multan.

Early in 1818, the Durbar resolved to put whatever it had into capturing Multan. The chain of small Muslim states round about the city had already been broken: all that remained was Multan itself. This decision was obviously influenced by the preoccupation of the Afghans with the Persians on their western front. An indecisive engagement was reported to have been fought at Khorassan; Wazir Fateh Khan was reported to have been injured and likely to remain out of action for some time.

A force of 20,000 men under Misr Diwan Chand was ordered to Multan. To avoid bickering between the Sardars who looked upon Diwan Chand as an upstart, Prince Kharak Singh was made nominal commander to the army. Artillery, which had to play a major role in reducing the fort, was under the command of Ilahi Baksh.

Preparations were made on an elaborate scale. All the boats on the Sutlej and the Ravi were commandeered to ensure a regular supply of provisions. Depots were opened along the route. The overall charge of maintaining a free flow of war material and food grains was given to Kharak Singh's mother, Mai Nakkain, who set up her headquarters at Kamalia. The big Bhangi gun Zam Zama was ordered down to Multan. So also were platoons of Nihangs.

The Maharaja stayed on at Lahore. A dispatch rider was posted at every third mile between the capital and the army camp at Multan so that the Maharaja could obtain the latest information and be able to transmit orders.

Nawab Muzaffar Khan was aware of these large-scale preparations and realized that this time he would not be able to bribe or buy off the Durbar. He roused the populace of the countryside to fight a holy war and prepared the city and the fort for a long siege.

Nawab Muzaffar Khan had planned to defend himself in three stages: in the countryside, in the city and in the fort. The first engagement was in the open where he let his Ghazis do most of the fighting. This battle lasted only one day and the Ghazis gained the martyrdom they sought: they were a rabble armed with swords or spears and had to contend with a disciplined army equipped with muskets and field batteries. Muzaffar Khan withdrew his regulars intact behind the city walls as he had planned. The second round began by the Lahore troops surrounding the city and bombarding its walls. The defenders held them at bay for a couple of weeks till the city wall was blown up at several points. The defenders retreated into the fort to fight the third and last round.

The fort was surrounded by a large, deep moat. Although at that time of the year (March) there was no water in the moat, it prevented cannon from being brought close enough to do any serious damage to the walls and it seriously impeded the laying of a mine under the battlements. For a whole month Ilahi Baksh's batteries pounded the mud and brick without making any impression. March turned to April and the heat became unbearable. Ranjit Singh's messages became angrier.

He told Diwan Chand how much money the State had put into the venture and what disgrace it would be if they did not succeed. Diwan Chand also knew that if he did not capture the fort before the monsoons, he would never do it for the moat would be filled with water.

Ilahi Baksh redoubled his efforts and subjected the fort to intensive bombardment. The Bhangi cannon arrived in April and with each shot it sent 80 lb. of solid metal hurtling into the wall and tore huge holes in it. A spy sent out by Muzaffar Khan into the Durbar lines saw something of the enthusiasm with which the Sikh gunners under Ilahi Baksh fought. When a cannon lost one of its wheels and could not be properly fired without support, soldiers wrangled amongst each other for the privilege of having it rest on their shoulders. Many were killed with the recoil of the gun.[1] The defenders' energies were concentrated on blocking the damage done by the cannon, when a party of Nihangs stole down the moat under cover of darkness and laid a mine under another portion of the wall. Next morning a huge segment of the battlement was blown sky high.

Muzaffar Khan had had enough of fighting and sent his envoy to discuss terms of surrender. He was offered Shujabad, Khangarh and a big *jāgir* if he gave up the fort. Muzaffar Khan accepted the terms and asked for a treaty to be drawn up.

The news of Muzaffar Khan's acceptance of the terms offered made Ranjit delirious with joy. Cannons were fired to celebrate the victory and Lahore was illuminated at night. But when the draft treaty was presented to the Khan in Multan, he was dissuaded from signing it. 'It is better to die in honour than live in shame,' said his soldiers. 'We will fight the Sikhs to a finish.'

Ranjit was angered by this sudden turn of events. He sent Jemadar Khushal Singh from Lahore to tell Diwan Chand and the other generals that if Multan did not capitulate in the next few days he would want to know the reason why. He also wanted the generals to give him full details of individual acts of valour performed by his soldiers.

The Maharaja's taunts stung the soldiers to fury. The battle recommenced. The cannon blew up the bags of earth which had

[1]Ghulam Jilani in *Jangi-Multan*.

been hurriedly placed to repair the breaches. The Nihangs came to the fore again. Their leader, Sadhu Singh, led his band in a desperate charge through one of the breaches and closed in on the defenders.[1] They drove the Multanis back till they came to the steps of the Khan's place. The old Nawab and his sons donned the green garb of the Mohammedan faith, perfumed their beards and with drawn swords 'came out to answer the call of the angel of death'. Nawab Muzaffar Khan, his two sons and a nephew were killed; his two younger sons were captured alive.

The fort capitulated on June 2, 1818. The news reached Lahore three days later. This time nothing could contain the Maharaja's joy. He gave the messenger who brought the news of the victory a pair of gold bracelets and rode out on the back of his elephant to shower his people with gold and silver. Misr Diwan Chand was honoured with the title of *Zafar Jang Bahadur*—Brave Victor of Battles.

Some days later one of Muzaffar Khan's sons was brought into court. The Maharaja had heard of the valour of the old Nawab and since he admired bravery above all manly virtues, he got up from his seat and took the young Nawab in his arms. Five days later, Misr Diwan Chand arrived in Lahore with the second of Nawab Muzaffar's captive sons. The Maharaja embraced the boy and made him sit beside him. While the lad poured out his heart about the perfidy of the Durbar troops to Ranjit, the palace guns roared their welcome to the victor of Multan.

The conquest of Multan ended Afghan influence in the Punjab and broke the solid phalanx of Muslim states in the south. It subdued the chiefs of Bahawalpur, Dera Ghazi Khan, Dera Ismail Khan and Mankera. And it opened up the road to Sindh. In addition to all these military and political advantages, Multan was a valuable acquisition. It yielded an annual revenue of nearly

---

[1]Many accounts, including that of Prem Singh, give the credit of the victorious assault to Phula Singh. Sohan Lal correctly states the Phula Singh was in Attock at the time.

Ranjit Singh told the English traveller William Moorcroft that the lives of five hundred of Muzaffar Khan's men who surrendered were spared. Griffin, *Ranjit Singh* (p. 187), disbelieves this and states (without quoting his source) that the entire garrison was put to the sword. He also states that Multan was plundered and yielded two million sterling, of which five lakhs was recovered by the Durbar.

Rs. 7 lakhs.[1]

Three weeks after the victory at Multan came the Muslim festival of *Idul Fitr*. The Maharaja thought it the best occasion to pay homage to the memory of his faithful servant, Mian Ghausa, who was also the father of the Durbar artillery to which Ranjit owed many of his victories including that of Multan. He went to the mausoleum of Shah Abdul Maali which had been built by the late commander and spent some time in silent prayer amongst his Muslim subjects.

It was fortunate that Multan capitulated early in June because a few days later the monsoon burst in all its fury and it continued to rain for several days. Ranjit Singh could never resist the monsoon and loved to ride out in a downpour to see the flooded countryside and the rivers in spate. The victory of Multan had already put him in high spirits. He suspended work and spent many days in the country with his companions and watching the nautch girls perform. His favourite music for the monsoon season was the flute; and when he was tired of his boisterous parties, he dismissed the nautch girls and sat alone for several hours to listen to the flautist, Attar Khan. This carefree mood came to an abrupt end on September 28 when he nearly killed himself. He had gone to see the Ravi in flood and in a mood of exaltation plunged his horse in the river. The powerful current swept the horse and rider into midstream. Ranjit Singh was just able to get his feet out of the stirrups and swim ashore before the horse was sucked under water by a whirlpool.

The news of the Maharaja's narrow escape spread in the city. Prayers of thanksgiving were offered at the mosques and temples. Nobles and commoners waved handfuls of gold and silver round the Maharaja's head (*sir wārna*) and gave it away to beggars.

Ranjit Singh could not remain inactive for long. Since it was too early to start on another campaign, he turned his attention to problems of administration. Some ministerial changes had been

[1]According to Sohan Lal, Multan was leased out to one Diwan Sham Singh of Peshawar at Rs 6 lakhs per year; the remaining lakh being appropriated toward expenses of administration. The exact figure of income from Multan in the second year after its conquest, according to Sita Ram Kohli, was Rs. 6,80,975 (*Maharaja Ranjit Singh*, p. 148).

long overdue. He had many reports against Bhawani Das; the
most serious being that in 1817 the hunchback had taken money
from Nawab Muzaffar Khan to call off the siege of the fort of
Multan. At the time Ranjit Singh had disregarded these stories.
It is not unlikely that with the capture of Multan and the two
sons of Muzaffar Khan, Ranjit got concrete evidence of the
Minister's dishonesty. Bhawani Das was dismissed without ceremony. The other person whose presence in court had become
too irksome was Jemadar Khushal Singh. The Jemadar had
suffered a nervous breakdown and had developed an irascible
temper which led to many unpleasant exchanges in the Durbar.
He had become in Ranjit's own words a *dungāwālā*, which was
an absolute anathema to Ranjit Singh. Khushal Singh was removed from his post of Chamberlain and in his place was
appointed Dhian Singh Dogra—a man of great charm and courtesy. The Dogra introduced two other brothers in the Court. The
elder, Gulab Singh, was a smooth spoken man. The younger,
Suchet Singh, who was appointed conveyor of petitions, was in
addition to his native courtesy, strikingly handsome. The year
marked the beginning of the ascendancy of the Dogra family in
the affairs of the Lahore Durbar.

CHAPTER XIII

THE CAPTURE OF PESHAWAR
AND KASHMIR

IN THE SUMMER of 1818, Ranjit Singh got the opportunity he was waiting for to extend his kingdom in the north-west. In August, Wazir Fateh Khan was murdered by Prince Kamran, whose father Mahmud had been raised and kept on the throne of Kabul for many years by the Wazir. The Wazir's numerous brothers, who were spread out in different parts of Afghanistan, Peshawar and Kashmir called for vengeance and Afghanistan was plunged into civil war. The Maharaja sent for Akali Phula Singh, who knew the north-west frontier well, and questioned him about Attock and its environments. Phula Singh told him that Attock was like a small island in the midst of a sea of turbulent tribesmen. If the north-western bastion was to be made secure against the Afghans and Pathans, the frontier would have to be pushed further north to Peshawar, or better, up to the entrance of the Khyber Pass. The close alliance between the Afghans and Pathan tribes-men would then be broken and the most important gateway into India be slammed in the face of the invaders. There was no time to lose. The strife between the Barakzai brothers of the late Wazir and Mahmud's branch of the Saddozais had begun. In their anxiety to occupy Kabul, the rival factions had left their south-eastern frontier with the Punjab practically undefended.

On October 15, 1818, Ranjit Singh marched out of Lahore at the head of his troops. Amongst the generals with him were two who knew these lands and the people, and whose names were becoming a terror amongst the tribes, Hari Singh Nalwa and Akali Phula Singh.

The Durbar army passed through Rohtas, Rawalpindi, Hassan Abdal and arrived in the plains of Hazara. A reconnaissance party was sent across the river Attock by boat; the rest of the army halted on the eastern bank till scouts could locate a suitable ford.

The reconnaissance party was ambushed by Khattak tribesmen and completely destroyed. The place where the ambush took place was within the Durbar's territories and the Khattaks paid tribute to the Maharaja. Their dastardly attack was therefore not an act of war but one of treacherous rebellion. The news of the disaster infuriated Ranjit Singh. He ordered the troops to be lined up along the river bank and after hurling a trayful of gold coins into the stream as an offering, he rode his elephant into the whirling waters.[1] The melodramatic gesture had its effect. The men plunged their horses in the river or swam across.

The Khattaks did not put up much resistance. Their strongholds at Khairabad and Jahangiria were occupied and the Durbar troops were given permission to plunder Khattak villages. Ranjit Singh pressed on to Naushera.

The defeat of the Khattaks disheartened Mohammed Khan, the Afghan Governor of Peshawar; he fled the city leaving fourteen big guns and other war equipment intact. On November 19, 1818, Ranjit Singh entered the famous citadel of the Pathans. Contrary to the traditions of most of the Afghan and Pathan conquerors who had always plundered the towns and cities of Northern India, Ranjit Singh forbade his soldiers to lay their hands on any person or property. A proclamation was made by beat of drum assuring the citizens that they would not be molested and advising them to carry on their occupations as usual. The next morning the Maharaja rode on his elephant through the bazaars of Peshawar. It was the first time in 700 years that the city saw an Indian conqueror ride through its streets.

Ranjit Singh stayed in Peshawar only for four days. He appointed Jahan Dad Khan (who had five years earlier given him the fort of Attock) as Governor of Peshawar and returned to Lahore. Yet once again he was welcomed by the jubilant crowds as the victor of battles. The cannon of the fort barked out its welcome.

---

[1] One of the legends which became current in the Punjab and on the North-West Frontier was that as soon as Ranjit's elephant stepped into the river, the flood subsided. The legend had enormous psychological value as it gave currency to a saying among the tribesmen: 'Khudā hum Khālsā Shud'—God is on the side of Sikhs.

There was little respite for Ranjit Singh. He had hardly time to unbuckle his sword when he heard of the expulsion of his nominee Jahan Dad Khan from Peshawar by Dost Mohammed, one of the Barakzai brothers who had now become the chief actor on the Afghan stage. Before he could take any steps to restore Jahan Dad, envoys from Dost Mohammed arrived at Lahore, offered to pay a revenue of Rs. 1 lakh per year and accepted the Durbar's title over the city. The Maharaja wanted to spare his troops another troublesome campaign and being more concerned with the submission of Peshawar than with its administration, accepted the offer.

No sooner had Ranjit Singh returned to his capital than he began to talk openly of an all-out campaign in the following spring to wrest Kashmir from the Afghans. The information was conveyed to Azim Khan, the Afghan Governor of Kashmir, who sent his agents to Delhi to solicit help from the English. They were received by Colonel Ochterlony and asked to state their purpose. They lauded the greatness of Azim Khan and suggested that an alliance between him and the English would be to their mutual advantage. Ochterlony, who had received advance instructions on the subject, told them that his government could not consider it. Then, reports the Colonel, 'their tones lowered and terminated in an earnest request that Kashmir be taken under our protection'. To reconcile the two statements, the envoys explained that powerful as their master was, he wanted to go to Kabul to avenge the murder of his brother, Wazir Fateh Khan, and feared that in his absence Ranjit Singh might make an attempt on Kashmir.[1] Ochterlony explained that the British Government was bound by treaty not to interfere in the affairs of the regions west of the Sutlej and dismissed the Kashmirian envoys.

Despite the diplomatic failure at Ludhiana, Azim Khan took a chance in leaving Kashmir and going away to Afghanistan. He left his younger brother, Jabbar Khan, with a force he considered adequate to defend the valley. Jabbar Khan taught that the best policy under the circumstance was to rule with an iron hand and keep any likely collaborators of the Durbar in terror. His treatment of the non-Muslim Kashmiris became very harsh and many Hindus were compelled to leave the valley. Amongst the

[1] Ochterlony to the Governor-General (PC$_{15-16}$ of March 20, 1819).

refugees was Jabbar Khan's own Revenue Minister, Pandit Birbal
Dhar. The Pandit came to Lahore and advised the Durbar that
it was an opportune moment to invade Kashmir. Agar Khan, the
chief of Rajauri, who was in Lahore agreed that it was the right
time for an invasion. He dipped his hand in saffron (a product
of his country), put its imprint on the holy Koran and swore to
help Ranjit Singh in every way he could. By his earlier campaign
in the north-west, Ranjit Singh had snapped the link between
Kashmir and the western hinterland of Afghanistan and the
Pathan tribal territory; there was now little danger of any sizeable
force coming from those regions to oppose him. Everything
seemed propitious.

Ranjit Singh went to Amritsar to pray for success. He was
back in the capital in time for the Holi festival, which was
celebrated with greater zest that ever before. Sohan Lal waxes
lyrical in the description: 'For one quarter of the day, the
assembly of merry-making was on and the market of pleasure
remained brisk. The moon-faced beauties with their melodious
songs and blandishments made stony hearts melt like wax; the
music of joy and jollity reached the very top of the seventh
heaven.'[1]

By April, the snows had melted, the passes to the valley of
the Jhelum were clear and the forces had assembled at
Wazirabad, which had been selected as the main base of operations and the headquarters of the Maharaja. The army was
divided into three parts. One under the Maharaja's command was
to stay at the base to send assistance to the forward columns
and organize the supply of rations and war material. A column
under Misr Diwan Chand and another under Prince Kharak Singh
were to march together as far as Rajauri and thereafter they were
to divide and make a pincer movement on Shupaiyan where they
expected to meet the Afghan army.

After the two columns left for Rajauri, the Maharaja got secret
information that Agar Khan was likely to defect. To forestall the
danger he ordered the release of Sultan Khan, Chief of Bhimbar
(who had been in prison for seven years), and offered to reinstate and reward him if he undertook to guide the Durbar troops
over the mountain routes. Ranjit Singh was correct in his judg-
ment of the two men. As soon as advance columns of the Durbar

[1]*Daftar* II, p. 247.

had their first skirmish with the Afghans, Agar Khan went over to the enemy and the Durbar army had to rely on Sultan Khan of Bhimbar.

Kharak Singh's column advanced without much opposition up to Baramgulla and, directed by Sultan Khan, was able to side-track the Poonchis and reach Shupaiyan. From the other end, after crossing the Pir Panjal range, Diwan Chand despite losses inflicted on him by Afghan snipers, pushed on and the two columns came in view of each other and of Jabbar Khan with 12,00C Afghans in battle formation on the plain of Shupaiyan.

Diwan Chand let his troops rest for a few days. When the men were refreshed, he quietly surrounded the Afghan host. In the early hours of the morning of July 3, Durbar batteries opened up on the Afghans. Jabbar Khan, who did not have as many guns as the Punjabis, ordered his cavalry to charge. Afghan horsemen captured many Punjabi guns. Akali Phula Singh flung his Nihangs against the Afghan horsemen and infantry. The Afghans recoiled from the shock of the Nihang charge, turned and fled into the hills. Jabbar Khan was severely wounded and barely escaped with his life.

News of the victory reached the Maharaja the next day whilst he was marching forward to the help of his troops. Sohan Lal who was with Ranjit Singh at the time describes the scene:

'At noon an angel from the Unknown brought the news that the paradise-like Kashmir had come within the possession of the well-wishers of the powerful state. From all sides arose the voice of congratulations and Wah Guru Ji ki Fateh.'

Prince Kharak Singh and Misr Diwan Chand entered Srinagar the next day and received the victors with acclaim. The Prince issued strict orders against looting or molesting of citizens.

The Maharaja returned to the plains. He first went to Amritsar for thanksgiving and the city abandoned itself to a riotous celebration. On September 22 he was back in Lahore where he rode through triumphal arches set up in his honour.

Fakeer Azizuddin was instructed to make a detailed report on the people, climate, produce and general conditions of Kashmir. Moti Ram, the son of the late Diwan Mohkam Chand, was

appointed Governor. Troops were billeted in different towns to
mop up pockets of Afghan resistance and to extend the control
of the government to its furthest borders. Kashmir was an
important acquisition for the Punjab. Apart from the Rs 70 lakhs
it fetched every year in revenue, it extended the frontiers of the
State to the borders of China and Tibet.

In February 1820, Ranjit Singh toured his southern dominions.
His first long halt was at Multan and his first public act was
to pay homage at the tomb of Nawab Muzaffar Khan. He
celebrated Holi in Multan with his usual zeal, riding out on his
elephant into the steets and spraying coloured water and powder on the crowds. The gaiety of Holi was prolonged by the
news of the birth of sons to two of his wives, Daya Kaur and
Ratan Kaur.[1] He decided to name the boys Peshaura Singh and
Kashmira Singh in commemoration of his latest victories.
    From Multan Ranjit Singh sent Jemadar Khushal Singh against
Nawab Zaman Khan of Dera Ghazi Khan. The Nawab was expelled from the city and the district was assigned to the Nawab
of Bahawalpur at an annual payment of Rs. 3 lakhs per year.

Ranjit Singh had to cut short his stay in Multan on account of
reports of widespread disturbances in the north-west. Ever since
Kashmir had passed into Punjabi hands, Pathan tribesmen in
Hazara had been restive. Prince Sher Singh, who was becoming
popular with the soldiers, was ordered to conduct the operations
against the tribes. With him was his grandmother, Sada Kaur,
Fateh Singh Ahluwalia, Gunner Ilahi Baksh and the youthful Ram
Dyal, the grandson of Diwan Mohkam Chand. The pacification
of Hazara was in the nature of mopping up of scattered tribal
concentrations. In one of these operations, Ram Dyal, who was
chasing a party of tribesmen, was caught in a blinding dust storm
and separated from his troops. The tribesmen captured and
murdered Ram Dyal.
    This news was a great shock to the Maharaja who had seen
signs of Mohkam Chand's greatness as a military leader in his

[1]These two were widows of Sahib Singh Bhangi of Gujerat who died in 1811;
Ranjit Singh took them under his mantle (*Chaddar andāzi*), as was customary
among the Jat tribes of the Punjab.

young grandson. Moti Ram was prostrated with grief at the loss of his son and retired to Benares to pray and meditate. In Moti Ram's absence, Hari Singh Nalwa was appointed Governor of Kashmir.

The administration of Hazara was entrusted to Fateh Singh Ahluwalia and Kirpa Ram. To keep the tribes in check, they began to build a chain of forts and garrisoned them as police posts. Despite these measures, the tribes remained a major problem for the Lahore Durbar.

In the summer of 1821 an English horse merchant, William Moorcroft, arrived in Lahore with letters from senior officials of the East India Company and waited on Ranjit Singh. The Maharaja received him with courtesy and gave him the permit to travel to Kashmir and Ladakh that he had asked for. At Ladakh, Moorcroft instigated the chiefs to reiterate their loyalty to the Mughal Emperor on the grounds that they had always owed allegiance to the Delhi Durbar (which was under the control of the English). Moorcroft had the impudence to address Ranjit Singh and tell him that the people were ready to revolt if he tried to make his control more effective.[1] The Maharaja passed this letter on the the British Government which censured Moorcroft for his 'act of singular indiscretion'[2] and clearly informed him that he had not diplomatic or representative status. Ranjit Singh was not convinced[3] by the explanation as Moorcroft continued to operate in Central Asia till he was murdered, presumably by the Afghans. It is not unlikely that the Maharaja's subsequent reserve in taking Englishmen and Anglo-Indians into his service and his eagerness to employ men of nationalities inimical to the English sprang from his experience of William Moorcroft.

Ranjit Singh caught a bad cold that summer. He tried to shake it off by hard exercise but his craving for ice-cold water after

[1]Moorcroft, vol. 69a of July 29, 1821.
[2]PC$_{93}$ of October 27, 1821.
[3]Nevertheless the Maharaja thanked the Governor-General for his action against Moorcroft (letter dated February 2, 1822, vol. 70 Persian letters) and wrote that: 'Friendship was refreshed with a fragrant drop of dew...it gave me delight as the rose-petal in the beak of the bulbul on the dawn of accomplished hopes.'

a long ride prolonged the cold brought on a cough and fever. Owing to this illness, he started taking opium. He found it soothed his nerves and continued taking it even when it was not necessary.

The Maharaja was not fully recovered from his illness when a domestic issue which had been brewing for some years came to the boil. His relations with his mother-in-law, Sada Kaur, had been strained for many years. She had been hostile to him during his negotiations with Metcalfe; she had later refused to come to the wedding of Prince Kharak Singh and forbidden her grandsons Sher Singh and Tara Singh to attend. Since the investiture of Kharak Singh as heir-apparent she had been complaining bitterly that while many jagirs had been conferred on Kharak Singh, nothing had been given to the sons born to her daughter, Mehtab Kaur, who had died some time earlier. The Maharaja lost patience with Sada Kaur's constant bickering and decided to settle the matter once for all. Sada Kaur was in her seventies and had no heirs apart from Sher Singh and Tara Singh. He told her to let Sher Singh take over the administration of her estates. Sada Kaur knew Ranjit Singh well enough to guess that this was not an idle suggestion. Could she persuade the English to save her from her son-in-law? She had estates on both sides of the Sutlej (Whadni in Ferozepur had been given to her by Ranjit Singh) and decided to cross the river on the pretence of seeing how her lands were being managed. When Ranjit Singh heard of her plans, he invited her to Lahore to discuss the matter of jagirs for the two boys. Sada Kaur did not suspect that a man whom she had dominated for so many years would ever dare to treat her with any thing but deference, and accepted Ranjit's invitation. Once she was in Lahore, the Maharaja's tone changed. He told her bluntly that he had conferred her estates on her grandsons and that she was to retire. Sada Kaur raved and ranted but Ranjit Singh was unmoved. She realized that in Lahore she would get no help, but if she could get back to Batala, she might be able to resist the Durbar's troops for some time and, if compelled to do so, cross the Sutlej and appeal to the English. She quietly slipped out of the capital, but her disappearance was noticed before she had gone very far. A body of horsemen was sent after her and she was brought back to the city as prisoner. Misra Diwan

Chand and Sham Singh Attariwala were instructed to sequester Sada Kaur's estate. Kanhaya forts were occupied and their militia incorporated in the State army. Batala, which had been the ancestral home of the Kanhaya Sardars, was given to Prince Sher Singh as a jagir; the rest was joined onto the district of Kangra.

Sada Kaur was understandably bitter against her ungrateful son-in-law. The Lahore Akhbars of May 1822 describe a touching scene between two of her maidservants and Ranjit Singh. They came to Ranjit's tent and greeted him on behalf of their mistress. Ranjit replied to their greeting with the words: 'Sada Kaur is not my mother nor I her son.' The maidservants asked the Maharaja if he had forgotten how their mistress had helped him on the battlefield and made him what he was. Their mistress had wanted it conveyed that instead of imprisoning her and having her watched by women of low caste, she wished to be put to death. If Ranjit Singh wanted Whadni back, she would be willing. (Since Whadni was on the British side of the Sutlej, Ranjit could not get it without Sada Kaur giving it to him.) The maidservants broke down and wept. There were also tears in Ranjit's eyes. He promised to call on Sada Kaur but was noncommittal in his reply to the other complaints. He dismissed the maidservants with a sigh: 'Such has been the will of God.'

Ranjit Singh never went to see Sada Kaur. She died in confinement full of angry recriminations against the Maharaja.

While Diwan Chand was engaged in taking over Sada Kaur's estates on behalf of the Durbar, Ranjit Singh went southwards towards Mankera. The estates of Nawab Hafiz Ahmed Khan lay on both sides of the Indus and included important towns like Leiah, Bhakkar and Dera Ismail Khan. There was considerable mercantile traffic on the river and the caravan route from Persia and Baluchistan to India passed through his territory. Despite the barren nature of the land, Mankera was worth Rs. 10 lakhs a year in revenue. It was also politically important. The Nawab, like other Muslim chieftains of the region, had become independent. When forced by circumstances he preferred to pay tribute to the ruler of Afghanistan, from whose ancestors his forefathers had acquired their title, rather than to the Punjab to which the region belonged both historically and geographically.

In October 1821 Ranjit Singh crossed the Jhelum into Khushab
and was joined by Ahmed Yar, the Chief of the Tiwanas. The
fort of Bhakkar capitulated without firing a shot. Ranjit Singh
stayed on at Bhakkar and sent out two forces in different directions. One division consisting of 15,000 men under Jamadar
Khushal Singh and Dal Singh captured Dera Ismail Khan. The
other force under Misra Diwan Chand (who had come down after
sequestering Sada Kaur's estates) took Leiah and Khangarh and
then the three armies converged and marched on to Mankera.

Mankera lay in the midst of a sandy desert with no
stream or water tank for miles around. The Nawab's only hope
was to hold out until the water supply of the Durbar troops ran
out. Ranjit Singh had anticipated such a situation and in three
days enough wells were dug to provide drinking water for the
soldiers. The siege only lasted a fortnight. The Nawab accepted
the offer of a jagir and safe residence at Dera Ismail Khan and
handed over the fort with its arsenal intact. With the fall of
Mankera, the huge tract of land between the Jhelum and the
Indus, the Sind Sagar Doab, was added to the Punjab.

On February 22, 1822, Ranjit Singh became a grandfather. A
son was born to the wife of the heir-apparent, Kharak Singh,
and given the name Nau Nihal Singh. The Maharaja had a
special tent with poles of solid gold erected to receive felicitations from his nobles. They came one by one and presented
nazars. Diwan Chand and Jemadar Khushal Singh took handfuls
of gold coins, waved them round Ranjit's head and gave them
away to charity.

CHAPTER XIV

RANJIT SINGH AND HIS FERINGHEES

A FEW DAYS after the birth of Nau Nihal two Europeans[1] arrived at Lahore. The Maharaja received the feringhees (foreigners) in his usual courteous manner and asked them to be seated beside him on the carpet. Through an interpreter he inquired after their health, from where they had come what their plans were and whether they had any knowledge of military matters. They explained they were soldiers and had travelled through Constantinople, Baghdad, Persia, Kandahar, Kabul Peshawar and Attock to come to Lahore. The Maharaja then asked them about their views on the armies of these countries, the relative merits of French and English as soldiers, the fighting qualities of the Sikhs. He listened to their answers and then asked them if it was their pleasure to stay with him. They replied that they were not looking for service but only meant to pass the hot season at Lahore; then added significantly—they would proceed where their *Kismet* led them. The Maharaja knew precisely what they wanted.

That afternoon he tried to test their military skill by asking them to put one of his battalions through some movements. They refused to submit to the trial. 'What your battalions have learnt they have learnt; we are not able to teach them,' they replied, and added, 'a shawl once woven, cannot be woven in another fashion.' They asked the Maharaja to give them raw recruits, whom they could teach, and offered to train a battalion free of charge. They had it tactfully conveyed to the Maharaja that they

[1]Ranjit Singh had been kept informed of their progress towards Lahore by his agents in the neighbouring states. On March 12, 1822, he sent a note of reprimand to the newswriter at Peshawar for not sending word of the ingress of these men across the frontier and demanded an explanation from the Lahore newswriter for having failed to note the arrival of the feringhees at Shahadara.

had been colonels in Bonaparte's army drawing fifty gold *mohurs* per day. However, as a special concession, they would be willing to accept only 'ten gold mohurs each per diem, independent of the keep of their horses and servants', The Maharaja made no further observation but decided to find out more about the visitors. Their manner of speech convinced him that they were men of rank and consequence. He asked them to address an application to him in French and send it to Delhi for translation; he also wished to be advised whether it was the sort of language a real Frenchman would write under the circumstances. At Lahore the negotiations were kept up; the Maharaja started with an offer of Rs. 10 per day, the Europeans protesting that they had drawn fifty times as much from Napoleon, whose friendship they had also enjoyed. They showed the Durbar's agent a tray full of gold coins to prove that they were well off and did not really need employment.

At the end of two months Ranjit Singh had satisfied himself that the two were genuine Frenchmen and not English passing for French; that they had in fact been officers in Napoleon's army and knew a great deal about military matters. Then with his usual generosity he gave them the money they wanted, and even more. Jean Francois Allard was required to train the cavalry. Jean Baptiste Ventura was instructed to raise battalions of infantry.

Allard and Ventura were not the first Europeans to join Ranjit Singh's service; the first was a foreigner called Price, who deserted from Ochterlony's unit and joined up at Lahore in 1809. Thereafter there was a steady stream of one or two showing up every other month. Most of them were half-castes, being the illegitimate offspring of Englishmen through native women. Some bore famous names, e.g. Van Cortlandt, son of Colonel Van Cortlandt of the 19th Dragoons; Robert Dick, son of Major General Sir Robert Dick of the 42nd Highlanders; Jacob Thomas, son of the famous adventurer, George Thomas; others of similar parentage bore unknown names. The Maharaja was, however, anxious to keep the number of English and Anglo-Indians in his service as low as possible, because he could not rely on their loyalties in the event of a conflict with the Company's forces. He had also reason to suspect that some of these men had been planted on him so that the English might be kept informed of military movements and the state of preparedness. The only foreigners upon whom he could rely were the French, or those who at one time or another had fought the English.

The employment of Allard and Ventura is significant as thereafter it became the policy of the Durbar (largely Ranjit Singh himself because most of the ministers were opposed to it) to take in as many qualified foreigners as possible. Within a few years there were over fifty of various nationalities—French, English, Italian, Spanish, Greek, American and Eurasian—on the payrolls of the Durbar.

Ranjit Singh was liberal in the terms he offered the foreigners. They were given higher wages than Indians of similar rank and treated with greater consideration than other subordinates. But he never really trusted any of them.

By the terms of contract the feringhees undertook for the period of their service to 'abstain from eating beef and smoking or shaving' (these practices being forbidden by the Sikh faith) and promised that they 'would domesticate themselves in the country by marriage, would never quit service without formal permission from the Maharaja and would engage to fight any nation against whom the Maharaja declared war, even should it be their own'.

Ranjit Singh was only partially successful in persuading this flotsam and jetsam of Europe to make permanent homes in the Punjab. Although they showed no reluctance in conforming to the outward practices of the Khalsa and enthusiastically 'domesticated' themselves by taking on harems of native women, it did not make them put out roots in the soil or develop loyalty to the master whose salt they ate. When they had made their pile, they left their wives, mistresses and children frequently unprovided for — and returned to their homelands to lead respectable 'Christian' lives.

Ranjit Singh looked upon his European officers as highly paid drill-sergeants. Most of his conquests had been made before 1822 by men like Mohkam Chand, Hari Singh Nalwa and Misr Diwan Chand. Even after 1822 the real commanders of the Durbar army were Punjabi officers or the Maharaja's own sons, Kharak Singh and Sher Singh. Ranjit Singh also took precautions against the foreign officers ganging up against him by never allowing more than one to be in the capital with his troops. The

distance at which Ranjit Singh kept his Europeans was evidenced
by the protocol observed at Court. Although some of them
attained the rank of general and were made governors of important districts, not one was ever allowed the privilege of a seat
at formal functions. And there were times when Ranjit Singh let
loose his temper on them. The Lahore Akhbar of January 13,
1825, mentions an incident when the Maharaja had requested
his French officers to contribute two months of their salary to
meet the heavy deficit incurred in the campaign against the
Yusufzais. The Frenchmen told the Maharaja's messenger curtly
that they would not give a pice. Ranjit Singh sent for them.
When they appeared,

'the Maharaja boiling with anger drew his sword and rising from
his seat ran to the officers with the intention of destroying them.
But Sardar Himmat Singh and other officers present took the
weapon from his hand and caused him to be again seated. Then
he gave the French officers gross abuse and again rising and
drawing his dagger he flew at them several times until his officers with folded hands begged him to forgive their faults.'

Such outbursts of rage were rare. But Ranjit Singh's attitude to
his European officers was consistently distrustful. Once when sack-
ing the German Mevius (self-styled Baron de Mevius) he ex-
ploded: 'German, French or English, all these European bastards
are alike.'

The careers of these European adventurers are colourful enough
to permit a little diversion.

Allard became Ranjit Singh's favourite European officer. He
was perhaps the only one of the foreigners who had genuine
affection for his master. The French traveller-botanist Jacquement
noticed the hold he had on the Maharaja. 'M. Allard is quite
the Suleiman Bey of Ranjit Singh,' he wrote. Masson, who met
Allard in 1829, noted that

'the establishments of the general are on the most splendid scale,
for the liberality of Ranjit Singh, who appreciated his merits,

enabled him to enjoy all the luxuries of a refined state, and to amass wealth besides.'

Allard was a much-decorated man. He was a Chevalier of the Legion of Honour and the recipient of the Order of the Durrani Empire. To these Ranjit Singh added the Order of the Star of the Prosperity of the Punjab.

The Maharaja was reluctant to let his European officers go on leave to their countries as there was no guarantee of their ever coming back. He was particularly averse to letting Allard go. Nevertheless when in one year Allard lost all his money due to the crashing of the English bank in which he had invested it, and his daughter died, the Maharaja sanctioned leave. Allard took his Kashmiri wife and her remaining children to France.

While on leave, Allard had called on King Louis Phillipe and conveyed the compliment of his adoptive sovereign to his natural one. The latter returned the gesture and gave Allard a letter appointing him as France's representative to the Durbar. As a matter of course, a copy was forwarded to the Governor-General. The British Government objected to any foreign country opening diplomatic relations with Ranjit Singh without first consulting it. Ranjit Singh dealt with the crisis by explaining that the letter was mostly an expression of friendship. Louis Philippe had written: 'Although long distances and oceans part the Kingdom of the Punjab from that of France, there is no bar to the love that binds our hearts together.'

Allard brought a large consignment of French cuirasses, carbines, pistols and other arms for the Maharaja. Ranjit Singh was very pleased with Allard and in addition to paying for the arms, gave him Rs. 30,000 as leave pay. The Frenchman burst forth in poetic rapture and recited a Persian poem he had composed in praise of his master.

> 'O God, may my King live long,
> May the firmament be as a slave in his service,
> May I reach his royal court and be honoured,
> And should I ever disobey his command, may
>   death come over me,
> When I die let my grave be in Lahore
> And my remains be interred in Anarkalee.'

Allard served Ranjit Singh another five years before he suc-
cumbed to a heart attack at Peshawar in January 1839. His body
was embalmed and brought to Lahore. As the bier passed
through the cities, people came out to pay homage and salutes
were fired. From Shahadara the entire three mile route from
across the river to Allard's residence in Anarkali was lined with
soldiers. His body lay in state in a room decorated with flags
and flowers and thousands of citizens filed past. Barr, who
happened to be present in Lahore at the time, records his
impressions:

'He (Allard) was beloved by both European and Indian alike.
He was much loved by the Maharaja and they were afraid to
tell him of Allard's death, his own health being precarious. The
portrait of Allard bespeaks him a man of firmness and decision
of character and a handsome and benevolent man. He wore a
uniform somewhat resembling that of our horse artillery, with
two orders, one being the Legion of Honour, and the other
Ranjit's new order. In another picture were the pretty faces of
his Kashmiri wife and his children who were dressed in the
costume of the country, and drew the admiration of all.'

Jean Baptiste Ventura was the most eminent of the Durbar's
European officers. Murray, who met him in 1827, described him
as a fine looking young man, about 33 years of age, 'very neat
in his person and dress, and wearing his beard long'. Ventura
trained the best of the Durbar's infantry divisions, particularly
the Gurkha units. The uniform that he designed for his Gurkhas
was taken over by the British and is to this day worn by troops
of that race.

Although Ranjit Singh had a very high opinion of Ventura's
ability, and, in his later years, entrusted him with any difficult
missions, he never warmed towards him. This, however, did not
prevent Ranjit from being extremely generous towards him. Only
three years after joining his service, Ventura was given permission to go to Ludhiana to marry an Armenian woman. On the
return of the couple to Lahore, the Maharaja and the noblemen

---

[1]Allard's house still stands in Lahore—a miniature Versailles in the midst of
an Oriental bazaar. One mound is the dilapidated grave of his daughter,
Charlotte. He lies buried in a cemetery outside the city wall.

loaded them with presents estimated to be worth Rs 40,000.

The Christian marriage did not change Ventura's style of living in Lahore. He continued to maintain a harem of Kashmiri and Punjabi women in the city. When he returned to France, he left his wife in Ludhiana and only took his daughter with him. Ventura returned to the Punjab a few months before the Maharaja's death. Being a close friend of Prince Sher Singh he played a very important role in the affairs of state in the years that followed. He left the Punjab soon after Sher Singh's assassination but returned once again to claim compensation for his confiscated jagirs, he was given the title of the 'Count of Mandi' before he died in Paris.

Two other Europeans who came to the Punjab together and rose to positions of importance were the Frenchman, M. Henri Court, and the Italian, Paolo de Avitabile. Apart from having been travelling companions, they were utterly unlike each other. Court was a man of noble birth and had been educated at the Military Polytechnic; he was correct, courteous and cold. The Italian had risen from the ranks and was a rough and rude soldier. Court was content to travel in modest comfort; Avitabile liked to travel ostentatiously and met the expenses of his journey by selling artificial jewellery, watches, musical boxes and obscene pictures.

They joined the Durbar's service in 1827. Within a few years Avitabile was drawing Rs. 5,000 per month, with jagirs thrown in. Court was given Rs. 2,500 per month but was able to make up with the expensive presents the Maharaja gave him. They both lived in style. Avitabile in a gaudily done-up house: the walls of his bedroom covered with pictures of underclad nautch girls, his 'angeli custodi' (guardian angels), as he called them.

Three years later, Avitabile was made Governor of Wazirabad. Since he was a ruthless administrator he was transferred to Peshawar to control the Pathan tribesmen who had in one year alone murdered more than one hundred Sikh soldiers in cold blood. The way he subdued the tribesmen is described by him in his own words: 'When I marched into Peshawar, I sent on in advance a number of wooden post which my men erected around the walls of the city. The men scoffed at them, and laughed at the madness of the feringhee and harder still when my men came in and laid coils of rope at the foot of the posts. Guns and swords, said they, were the arms to rule the city and not sticks and ropes. However, when my preparations were completed and they found one fine morning dangling from these posts, fifty of the worst characters in Peshawar they thought differently. And I repeated the exhibition every day till I had made a scarcity of brigands and murderers.

'Then I had to deal with the liars and tale bearers. My method with them was to cut out their tongues... and when a surgeon appeared and professed to be able to restore their speech, I sent for him and cut out his tongue also. After that there was peace, and in six months there was no crime in Peshawar.'

This flamboyant, stout man, upwards of six feet high was, despite his morbid pastimes, clever and full of fun. He organized assistance to the English in the Kabul campaign and stayed on in Lahore for a few years after Ranjit Singh's death. When he left the Punjab he fixed a pension for all the women in his harem and married off his favourite daughter (born of a Pathan woman) to his cook.

Avitabile had a royal reception on his return to Europe. He was received by King Louis Philippe of France who awarded him the Cross of the Legion of Honour and honorary rank of General of the French Army. In London, the East India Company gave him a banquet and presented him with a sword of honour. The man who had bullied the Pathans of Peshawar was cuckolded by a village wench. He died soon after his marriage in circumstances which caused considerable speculation in the Italian countryside.

Court was made in an altogether different mould. Although a soldier of distinction (he held the honorary rank of General in the French Army), he was essentially a man of scholastic tastes. He was a fellow of the Royal Geographical Society and a member of several scientific societies. He is described as a 'very well dressed, short, thick man pitted with small-pox', looking like a rough and ready sailor. What he lacked in looks, he apparently made up in ability. In a Persian inscription on one of the many guns cast by him, he is described as a 'Sahib possessing wisdom like Aristotle and Plato of the age'. As ordnance officer he cast many cannon in the foundry at Lahore and trained an excellent set of gunners. European writers are wont to give him credit for the superiority of Sikh artillery over the British. The brains behind Ranjit's ordnance works were not Court's but Lehna Singh Majithia's. It was to Majithia that Ranjit Singh turned whenever he saw a new and powerful weapon and it was Majithia who invariably succeeded in producing something better. Court was essentially an administrator—and not a very successful one at that. He was about the most unpopular European officer in the Durbar's army and had many times to be rescued from the wrath of his men.

Court's scholastic bent of mind did not prevent him from maintaining a harem. His house (which was a mausoleum converted to a residence) still stands in Lahore. It has a small mosque which he built for his Kashmiri wife who now sleeps under its floor. When he left the Punjab in 1845, he took a considerable amount of wealth (he was drawing Rs. 40,000 a year) and a Kashmiri woman whom he later married in France.

An officer who might have risen high in the Durbar army if he had lived longer was a Spaniard, Señor Oms. Ranjit Singh was very taken up by 'Musa Sahib's' energy and enthusiasm and started him on a salary much higher than the initial salaries given to Court or Avitabile. He also allowed him to convert the vast gardens surrounding Jehangir's tomb at Shahadara for his residence. Oms fell a victim to the cholera epidemic which broke out in the autumn of 1828. Superstitious Muslims ascribed his health to the shade of Emperor Jehangh whose rest he had disturbed by squatting on his premises. Under the Maharaja's orders Oms was buried in the same mausoleum (so that the shade of the Señor could contend with that of the Mughal).

An American who flitted across the pages of Ranjit Singh's life for a few memorable years was an incredible wind-bag, Josiah Harlan, who posed successively as doctor, scholar, statesman and soldier. He was, surprisingly, able to worm his way into the favour of so shrewd a judge of men as Ranjit Singh. Harlan served as a 'doctor' with the British Army in the Burmese wars. After an inglorious discharge he crossed the frontier into the Punjab and was hired by Ranjit Singh in 1829. Within a few months of his arrival he was made Governor of Nurpur and Jasrota and three years later, Governor of Gujerat. Dr Wolff gives a delightful picture of his meeting with the American. Whilst waiting in the entrance hall, he heard someone singing 'Yankee Doodle' with the true American snuffle. Presently in came the Governor himself, who was a fine tall man, dressed in European clothing and smoking a hookah. Wolff asked him how he came to know 'Yankee Doodle'. The American answered in his nasal tone: 'I am a free citizen of the United States, from the city of Philadelphia. I am the son of a Quaker. My name is Josiah Harlan.'

Harlan tells of how he came to be employed by Ranjit Singh. He was (according to himself) engaged in making himself king of Afghanistan when he was defeated by the Durbar Army and taken prisoner. Ranjit Singh, seeing how talented he was, said to him: 'I will make you Governor of Gujerat. If you behave well, I will increase your salary. If not, I'll cut off your nose.'

When Harlan was sworn in as Governor of Gujerat he took a solemn oath on the Bible that he would serve Ranjit Singh faithfully for the rest of his life even to fighting against his own country if ordered to do so. This did not prevent him from intriguing with Ranjit Singh's bitterest enemy, Dost Mohammed. Later when Ranjit Singh was stricken with paralysis and rendered speechless, Harlan had it conveyed that he had medicine which could cure him. The Maharaja sent a courtier to fetch the concoction. Harlan blandly demanded Rs.1 lakh in advance. Ranjit Singh had him stripped of all his possessions and put across the river Sutlej without any ceremony. The outraged Harlan proclaimed his intention of joining Dost Mohammed and bringing down an army on the Punjab.

Harlan's post as Governor of Gujerat was filled by Holmes, an Anglo-Indian who had risen from bandmaster to colonel. Holmes was later suspected of treason against the Durbar and was shot and beheaded by his own men.

CHAPTER XV

THE BATTLE OF NAUSHERA

A FEW MONTHS after Ventura and Allard had joined service, their newly-trained platoons were called upon to show their mettle on the field of battle. Trouble had been simmering on the North-West Frontier all through the summer. Fakeer Azizuddin's visit to Peshawar to collect revenue owing to the Durbar; the ceremonial reception accorded to him by Yar Mohammed who ordered the city to be illuminated in the Fakeer's honour, further irritated the tribesmen. Yar and his brother, Dost Mohammed, expressed their loyalty to Ranjit Singh and Yar Mohammed paid what was due from him in cash and horses. He politely expressed inability to obtain the fleet-footed Persian horse, 'Gauharbar', which Ranjit Singh had specially asked for. Azizuddin returned to Lahore reasonably satisfied with his mission.

The Fakeer had hardly turned his footsteps homewards to Lahore when the Pathan tribes flared up in open revolt against Yar Mohammed. The chief instigator was Yar's elder brother, Azim Khan, who exploited the religious sentiments of the tribesmen to his own advantage by proclaiming his intention of liberating the Pathans from the yoke of the infidel. The cry of Jihad once more echoed in the barren defiles of the Khyber and within a few days over 25,000 Ghazis, mostly of the Yusufzai and Khattak tribes, volunteered to fight under the green banner of the Prophet and gain either victory or martyrdom. Yar Mohammed abandoned Peshawar and went into hiding in the neighbouring hills. (It was conjectured that he was not altogether unwilling to hand over Peshawar since otherwise he might have sought refuge with Ranjit Singh.)

The Durbar ordered the army northwards. Misr Diwan Chand, Hari Singh Nalwa and Akali Phula Singh were amongst the Punjabi generals. With them were Allard, Ventura and the

Gurkha Balbhadra, leading their newly-trained battalions.

Prince Sher Singh and Hari Singh Nalwa led the advance columns. They spanned the Attock by means of a pontoon bridge and came up to the fort of Jahangiria. The Maharaja followed in easy stages hunting wild boar and waterfowl on the way and arrived on the eastern bank of the river by the end of January. To his dismay he found that the Afghans had destroyed the pontoon bridge. His son, who had taken Jahangiria, was now besieged with the entire country round about thirsting for his blood. Conducting the siege operations were Azim's brothers, Dost Mohammed (who had more than once paid tribute to the Durbar) and Jabbar Khan, who had been ousted from Kashmir four years earlier.

The early thaw in the mountains made the Attock impassable and Afghan snipers would not allow the engineers to lash boats together. Sher Singh was in a precarious position.

One evening an informer brought intelligence that the Afghans planned to annihilate Sher Singh's force at Jahangiria next day. There was no time to lose. In the early hours of the morning Ranjit Singh ordered his soldiers to cross the Attock as best they could. He was the first to plunge his horse in the stream; the rest of the army followed: elephants, camels, horses and mules with men clinging to them. Many were carried away by the current and much valuable equipment was lost. Nevertheless before the Afghan snipers could arrive on the scene the Punjabis had control of the western bank. The Ghazis were taken by surprise and retreated. The gates of Jahangiria fort were thrown open and Prince Sher Singh welcomed his father with filial gratitude.[1]

The Ghazis who had retired from Jehangiria entrenched themselves in the plain outside Naushera. Between Naushera and

[1] A dramatic episode took place one night at Jahangiria. Jai Singh Attariwala who had deserted two years earlier and joined the Afghans, suddenly arrived in the fort, and being conducted to the Maharaja's presence, fell at his feet craving forgiveness. Ranjit Singh took the errant Sardar in his embrace and forgave him. Jai Singh narrated the incident which had caused him to desert the Afghan camp. He was in Peshawar with Azim Khan when the heads of thirty Sikh soldiers were brought into the Afghan court. A courtier contemptuously kicked one of the heads with his foot. This was too much for Jai Singh and he took the first opportunity to escape and rejoin his countrymen.

Peshawar ran the stream Landai; on the western bank of the Landai were the Afghan regulars. Ranjit Singh consulted his generals. Ventura advised an immediate attack: 'Today the strength of the Maharaja would prove ten times greater than the Afghans. Tomorrow the situation may be reversed', he said. He explained that if the Afghan regulars on the western bank of the Landai were allowed to cross the stream and join the Ghazis at Naushera, the enemy would become far too numerous for the Punjabis.

The Durbar artillery flanked Naushera, reached the bank of the Landai and trained its guns on the opposite bank where the Afghan regulars were lined up. The infantry and the cavalry faced the Ghazis entrenched on a hillock called Pir Sabak, which the Punjabis called Tibba Tiri.

When Azim Khan was apprised of the Punjabi manoeuvre, he hurried from Peshawar and joined his brother on the bank of the Landai. The guns across the stream made it impossible for them to go to the help of the Ghazis. Meanwhile Ranjit Singh prepared to take the offensive. He rode up to a mound and took the salute from the troops going into action. The cavalry galloped past him dipping its colours and shouting 'Sat Sri Akal'. The Maharaja acknowledged the salutation by raising his unsheathed kirpan to his forehead. And so the battle commenced. It was an unequal fight, Moorcroft, who was present, sent an account to the Governor-General.[1] He wrote:

'The matchlock, the bow, the spear, the sword, the knife and even the staff of an undisciplined multitude were about to be opposed by the cannon, the musket, the matchlock and the sabre directed by disciplined artillerists... under the command of Ranjit Singh himself and consisting of the flower of the Sikh army.'

The attack was opened by the infantry but their fire proved ineffective against the Ghazi stockades. The Sikh cavalry was ordered to charge. Moorcroft describes how one line of horsemen galloped up to the enemy, fired, wheeled and turned back and were followed by another line doing precisely the same thing. The Ghazis realized that this sort of distant combat would go

[1]SC$_9$ of October 29, 1824.

against them. They came down from Pir Sabak hill and made a wild charge on the Punjabis. They captured two of the Punjabi's guns; but before they could discover how the guns were fired or spiked, the Sikh cavalry recaptured them. Then the Durbar's Mussulman Najibs and Gurkhas counter-charged and drove the remaining concentration of Ghazis on the eminence of Pir Sabak westward till they were within range of the Durbar's artillery on the Landai. The guns wheeled round and opened fire. The Ghazis made a desperate bid to get away but the Sikh Nihangs led by Akali Phula Singh burst on them and for one hour the rival bands of fanatics were locked in a deadly hand-to-hand combat. Phula Singh's horse was shot under him. He took an elephant and pressed on. The Ghazis were able to see the man who had so often humbled them and trained their muskets on his howdah. Phula Singh's body was riddled with bullets and he collapsed on his elephant. The news of his death further infuriated the Nihangs who gave no quarter to the enemy. The annihilation of the Ghazis began in the afternoon when the Sikh cavalry rode into disorganized masses of Ghazis and transfixed them with lances. Mohammed Azim Khan watched the massacre from the other side of the stream. As the shades of twilight fell he saw some of the Ghazis who had broken through the Punjabi cordon floundering in the Attock; over 300 were drowned in the attempt to swim across. Azim Khan was too ashamed to face the people of Peshawar and turned his footsteps to Afghanistan.[1]

Moorcroft's estimate of casualties was 4,000 Afghans dead. The Durbar losses, though much less, included besides Akali Phula Singh, the Gurkha Commander Balbhadra. It was a crushing defeat for the Afghans and convinced the frontier tribesmen of the superiority of Punjabi arms over those of the Afghans.

Three days later the Maharaja entered Peshawar at the head of his victorious troops. The citizens welcomed him and paid him tribute with gifts. At night the bazaars were illuminated in his honour. But the Maharaja's sojourn was not peaceful. What the tribesmen could not achieve in open combat, they tried to do by cold-blooded murder of sentinels under cover of darkness.

[1] Sir Olaf Caroe gives a different version of the battle. See *The Pathans*, p. 269.

Moorcroft describes the tactics employed by the tribesmen to harass the Punjabis. They would tie hundreds of stakes to a long rope and set fire to the tops. Then two men would hold the rope from either end and advance towards the Punjabi encampment. The Durbar artillery would blaze out, the infantry fire volleys, and since there was no return fire, the cavalry would charge the row of lit up stakes. While the Durbar troops were thus employed fighting two men, the tribesmen would come in from the rear and plunder their baggage.

Ranjit Singh wearied of these tactics. A few days later when both Yar Mohammed and Dost Mohammed presented themselves and craved his pardon, he forgave them readily and accepted their tribute of presents and horses (including the famous 'Gauharbar'). Yar Mohammed was reinstated Governor of Peshawar on promising an annual revenue of a lakh and 10,000 rupees to the Lahore Durbar. Ranjit Singh turned homewards with evident relief.

The Maharaja arrived back in Lahore on the Muslim festival of *Shabi-i-barāt*. Hindus and Sikhs joined their Muslim brethren in the celebration and greeted their victorious monarch with songs of welcome. Once more it was roses, roses all the way with Ranjit Singh showering gold and silver on the crowds. The dark nights were made bright with myriads of oil lamps and rent with the explosion of rockets and salvos.

The Durbar's conquests had reached the furthest geographical limits of the Punjab in the north and north-west. Beyond were impassable mountains and inhospitable, unprofitable regions. If the Punjabi empire was to expand any further, it could only be over the Sindh desert to the sea or across the Sutlej to India. The latter alternative was not possible for the simple reason that the English with the whole of Hindustan behind them were far too strong for the Punjabis. Ranjit Singh's mind had been turning towards Sindh for some time. But before he could take any steps in that direction, the English sent their agents to the Amirs or Sindh. When news of the Anglo-Sindhian negotiations reached Lahore, there was loud talk in the Durbar of settling the issue with the English once and for all. The Punjabis were flushed with victories over the Afghans and Pathans and sabre-rattling was natural to their temperament. Newswriters posted by the English at Lahore began to send reports of an impending Punjabi invasion of Hindustan to the English Agent at Ludhiana. The Agent added comments of his own to the despatches he forwarded to the Governor-General. Within a few months, the whole of British India began to buzz with rumours of Punjabi troop concentrations on the Sutlej and Ranjit Singh's plans to extend his arms over the sub-continent. When war started on the Burmese front, there was considerable uneasiness in English circles over what the Punjabis might do when the Sutlej frontier was left unguarded. Begum Samru was said to be in communication with the Lahore Durbar; the exiled Raja of Nagpur was said to have offered Ranjit Singh large sums of money if he went to war against the English; envoys sent by the Gurkhas and the Marthas were reported to have been seen in Lahore. The English Agent at Ludhiana addressed a note to the Maharaja asking him to explain the troop movements and the massing of arms. Since there was no massing of arms or men nor any other kind of preparation for war in the Punjab, Ranjit Singh answered with a gentle rebuke that the Agent should not lend a ready ear to gossipmongers; if he had any suspicions he should first have a word with the Durbar's representative in Ludhiana. The note ended with the advice, 'Let the mirror of friendship be kept clear and polished.'[1] The British Government despite the protests of their agent in Ludhiana that the English never listened to gossip took the rebuke with a sigh of relief.

Ranjit Singh might well have utilized the British preccupation on the Burmese front to forward his ambitions in Sindh if he had been physically capable of undertaking it himself. That year he suffered the first of the series of ·attacks of paralysis which ultimately shattered his iron constitution. Besides this personal incapacity, the campaign on the North-West Frontier had been ruinously expensive and the pay of the army was heavily in arrears. (The request for contributions from the French officers was made at this time.) Partial relief (Rs. 20 lakhs) came from

[1]PC$_{23}$ of October 11, 1822.

the estate of Ramanand Saraf,[1] a millionaire banker of Amritsar who died intestate in September 1823. But this was not enough to meet all the State's obligations or finance another major campaign. Consequently the first priority was to raise money.

After the usual muster of forces at Dussehra, the Maharaja toured South-Western Punjab and realized dues from the Muslim chiefs. He spent Diwali at Khushab. Early in November he crossed and recrossed the Indus at Attock and with short halts passed through Bannu, Dera Ismail Khan, Bhakkar, Leiah and Dera Ghazi Khan. By December he was back in his capital with the coffers of the treasury fuller than they had been for a long time. That month there was another small windfall. Raja Sansar Chand of Kangra died and his son Anirudha Chand paid a lakh of rupees to the Lahore Durbar as succession duty.

In July 1825 Misr Diwan Chand died. His death was a grievous loss to the Durbar which was left with very few Punjabi generals of any ability. As a result the Maharaja began to turn more and more to his European officers, particularly to Ventura, to plan his strategy. The nominal command was, as before entrusted to one of his sons, Kharak Singh, or more often to Sher Singh who had begun to attract his father's attention as an up and coming army commander who was also popular with the rank and file.

Sher Singh's growing popularity began to worry Kharak Singh and his mother, Raj Kaur. In January 1826 when Ranjit Singh went on tour he appointed Sher Singh to deputize for him at Lahore. Kharak Singh took the appointment as a personal snub. Later that year when Ranjit was taken seriously ill, Kharak Singh opened communication with the British to elicit their support for his succession. It was through these communications that Kharak gave currency to the gossip that neither Sher Singh nor Tara Singh were the real sons of Ranjit Singh but foundlings planted on the Maharaja by Sada Kaur.

The filial situation was still brewing when Ranjit Singh's old friend and brother-in-arms, Fateh Singh Ahluwalia, suddenly panicked and fled across the Sutlej. His nervousness was not

---

[1]Ramanand's frugal habits made him a legend. People would not mention his name in the morning for fear of going hungry for the rest of the day.

altogether unreasonable. Ranjit Singh had liquidated all the misls and principalities in the Punjab under his control one after another till only two of them were left. Then Sada Kaur had also been eliminated and only the Ahluwalia household remained. People began to say it was only a matter of time and Feteh Singh would go the way of the other Sardars. The chief mischief-makers were Fateh Singh's own agents at Lahore. These men tried to prove their loyalty to Fateh Singh by suggesting that he would be safer across the Sutlej. They played on his fears till he packed up bag and baggage, crossed the Sutlej and asked the English Agent for protection.[1]

The English were as embarrassed with their guest as Ranjit Singh was pained to find that one of his closest associates should have distrusted him. Fortunately neither party tried to exploit the situation. The English could have kept Fateh Singh and used him against the Durbar at a later date. And Ranjit Singh could certainly have profited by taking over the entire Ahluwalia estate. The English Agent tried to persuade Fateh Singh to go back and make his peace with the Maharaja. Ranjit Singh sent his envoys to convince him that his fears had been absolutely imaginary. The crestfallen Fateh Singh returned to his home in the Punjab. Ranjit Singh sent his grandson, Nau Nihal Singh, and Dhian Singh (who had only a few days earlier been given the title of Raja and had become the Chief of the Council of Ministers) to receive him and escort him to Lahore. The meeting between the two friends was full of melodrama. Fateh Singh placed his unsheathed sword at the Maharaja's feet, knelt down and asked Ranjit Singh to behead him as punishment for the act of treachery. Ranjit Singh took Fateh Singh in his arms and the two men burst into tears. Fateh Singh's estates were guaranteed for ever, and he was loaded with expensive presents including an elephant with a highly ornamental howdah.

In the summer of 1826, Ranjit Singh was again taken ill. 'According to the revolution of the tyrannical heavens, the disposition of the Maharaja got adrift from the pivot of normality,'

---

[1]The actual 'incident' which precipitated Fateh Singh's departure was an order from Ranjit Singh to the Sardar that he should stop building a fort (which he was doing) as the Maharaja did not like chiefs to have too many forts.

recorded Sohan Lal. Rumours got round that the Lion was mortally stricken. People began to prepare for the eventuality. 'People who were fond of sensational news began to talk much nonsense,' wrote Sohan Lal, 'but the sincere wellwishers, faithful servants and old attendants were lost in restlessness and prayed for help from the Lord Most High.' Ranjit Singh himself felt that his days were numbered and asked to be taken to Amritsar where he spent the whole afternoon at prayer in the Harmandir. Fakeer Imamuddin was sent to Ludhiana to fetch an English physician. The Governor-General lent the services of Dr Murray. The doctor persuaded the Maharaja to move out of the city to the Shalamar Gardens. There, according to Sohan Lal,

'The sweet-smelling breeze of health and normality blew upon the garden of his blissful temperament...trees of pleasure and mirth put forth fruits of happiness and merriment and the bud of the heart of the people, which had become wilted, blossomed.'

By Dussehra the Maharaja was on his feet. Dr Murray was handsomely rewarded with money and presents and allowed to leave. Ranjut Singh went to Amritsar to celebrate Diwali and give thanks to the Guru for having spared his life.

CHAPTER XVI

WATERING THE SAPLING
OF FRIENDSHIP

THE LONG ILLNESS did not dim any of the fire in the Maharaja. He was barely able to get back into the saddle when his mind turned once again towards Sindh. The English had until then done little more than sound the different Amirs with proposals for treaties of commerce. What Ranjit wondered was whether trade was only a veil to cover political design, the thin end of the wedge to open the way to outright annexation. He pinned his faith on the treaty of 1809 whereby the English had solemnly undertaken not to interfere in the affairs of countries west of the Sutlej. Nevertheless he wanted to be reassured that they would abide by the terms of their agreement before he embarked on the venture. There were other minor matters connected with his possessions in Malwa which needed clarification.

The Governor-General, Lord Amherst, had left Calcutta and was making his way through the hot, dusty plains towards the cool heights of Simla. Ranjit Singh sent him a message of greetings couched in florid orientalese on his approach to the Punjab frontier. 'God knows how great a desire for a meeting has circumambulated the mansions of my heart,' he wrote. He regretted that Dr Murray had forbidden him to undertake the journey and his sons, Kharak Singh and Sher Singh, were engaged in military campaigns a long way away. He was consequently compelled to have his good wishes conveyed through his trusted servants, Diwan Moti Ram and Fakeer Imamuddin. Lord Amherst reciprocated the Maharaja's sentiments and invited the two envoys to meet him at Simla.

Moti Ram and Imamuddin were received by the Governor-General at a ceremonial Durbar attended by senior British officers and the Rajas of the neighbouring states. Captain Wade, the Agent at Ludhiana, acted as liaison officer. The envoys presented the Governor-General with expensive Kashmir shawls, a string of thoroughbred horses and an elephant. There was also a superbly embroidered tent made of the best Kashmir wool for the King of England.

In the speeches of goodwill the envoys referred to the Durbar's claim to certain towns across Sutlej and indicated that the Maharaja had his eye on Sindh. Lord Amherst's reply was restricted to expressions of friendship. He also announced that a delegation of senior officials of the Company would pay a return visit to Lahore.

The English delegation, consisting of Captain Wade, Captain Pearson, A.D.C. to the Governor-General, and surgeon Gerrard, was received by the Maharaja at Amritsar in the last week of May 1827. They presented a string of English thoroughbreds, an elephant, a bejewelled sword, guns, pistols and brocades from Benares on behalf of the Governor-General. Ranjit Singh again mentioned the fact that he had claims over certain towns in Malwa and was contemplating taking Sindh under his protection. The English envoys made no comment on either point.

There were other things besides the uncertainty of English reactions that made Ranjit Singh hold his hand on Sindh: an earthquake in Kashmir which caused heavy loss of life and property was followed by a failure of the monsoon and wide-spread famine in the valley; Lahore was stricken with cholera; Ranjit's own health was too delicate to risk his staying in the city and he sought refuge across the Ravi at Dilkusha. Besides the earthquake, famine and disease, there was trouble brewing in Kangra and a new menace had appeared on the North-West Frontier in the person of the Muslim fanatic, Syed Ahmed, who had again roused the tribesmen to a holy war against the infidel Sikhs.

The trouble in Kangra arose out of a simple misunderstanding. For some time past, the Dogra brothers, Gulab Singh, Dhian Singh and Suchet Singh, had become the dominant element in the Lahore Durbar. Of the three, Dhian Singh was pre-eminent. He had first replaced Jemadar Khushal Singh as the Lord Chamberlain (*deorhidār*) and then been elevated to the position of Chief Minister. In March 1828, the Maharaja had formally invested him with the title *Rajā-i-Rājgān*—Chief among the Rajas.

Dhian Singh's son, Hira Singh, a precocious and handsome lad
for whom the Maharaja had conceived more affection than he
had his own sons, was allowed to take a seat on formal occasions when other courtiers, including his father, Dhian Singh,
were expected to remain standing. He was allowed to speak
without waiting for permission from the Maharaja; and he often
spoke his mind without fear of rebuke. He travelled with Ranjit
Singh in the same palanqin or howdah and rode beside him on
horseback when they went out hunting. On the Dussehra of 1828
the Maharaja put the saffron mark on the boy's forehead investing
him with the title of Raja. He was eager to find a suitable wife
for his protege. Of the aristocratic families of Rajputs of the hills
there was none more blue-blooded than that of Sansar Chand of
Kangra.

Sansar Chand had died in the winter of 1823 leaving behind
a large number of children through his wives and concubines.
His son, Anirudha Chand who succeeded him, had two real
sisters both unmarried. In 1825, when Ranjit was visiting
Jwalamukhi and Anirudha Chand came to call on him, he
mentioned the desirability of linking the Dogra household with
Sansar Chand's. Anirudha kept silent but had it later conveyed
to the Maharaja that he could not consider an alliance between
his family, which had a long proud lineage, and the Dogras who
were upstarts. Anirudha's mother, a fiery old Rajput woman,
swore that she would rather see her daughter dead than let her
wed Hira Singh. When Ranjit Singh expressed his displeasure,
Anirudha Chand slipped across the Sutlej and sought the protection of the English. He gave away his two sisters in marriage
to the ruler of Tehri-Garhwal.

The Maharaja was very piqued at Anirudha Chand's haughty
behaviour. He sequestered Kangra and took two of Sansar
Chand's daughters who were famed for their good looks into the
royal harem. A year later, he found Hira Singh a bride and
arranged the wedding on a lavish scale as though the boy had
been his own son.

The period of military inactivity was utilized in carrying out public works and reorganizing the administration of justice. Roads
were constructed to link the bigger towns. The one from Lahore
to Amritsar was repaired; trees were planted on either side and

rest houses built along the route. Gardens were laid out in Amritsar and Lahore.

The Punjab had no codified law—except to the extent that the *Shariat* could be described as a code for the Muslims. But all Punjabis (including Muslims) were governed by well-recognized custom. This customary law was administered by a succession of courts, of which the village *Panchayat* (council of five elders) was the primary and the most important tribunal. If one of the parties was dissatisfied with the arbitration of the Panchayat, it went in appeal to the *Kardār*, or in larger towns to the *Nāzim*. In many towns the Durbar appointed officers' *adālatis* whose sole function was to hear appeals from *Panchāyats*. Lahore had an appellate tribunal, the *adālat-i-ālā*, of its own. The Maharaja and his Durbar acted as the Supreme Court where the decisions of the *Kardārs*, *Nāzims* and *Adālatis* could be impugned.

The aforementioned tribunals heard all kinds of cases: civil, revenue, matrimonial and criminal. Crime was punished by well-understood and generally accepted penalties. There was no capital punishment and except where the *Nāzim* enforced material law (as Avitabile did on the North-West Frontier) even murder could only be punished with fine or mutilation of limbs. Gaols were usually maintained only for political prisoners. Violence and theft were punished with a fine or corporal punishment, frequently by the cutting of the nose, ears or hands. Justice was crude—but it was cheap, expeditious and in conformity with tradition.

The Maharaja began to take more interest in the administration of justice and personally heard complaints of corruption against Judicial Officers. The mode of appeal was the one practised by the rulers of Northern India. Any person who had failed to get justice could come to the palace gates or stop the monarch on tour with the cry '*dohai, Mahārājā, dohai*' (mercy, Maharaja, mercy); and present his petition. Ranjit Singh disposed of such petitions summarily or passed them on to one of his ministers. He was not satisfied with the state of the law and in 1828 appointed Bahadur Singh Hindustani to prepare a Civil and a Criminal Code.[1] Prince Sher Singh was given judicial training.

[1] Sohan Lal Suri was appointed to assist Bahadur Singh. No record of the written code has, however, been found.

With the affairs of Kangra settled, the Maharaja turned his attention to the unrest on the North-West Frontier fomented by Syed Ahmed a native of Rai Bareilly in Uttar Pradesh. The Syed was a follower of a well-known Muslim divine of Delhi, Shah Waliullah, who had started the *Targhib-i-Mohammadiyya*, a branch of the Wahabi movement in India. Syed Ahmed met Waliullah and soon became the leader of the movement to expel the infidel from Hindustan. His two chief lieutenants were Shah Ismail and Maulvi Abdul Haye. Syed Ahmed went on an extensive tour from Delhi to Calcutta adressing mammoth meetings. Nearly 100,000 men volunteered to join his crusade and money poured in from all quarters. Amongst the patrons were the Mughal King of Delhi and the Muslim rulers of many states, particularly the Nawab of Tonk.

In 1822 Syed Ahmed went to Mecca to pray for success. He got in touch with the Wahabis and 'Whatever was dreaming in his nature now gave place to a fiery ecstasy, in which he beheld himself planting the crescent throughout every district in India.'[1] On his return to India Syed Ahmed proclaimed his crusade and asked the Muslims to join him. Although the English were as infidel in his eyes as the Sikhs, he made it clear that the war was against the Sikhs and not the English. The Government of India consequently made no attempt to check the movement.[2] On the contrary, it was allowed to gather strength, and thousands of armed volunteers were trained in India and then permitted to cross over to Sindh on the way to the North-West Frontier of the Punjab. Crusading centres which collected arms and money functioned without let or hindrance in all the big cities of India. A pamphlet widely circulated in Northern India throws light on the progress of the movement. It reads:

[1] W.W. Hunter, *Indian Mussalmans*, pp. 14-15
[2] Mirza Hairat Delhvi tells us in the *Itayat-i-Taiyaba* that, in consultation with Maulana Shah Mohammed Ismail, Syed Ahmed Shah informed the Lieutenant-Governor of the North-West Frontier Province through Sheikh Ghulam Ali Reis of Allahabad that he was preparing for a *Jihād* against the Sikhs and hoped that the British Government had no objection to it. The Lieutenant-Governor wrote back to him in reply that as long as the peace of their territories was not disturbed, they had nothing to say, nor had they any objection to such preparation. Ganda Singh, *Private correspondence in relation to the Anglo-Sikh Wars*, p. 30

'The Sikh nation has long held sway in Lahore and other places. Their oppressions have exceeded all bounds. Thousands of Mohammedans have they unjustly killed, and on thousands they have heaped disgrace. No longer do they allow the call to prayer from the mosques, and the killing of cows they have entirely prohibited. When at last their insulting tyranny could no more be endured, Huzrat Sayyid Ahmed (may his fortunes and blessings ever abide!) having for his single object the protection of the Faith, took with him a few Mussulmans, and going in the direction of Kabul and Peshawar, succeeded in rousing Mohammedans from their slumber of indifference and nerving their courage for action. Praise be to God, some thousands of believers became ready at his call to tread the path of God's service; and on December 21, 1826, the Jihad against the infidel Sikhs begins.'

The Indian crusaders were joined by the Pathan tribesmen, mainly the Yusufzais and the Khattaks, who were always on the look out for an excuse to loot the Punjab. Yar Mohammed, true to his fickle and dishonest nature, decided to throw in his lot with what he believed would be the winning side, and evacuated Peshawar.

Ranjit sent Budh Singh Sandha walia ('one of the ablest and most intelligent commanders in the Punjab service' — Wade) along with Ventura and Allard to recapture Peshawar. Syed Ahmed marched forward and met Sandhawalia's forces at Akora near Attock on December 21, 1826. Religious fervour proved a poor match for discipline; the crusaders were pushed aside and Peshawar reoccupied. Yar Mohammed was on his knees again craving for pardon. He sent his brother as hostage, paid tribute in horses[1] and goods and promised to be faithful.

The crusaders survived this setback. It was explained away as a reverse only for Yar Mohammed, who was denounced as a collaborator. Syed Ahmed retired to the hills from where he started harassing stray columns of Punjabi troops. These skirmishes were magnified into victories and the whole of Muslim India was kept in a state of jubilation. Metcalfe reported the

[1]According to Sohan Lal, Yar Mohammed surrendered Leili, the most famous horse in Ranjit's stables. Leili arrived in Lahore in October 1827. According to other historians, it was handed over by Yar's brother Sultan Mohammed to General Ventura. (Griffin, pp. 102-3. 1957 edition.)

repercussion in India to the Governor-General in the following words:

'Syed Ahmed, Maulvi Ismail and their colleagues have established a very extensive, if not universal, influence over the minds of our Mohammedan subjects. During the period of their recent attacks on Ranjit Singh's territories, the most fervent anxiety for their success pervaded the Mohamedan population at Delhi. A number quitted their houses and marched to join them, including some who resigned their employment in the Company's service, both the military and civil branches, for that purpose. It is said that the King of Delhi encouraged this spirit.'[1]

Syed Ahmed's bold tactics soon put the Durbar's forces on the defensive. The Durbar's envoys tried to buy off some of the tribes but the crusaders' influence overcame the temptation of the infidels' cash. They swarmed all over the country around Peshawar. In the summer of 1830 Prince Sher Singh took the initiative and inflicted a severe defeat on the crusaders. Even this did not hold them back. A few months later Yar Mohammed was slain in a skirmish and his brother had to evacuate Peshawar. Syed Ahmed entered the city as a conqueror and proclaimed himself Caliph. Coins were struck in his name bearing the inscription 'Ahmed the Just; the glitter of whose scimitar scatters destruction among the infidels.' Success went to the Syed's head. As Muslims from all over India, Sindh and Kashmir flocked to his banner, he began to assume the airs of a conquering hero. Pathan tribesmen became restive at the influx of foreigners on their soil and the demands they made for food and women—particularly women. Then the Durbar's rupee diplomacy began to pay dividends, Many tribes deserted Syed Ahmed; some turned against the Hindustanis and murdered them in cold blood. Syed Ahmed was compelled to retire from Peshawar and the city was reoccupied by Prince Sher Singh.

Syed Ahmed found himself sandwiched between the Punjabis and hostile tribesmen. Early in May 1831 Prince Sher Singh surprised a small band led by the Syed at Balakot near Mansehra and annihilated it. Alexander Gardner, who later became a

[1]PC$_{38}$ of June 6, 1827.

colonel in the Punjab army and was with the crusaders at the
time, gave an account of this skirmish in the following words:

'Syed Ahmed and the Maulvi (Abdul Haye), surrounded by his
surviving Indian followers, were fighting desperately hand to hand
with the equally fanatical Akalis of the Sikh army. They had
been taken by surprise and isolated from the main body of the
Syed's forces, which fought very badly without their leader. Even
as I caught sight of the Syed and Maulvi they fell pierced by
a hundred weapons. Those around them were slain to a man,
and the main body dispersed in every direction...I was literally
within a few hundred yards of the Syed when he fell, but I did
not see the angel descend and carry him off to paradise, although
many of his followers remembered afterwards that they had seen
it distinctly enough.'[1]

Sher Singh did not betray any fanaticism in his behaviour towards a man who had roused a million people against the Sikhs
and vilified their faith with contemptuous abuse. The Prince
himself draped the body of the Syed with an expensive shawl
before it was buried with the honours due to a brave adversary.[2]
When the news of the Prince's behaviour towards the dead
crusader reached the Maharaja, he fully approved of it. Syed
Ahmed was a good, if misguided, man.

The Jihad was fitfully carried on by one of Syed Ahmed's dis-
ciples, Nasiruddin, but met with little success. But soon after the
death of the Syed, the new Barakzai chief, Dost Mohammed,
who had come to power at Kabul, took up the cry. He, like
other members of his family, was an adept in double dealing.
Sometimes he acknowledged Ranjit Singh as his master 'almost
like a father'; at other times he condemned him as an infidel
who deserved to be killed.

[1]*Memoirs of Alexander Gardner,* pp. 171-2.
    Sir Olaf Caroe gives a slightly different version of this encounter in *The
Pathans,* pp. 301-5.
[2]*Umdat-ut-Tawarikh, Daftar* III, Part I, p. 35.

CHAPTER XVII

SINDH AND THE FIELD OF
THE CLOTH OF GOLD

BRITISH INTEREST in Sindh was both commercial and political. The Indus ran through Sindh and the mouth of the Indus was very much nearer than that of the Hooghly for English cargo boats bringing goods for the markets of Northern India. Politically Sindh was important as a springboard for the invasion of Baluchistan and Afghanistan. And in any case, since the disunity between the Amirs created a power vacuum in Sindh, the English felt it was better that they filled it rather than the Punjabis.

In 1829 a reconnaissance of the Indus zone was attempted by a young subaltern (who later became a famous traveller and diplomat), Alexander Burnes. His interest in the vital frontier was, as he said, 'stimulated' by the Commander-in-Chief, Sir Thomas Bradford. Burnes and another English officer went as far as Jaisalmer. They had planned to sail down the river but were dissuaded from doing so to avoid arousing the suspicions of the Amirs and prejudicing the chances of subsequent intercourse with them. It was decided to send Burnes out again under a pretext which would facilitate his passage. The King of England had sent a team of five massive dray horses as presents for Ranjit Singh. The Governor-General agreed to a suggestion that he should add a gift of his own—a large sized coach which, in the absence of proper roads, could only be transported by boat. Burnes was made the bearer of gifts and armed with complimentary letters to the Amirs through whose territories the Indus ran.

After a few mishaps, the convoy of boats began its journey up the river in March 1831. Burnes's companions were an ensign Leckie, a surveyor, and a Parsi doctor. The boats were equipped with instruments to record data for the navigation of bigger vessels. Burnes was also instructed to investigate the affairs of Sindh: its politics, the military strength of the Amirs, their views on opening up the river to regular traffic, etc. All this was to be done under the innocuous guise that he was conveying gifts from one king to another. Obstruction would be regarded as an act in bad taste likely to provoke Ranjit Singh.

Burnes was able to make the necessary contacts with the Amirs while his staff carried out depth soundings and prepared wind and temperature charts. Reports of the Englishman's activities left no doubt in Ranjit Singh's mind of the real reason for the envoy coming by river. Lehna Singh Majithia was sent to receive Burnes because he was the only man in the Durbar with a scientific bent of mind and could, if necessary, question Burnes on his survey records. Burnes, who had a very poor opinion of Orientals on such matters, was impressed with Lehna Singh's knowledge of mathematics, the movement of the stars, and his insatiable curiosity about the working of scientific instruments.

On June 7, 1831, Burnes entered the Durbar's territories and was welcomed as a royal emissary; with gun salutes and a guard of honour Lehna Singh held a durbar in the Englishman's honour and handed him letters of welcome from his master. Then he and the other Sardars presented *nazars* worth 1,400 rupees. The dray horses were exhibited to the assembled populace, and at Lehna Singh's request a shoe of one was sent to the Maharaja to give him an idea of the size of the beasts he was to receive. A newswriter was attached to the party to send a daily report of the progress it made up river.

An accident en route gave Burnes an idea of the mettle of the people whose kingdom he was visiting. The men whilst hauling the boats from the banks disturbed a tiger in a thicket of tamarisk. The animal attacked one of the coolies:

'The monster was speedily wounded by someone and several riders were unhorsed from the fright of their steeds. The Seikhs then advanced on foot, sword in hand, to attack the tiger. He sprang on one most fiercely; and as he fixed on his left shoulder, the poor fellow bravely struck his head by a well-directed blow. The contest was unequal and the man fell horribly lacerated. His comrades instantly ran up and with cuts and wounds the tiger soon fell. He was a large animal and measured 10 feet: his thigh was as large as that of a full-grown man. The coolness of the courage of the Seikhs surpassed belief.'[1]

Burnes had many more examples of this sort of courage and came to the conclusion that the Sikhs were 'the bravest of all Indians.'[2]

On July 18 Burnes came within sight of Lahore. Four miles away from the city, Fakeer Azizuddin and Raja Gulab Singh welcomed him on behalf of the Maharaja and invited him to stop at Allard's home for the night till all was ready for a ceremonial reception. Here, after many moons, Burnes and Leckie had *dejeuner a la fourchette* with champagne instead of the usual Indian meal washed down with tea or coffee.

Next morning the party set out to call on the Maharaja. Captain Wade arrived from Ludhiana with a platoon of sepoys to furnish the escort. The procession was formed with the coach in front, the drays following and Burnes's party bringing up the rear on elephant. The streets were lined with the Durber infantry to keep back the crowds which had collected to watch the procession. As the party entered the city walls, the guns began to boom in salute. At the palace gates they were received by Raja Dhian Singh who took them to the hall of audience.

'While stopping to remove my shoes at the threshold,' wrote Burnes, 'I suddenly found myself in the arms and tight embrace of a dimunitive and old-looking man—the great Maharaja Runjeet Singh.'[3] Leckie was greeted with similar effusion and the Englishmen were escorted to their seats. Then followed the conventional inquiries regarding each other's health. The carriage

---

[1]*Travels into Bokhara*, vol. I. p. 119.
[2]Another observation of Burnes on the Sikhs is worthy of notice: 'The Seikhs are doubtless the most rising people in modern India. Although they were unknown 400 years ago, the features of the whole nation are now as distinct from that of their neighbours as the Indian and the Chinese. With an extreme regularity of physiognomy, and an elongation of the countenance, they may be readily distinguished from the other tribes. That any nation possessing peculiar customs should have a common manner and character, is easily understood; but that in such a short period of time, some hundred thousand people should exhibit a strong national likeness as is to be seen among the children of Israel is, to say the least, remarkable. *Travels into Bokhara*, 1839, vol. I, p. 76.
[3]*Travels into Bokhara*, vol. I, p. 129.

and the horses were brought in. Burnes presented a letter from the Governor-General on behalf of the King of England. 'On this the Maharaja and his Court, rose up... His Highness received the letter, and touched his forehead to the seal,' writes Burnes. The letter was handed over to Fakeer Azizuddin who began to read the Persian text mentioning the gift of 'some horses of the gigantic breed which is peculiar to England,' and referring to the great friendship subsisting between the two nations. Ranjit Singh interrupted the Fakeer and said that the occasion called for a salute to the King of England. Once more the cannon roared: sixty guns firing twenty-one rounds each shook the walls of the palace and the people's homes in the city. Then the Maharaja stepped down to inspect the gifts.

'The sight of the horses excited his utmost surprise and wonder, their size and colour pleased him: he said they were little elephants. And as they passed singly before him, he called out to his different Sardars and officers, who joined him in admiration.'[1]

Ranjit Singh then had a string of his own thoroughbreds paraded for the benefit of his guests. After that followed an hour and a half of close questioning by Ranjit Singh. Was the Indus navigable throughout? What was the attitude of the people living along its banks? and so on. There was no doubt that Ranjit Singh knew the real object of Burnes's river journey.

The excitement of the ceremony was too much for Ranjit Singh and he retired after a couple of hours. Burnes penned his first impression of the Maharaja:

'Nature has indeed been sparing in her gifts to this personage and there must be a mighty contest between his mind and body.....he has but one eye, is pitted with small pox, and his stature does not certainly exceed 5 ft. 3 in. He is entirely free from pomp and show, yet the studied respect of his court is remarkable; not an individual spoke without a sign, though the throng was more like a bazaar than the court of the first native prince of India.'[2]

[1] *Travels into Bokhara*, vol. I. p. 132.
[2] *Ibid*, vol. I, p. 133.

The following day there was a review of troops and Burnes joined the Maharaja at an *al fresco* breakfast in the saddle. In the evening of July 25, Ranjit Singh asked Burnes to a private audience. It started as an ordinary party with courtiers and a band of Amazon nautch girls ('one of my platoons I cannot discipline', said Ranjit). Then the courtiers and the dancers were dismissed and Ranjit Singh spoke to Burnes as one man to another. He traced the history of the Punjabi-British relations; of Metcalfe's mission and the meeting with Ochterlony. He had done his duty as a friend. What did the British intend to do in Sindh? He too was interested in the country. He gave as broad a hint as he could, as a courteous host of how he meant to take Sindh. His strength did not lie in his allies, but in the strong right arm of the Khalsa. According to Burnes, Ranjit Singh said that—

'he owed all his success to the bravery of his nation, who were very free from prejudice, would carry eight day's provisions on their backs, dig a well if water were scarce, build a fort if circumstances required it.'[1]

After this disquisiton, the courtiers were allowed to return; dancing and drinking was resumed.

Before he took his leave Burnes was shown the royal jewels including the Koh-i-noor. Ranjit Singh slipped two rings on the envoy's fingers, one with a diamond, the other with an emerald, and gave him four other ornaments studded with emeralds and pearls. Burnes was also presented with a horse and robe of honour. Ranjit Singh put his letter to the King of England in a silk purse with two pearls on its string. Amongst other things, the letter referred to the size of the horse's shoes, which Lehna Singh had sent him: 'On beholding these shoes, the new moon turned pale with envy, and nearly disappeared from the sky.' Burnes saw a lot of the Maharaja during his stay at Lahore. 'Ranjit Singh is in every respect an extraordinary character,' he wrote. 'I have heard his French officers observe that he has no equal from Constantinople to India; and all of them have seen the immediate powers... The most creditable trait in Ranjit's character is his humanity; he has never been known to punish a criminal with death since his accession to power...cunning and

[1]*Travels into Bokhara*, vol. I, p. 140

conciliation have been the two great weapons of his diplomacy.'[1]

Burnes visited Amritsar and paid his respects at the Golden Temple. From there he went to Kapurthala where he was a guest of Fateh Singh Ahluwalia; and on to Phillaur from where he crossed over to British territory. One thing that struck Burnes in his journey across the Punjab was that there were so few Sikhs in the country. 'The paucity of Seikhs, in a country ruled and governed by them, is remarkable. The mother earth of the tribe is the Doab between the Ravi and the Sutlej; but there are few of them to be found thirty miles below Lahore, where they are said to predominate. There are no Seikhs westward of the Hydaspes (Jhelum); and to the eastwards of Lahore, where they are said to predominate they certainly do not compose a third of the population.' What did not occur to him was that Ranjit Singh's kingdom was not a kingdom of Sikhs alone, but all Punjabis, Hindus, Muslims, as well as Sikhs.

Burnes reported to the new Governor-General, Lord William Bentinck, that the Indus route was full of possibilities: that the Amirs of Sindh were terrified of Ranjit Singh and would be willing to allow the English rights of passage if guaranteed security against their Punjabi neighbours.

Early in 1831, Ranjit Singh had sent a delegation consisting of Fakeer Azizuddin, Moti Ram and Hari Singh Nalwa to Simla to welcome Bentinck on his first tour of Northern India. The delegates, especially Fakeer Azizuddin, made an extremely good impression on their English hosts.[2] While Fakeer Azizuddin charmed his audience with his euphemisms: 'the nightingales of esteem warble in the meadows of attachment...rivers of devotion rush into oceans of affection,' etc., Bentinck's mind was occupied with more practical matters. Burnes's report whetted his appetite. The problem was how to persuade Ranjit Singh to give up his design on Sindh, allow British vessels to navigate through all the six rivers in his domain and yet convince him that it was in his own interests. Bentinck desired to handle the matter personally. He instructed Captain Wade to go to Lahore and

---

[1]*Travels into Bokhara*, vol. I, p. 143.
[2]It was during this visit that an English officer asked Azizuddin of which eye the Maharaja was blind. 'The splendour of his face is such,' replied the Fakeer, 'that I have never been able to look enough to discover.'

suggest to the Maharaja that instead of having a delegation of English officials return the call made by the Durbar's Ministers, he could have the Governor-General himself call on him: only the invitation should come from Ranjit Singh (so that it should appear to the people that it was the Maharaja who was keen to meet the Englishman than the Englishman the Maharaja). The Durbar did not like this proposal, nor the suggestion that the Maharaja should be the first to call on a mere Governor-General.[1] However, Ranjit Singh waived protocol and agreed to meet Bentinck on Bentinck's terms. He wrote to the Governor-General that he had always been 'anxiously watering this sapling of friendship to see it rise into a thickly foliaged tree yielding luscious fruit and cool shade to both the parties.' Bentinck was not to be outdone in eloquence. 'The flowers of the garden of friendship and affection will be adorned with the verdure of perpetuity and cordiality, and mutual good understanding will always be cultivated with care....' It was agreed that the two should meet at Rupar on October 26, 1831.

The meeting at Rupar has been described by many eyewitnesses[2] as the Punjab's field of cloth of gold.

A large park on the bank of the river was specially laid out for the occasion. On top of a mound commanding a view of the countryside was erected a silver pavilion made in the shape of a Hindu temple. Next to the pavilion were the Maharaja's tents of deep red broadcloth with marquees of yellow silk and satin. About the enclosure was a garden where wheat had been ploughed in plots shaped to resemble birds, horses and other animals.

The Maharaja arrived at Rupar on the morning of October 25 with 16,000 of his cavalry. Next morning, accompanied by 1,000 horsemen in coats of mail covered with silk, he rode on

[1] The 'Lat Sahib was the servant of the company and the company was subordinate to the sovereign of England, so it did not behove the exalted position of the princely Ruler to meet the Governor-General on a footing of equality,' they said. Amar Nath, *Zafar Namah*, p. 205.
[2] The account of the meeting is based on the version of James Skinner or 'Old Sikundur,' as he was popularly known. Skinner was an Anglo-Indian who paraded a contingent of his famous Skinner's Horse or 'Yellow boys' (because of the colour of their uniform) before the monarch of the Punjab. *Military Memoirs of Lieut.-Col. James Skinner*, by Baillie Fraser, 2 vols., 1851.

his elephant along a road lined on either side by British troops. The Governor-General's party came out to receive him. Bentinck embraced Ranjit and escorted him inside his tent. 'After going through the ceremony of asking about each other's health,' writes Skinner, 'two hundred trays containing gifts which included silk, double-barrelled guns and pistols, were presented to the Maharaja.' A string of horses and two elephants also meant for Ranjit Singh were filed past. The meeting lasted an hour without anything serious being discussed. Since Bentinck spoke no Punjabi and none of the courtiers could speak English, the conversation had to be carried on through Fakeer Azizuddin and Captain Wade 'who like a candle lit the Chamber of friendship and like a rose perfumed the garden of unity.'[1] The meeting concluded with some dancing by nautch girls who had been brought by the English party. English ladies accompanying the Governor-General's party also gave a demonstration of an English folk dance which pleased the Sardars immensely. 'The desert of ill-will changed to an orchard of goodwill and the rust of anxiety was erased from the hearts of the people,' wrote Sohan Lal.

Next morning Bentinck, escorted by Prince Kharak Singh, paid his return visit. The Maharaja received him on the bank of the river[2] and the two rode on the same elephant the length of a mile-long lane flanked by the Durbar infantry and cavalry. Bentinck was taken up the mound to the silver pavilion: the scarlet tents alongside the pavilion had been draped with velvet embroidered with gold. On the floor were spread the finest carpets that Persia, Kashmir and the Punjab could produce. As the Durbar assembled, Punjabi artillery fired a twenty-one gun salute in welcome to Bentinck. Ranjit Singh introduced 300 of his 'good-looking men and richly armoured' Sardars. Bentinck then presented the Company's officers to Ranjit Singh. When they were seated, the Maharaja sent for his Kashmiri dancing girls,

[1] Sohan Lal, *Daftar* II, p. 89.
[2] Sohan Lal records the Maharaja's reactions to seeing Lord William help Lady Bentinck step off the boat: 'As soon as the Begum Lady Sahiba crossed the river by boat, Nawab Sahib (Lord Bentinck) personally went forward to receive her, and taking her by the hand, made her sit in a chair in such a way that it indicated his heartfelt love....The Maharaja said that at that moment he was reminded of Bibi Mohran for he had exactly the same kind of love and understanding with her that could not bear separation from her even for a monent.' Sohan Lal, *Daftar* III, p. 100.

'a band of about one hundred young women, well dressed and bejewelled, saluted and sat down; some had arrows in their hands, and some had bows—the commandant bore a staff of order. They all wore yellow turbans inclining to one side, which gave them a very imposing appearance. After singing a short while, they also retired; and then came the Maharaja's presents'— on a hundred trays containing all the best products of the Punjab (in addition to two fine horses and an elephant). Ranjit Singh put a string of large pearls round Bentinck's neck.

The formal meetings were followed by an inspection of troops, parades and tattoos, which were the things Ranjit Singh loved best. He carefully examined the British equipment and asked a hundred searching questions. He made the Company's troops repeat manoeuvres with which he was not familiar, particularly the square formation which was their speciality. 'They are like walls of iron,' he remarked. He was so pleased with their drill that he gave Rs. 11,000 to be distributed to the British soldiers. Skinner was most impressed with Ranjit's knowledge on military matters. 'In every way Runjeet proved himself to be a far superior soldier to any other native. He seemed as if gifted with the intelligence of an English Field Marshal and, in fact, he moved about as if he was himself in command of the troops.'[1]

Skinner was equally impressed with the review of Punjabi troops, which he and other British officers watched from the silver pavilion. 'It was as grand a sight as I have ever seen since I left the native service,' he wrote. Although the accurate firing of the Punjabi gunners surprised him, he did not think as much of their equipment. He formed a very low opinion of Allard's cavalry. 'The French lancers were only a mockery as to discipline, their horses were inferior and they were badly armed.'

Ranjit Singh's special interest was always the artillery. At his special request the Company's horse artillery was put through its paces. He watched the firing of howitzers and had targets put up to examine their marksmanship. 'There was no satisfying his curiosity,' wrote Skinner. 'Wishing to put their skill to a severer test, he required Lord William to have an umbrella put up as a mark near the target, a distance of about 1,000 yards,

[1]Skinner, vol. I, entries October 26 to 30.

and direct the artillery officers to fire at it with round shot. The first two or three discharges being ineffective, Runjeet Singh himself dismounted and laid the gun; but neither His Highness nor some of his best officers whom he desired to try their hand were any the more successful. Captain Campbell, of the horse artillery, then took their place, and the first shot he made rent the umbrella to pieces, on which a roar of applause arose from the Sikhs.'

Ranjit Singh got his cavalry to compete with the Company's at firing at a bottle while in full gallop and cutting a brass pot with the sabre. According to Skinner the Company's entrants were as good as the Punjabis, including Ranjit, who tried his hand at the brass pot but failed to cut it. (According to Sohan Lal, Ranjit succeeded where all others failed and the Punjabis completely outshone the Company's marksmen.)

In the evening, Ranjit Singh gave a party for Lord and Lady Bentinck. The royal tent was specially done up; a carpet of gold brocade was laid out on the floor and a gilded throne and two bedsteads studded with precious stones were put out for the guests. 'The whole inside of the tent was gorgeously decorated and formed a most perfect specimen of Indian luxury and extravagance,' wrote Skinner. While the fireworks lit the skies outside, the glittering jewels of the Kashmiri dancers lit the inside of the tent. There was music, dancing and much drinking of wine. 'Runjeet was very merry on this occasion and was most attentive to his noble guests, Lord and Lady William Bentinck....Wine was brought in and very freely ditributed in golden cups to all guests, Runjeet taking a pretty large allowance. After he had got somewhat inebriated, a quantity of gold dust was brought and placed before the Maharaja who ordered the nautch girls to throw it over the guests, in imitation of the festival of Hooly and seemed to enjoy the joke; for he also threw it at the ladies and gentlemen who sat near him, as well as at the dancing women.'

While Ranjit Singh was in this carefree mood, Bentinck and Wade introduced the business of navigation on the Punjab's rivers. The way they put it sounded a very profitable proposition. Ranjit, however, doubted their bonafides regarding Sindh. He asked them as tactfully as he could whether the English planned to extend their dominion over Sindh. No, assured Wade, the purpose was

purely commercial and the Amirs of Sindh had been persuaded
to see it in that light. And what, asked Ranjit Singh, was to
happen about his relationship with Bahawalpur who accepted the
Durbar's suzerainty and the Sindhians over whom he was pro-
posing to cast his mantle? Bentinck did not say so in so many
words, but he made it clear that the Durbar was now to consider its southern boundary as finally drawn. All that Ranjit Singh
got out of the week's extravagance at Rupar was a written assurance of perpetual friendship.

The Maharaja's carousal with the English was by no means
looked upon with favour by his people. Many courtiers were
critical of his behaviour and the Akalis were outspokenly hostile. Sohan Lal narrates an incident that took place soon after:

'Out of the adversity of his days and his evil character, one
Akali drew his sword out of its sheath and rushed towards the
Maharaja. The orderlies and State servants gathered on the spot,
held that Akali in the clutches of interference and restraint and
brought him before the Maharaja.'[1]

A sense of disappointment soon set in. Ranjit Singh had tried
to befriend the English in the open-hearted way Punjabis do; but
each time the English returned his embrace, they put a hand in
his pocket and took what was dearest to him—and left protesting their goodwill.

What Ranjit Singh really felt about the Rupar meeting was
expressed by him in a conversation he had with Dr Joseph Wolff,
a Jew-turned-evangelist, who visited him a few months later. The
doctor had heard of the name of 'Rundjud Singh, whose name
was a terror in Bokhara itself'.[2] He recorded the conversation

---

[1] Sohan Lal, *Daftar* III, p. 93.

[2] The doctor obviously was not frightened of Ranjit as the first thing he did
on arrival at Lahore was to paste posters on the walls warning the infidels
of the fires of hell, glorifying Christ as the only Saviour. Ranjit sent him a
mild reprimand: *Feen Sukhan nobayad guft nebayd shud*—such words must
neither be said nor heard—and invited him to the court for he loved to hear
people's views on God and religion. The doctor came with the growth of beard
he had acquired over his travels. ('Runjeet is very fond of people with fine
beards', his host Allard had advised.) When he arrived at court Ranjit was
entertaining. The puritan disdained the nautch as he was an 'English Fakeer'

LORD AUCKLAND,
GOVERNOR-GENERAL (1836-42)
(Oil painting by Simon Rochard, c.1840)
(Photo: Private collection)

4. LORD WILLIAM BENTINCK, GOVERNOR-GENERAL (1828-35)
(Engraving from a portrait by Thomas Lawrence)

5. SIKH SOLDIERY
(Photo: Punjab
Museum, India)

AN AKALI HORSEMAN
(Photo: India Office Library, Commonwealth

which took place at their first meeting. Ranjit Singh had been informed of the doctor's nervousness while crossing the Indus and his subsequent sermons to the 'infidel' on how people with religious convictions had no fear of death.

'Do you teach that we should not be afraid of anything?' asked the Maharaja.

'Yes.'

'Do you preach that we should trust in the Giver-of-All-Things? 'Yes.'

'Then why were you so afraid when you crossed the Indus over the suspension bridge on an elephant?' (Wolff had screamed with terror all the time.)

'Here your Majesty has certainly caught me; and all I can answer is, that I am weak, and I have daily need to pray that God will show His power in my weakness.'

'Now, I call this candour and uprightness,' conceded Ranjit; 'but answer me another thing; you say, you travel about for the sake of religion; why then, do you not preach to the English in Hindoostan, who have no religion at all?'[1]

The doctor tried to divert the conversation and asked the courtiers: 'How may one come nigh unto God?'

'One can come nigh unto God,' replied Ranjit Singh with biting sarcasm, 'by making an alliance with the British Government,

---

but did try some of Ranjit's brandy. 'Horrid stuff; hotter than any whisky, and it actually burns like fire.' *Travels and Adventures of Dr Wolff*, vol. II, p. 68.
[1]Wolff's biographer goes on to relate that when Wolff conveyed this last information to Lord Bentinck in Simla, the Governor-General replied: 'This is, alas! the opinion of all the natives all over India.'
Wolff was impressed with Ranjit's liberal views on religion and the futility of making forcible conversions. 'Randjud Singh has proved to the Mussulmans pretty well, that the edge of the sword is not always evidence of the truth of religion; for the name of Rundjud Singh is a terror from Lahore to the city of Bokhara—his sword having defeated the Mohammedans in every battle.'
Wolff had another and somewhat unexpected meeting with the Sikh ruler. Not expecting to see Ranjit again, he had shaved off his beard as soon as he left Amritsar on his way towards British territory. A messenger reached him on his way and imformed him that Ranjit desired to see him. The missionary retraced his steps with a certain amount of trepidation. Ranjit saw him and roared with laughter. 'Ho, ho, ho! where have you left your beard?'
'It is well taken care of in the house of your Majesty's General.'
'I shall cut off his nose, the first day I see the fellow.' *Travels and Adventures of Dr Wolff*, vol. II, p. 72 ff.

as I lately did with the Lord Nawab Sahib at Roopar.'[1]

A few months after the Rupar meeting, Alexander Burnes was sent to complete his investigation of the lands about the Indus. This time, his mission was to cover the tribal areas and Afghanistan. In order to allay suspicion, Burnes divested himself of his official status and gave out that he was taking the overland route to England. He, therefore, took the liberty of asking Ranjit Singh as an old friend for permission to pass through the Punjab. 'It would afford me the opportunity of renewing my friendship with a prince whose exalted virtues fill me with recollections of perpetual delight,' he wrote. The permission was immediately granted. Burnes was accompanied on this second exploratry mission by Dr James Gerard, a surveyor, and a staff of Indians including a young Kashmiri, Mohan Lal, as interpreter. The party entered the Punjab in 1832. They were welcomed by Sham Singh Attariwala and provided with an escort of 'four hundred Sikh horse'.[2]

Burnes met Ranjit Singh in a garden two miles out of Lahore, and presented him with a pistol. 'We found him in great spirits and continued with him for about two hours. His conversation ranged from points of the utmost importance to mere trifles,' he wrote. Burnes spent a month in Lahore during which he saw the Maharaja on several occasions. He accompanied Ranjit on a hunt and was present at the Basant celebrations to mark the advent of spring. Of both these he has left vivid recollections.

The Shikar was across the Ravi. 'The order of the march was very picturesque, and the retinue in every respect that of a soldier king. His horses were led in front of him, but the journey was performed on elephants. Two of these splendid animals bore howdahs of gold, in one of which His Highness sat. (The other

[1]*Travels and Adventures of Dr Wolff*, vol. II, pp. 71-2.
[2]*Travels into Bokhara*, vol. II, p. 14.

Some of Burnes's observations on the Punjab are illuminating. 'We passed innumerable villages, the houses of which are terrace-roofed, and formed of sun-dried bricks on a wooden framework. They had a clean and comfortable look, and the peasantry appeared well-clad and happy.' At Patti, Burnes visited Ranjit's stables where he saw Ranjit's Dhanni thoroughbreds. He also saw something of the Sikh attitude to their Muslim compatriots. The horses had been afflicted with disease which had been cured by a Muslim physician. The Seikhs have in gratitude repaired and beautified his temple (sic) which is now a conspicuous white building, that glitters in the sun. The Seikh people are most tolerant in their religion; and I have remarked in India generally much more of this virtue than people give credit for.' vol. II, pp. 9-10.

undoubtedly bore the Granth Sahib which invariably led all Ranjit's processions.) Six or seven others followed with his courtiers and favourites. A small body of cavalry and a field piece formed his escort; the carriage which he had received from the Governor-General drawn by horses completed the procession.'[1]

Throughout the journey, Ranjit Singh plied Burnes with questions. What was happening to the Rohilla leader, Amir Khan? How were the English treating him? How did the English maintain discipline in the army? and so on. 'The conversation could not, of course, conclude without his favourite topic of wine,' writes Burnes. 'And as he sat down, he remarked that the site of his tent was an agreeable one for a drinking party, since it commanded a fine view of the surrounding country. He inquired of the doctors whether wine was best before or after food; and laughed heartily at an answer from myself, when I recommended both.'[2]

Early next morning the actual hunt began. 'Runjeet rode his favourite bay horse, covered with an elegant saddle-cloth of the richest embroidery in its border, by almost every beast and bird which the sportman calls his own. Runjeet was dressed in a tunic of green shawls, lined with fur; his dagger was studded with the richest brilliants, and a light metal shield, the gift of the ex-King of Kabul, completed his equipment. Right in front of the party was the pack of hunting dogs of various breeds: Sindhian, Bokhara, Iranian and Punjabi. They were followed by elephants bearing the royal party. Alongside were the falconers on horseback with their hawks fluttering on their wrists. Several wild boars were beaten out of the pampas grass. The swords of the Seikhs glittered in the sun; and in the course of half-an-hour, eight monsters had bitten the dust, and many more were entrapped by snares. Most of the animals had been slain by the horsemen with their swords.'

Live hogs were brought to the camp and baited by hunting dogs. For some time the party watched the contest between boar and hound; and when they had had enough, the remaining hogs were set at liberty and scampered away into the jungle.

[1]*Travels into Bokhara*, vol. II, p. 18.
[2]*Ibid*, vol. II, p. 19.

In the evening, the tired huntmen gathered in the royal tent over their cups of wine. The English complimented the Maharaja on the courage of his Sikhs. Ranjit Singh warmed to the subject and told them of the exploits of Akali Phula Singh at Naushera: how when he had been wounded in the leg and could not stand, he had bandaged his wound and ridden back into the thick of the battle on horseback; and when additional injuries had further incapacitated him, he had got into a howdah and driven the elephant into the midst of the enemy; and how he had met his end roaring like a lion. 'He was a brave man but a great villain,' concluded Ranjit. 'And had he not fallen that day, I must have imprisoned him for life as he wished to cross the frontier and set fire to some British cantonments.'

There was no stopping the Maharaja when it came to talking of battles. 'It was quite delightful to hear Runjeet speak of his charges, his squares, his battles, and his successes; and his only one eye brightened with the description.'

The party returned to Lahore in time to celebrate Basant. It was one of the festivals which Muslims, Hindus and Sikhs celebrated in common, when all men and women wore yellow in honour of the mustard flower. Early in the morning Ranjit Singh rode down a street through a line of infantry all dressed in yellow uniforms. He entered a tent lined with yellow in which the Granth had been placed; the holy book was also draped in silks of the same colour: the canopy above it was covered with pearls and its border sagged with the weight of precious stones. 'Nothing can be imagined more grand,' commented Burnes. Ranjit Singh listened to the recitation from the Granth, made his offering 'and the holy book was borne away wrapped in ten different covers, the outside of which, in honour of the day, was of golden velvet. Flowers and fruits were placed before His Highness; and every kind of shrub or tree that produced a yellow flower must have been shorn of its branches that day.'[1]

The courtiers and visitors were presented; amongst them were the sons of Shah Zaman and Shah Shuja and the sons of the late Nawab of Multan. When the agents of Bahawalpur and the Amirs of Sindh made their bow, the Maharaja questioned them closely on the British proposals about the Indus. After the busi-

[1] *Travels into Bokhara*, vol. II, p. 23.

ness was over, arrived the nautch girls—all clad in yellow silks. Ranjit Singh had a heap of gold and silver coins placed before him which he gave to them in palmfuls.

In the evening there was a party at Musummum Burj. The place was 'superbly illuminated with waxen tapers-bottles with different coloured water were placed near the lights and increased the splendour.' The reception hall was one mass of mirrors and chandeliers. The guests, who included Captain Wade and Dr Murray, were shown Ranjit's bedroom. Its walls were gilded; the bedstead and the chair alongside it were of solid gold. The drinking and dancing went on late into the night. Burnes noticed that despite the praise Ranjit bestowed on wine, he did not drink much. 'Ranjeet drinks by the weight, and his usual dose does not exceed that of eight pice.' Nevertheless, he pressed it generously on his guests. Burnes and his companions did themselves well. 'The glorious Sahibs indulged in drinking wine with the dancing girls and were lost in the ocean of intoxication,' wrote Sohan Lal.[1]

The question of navigation on the Indus was brought up. Ranjit Singh conceded that although some benefits might accrue to him, 'he did not relish the idea of vessels navigating all parts of his territories. He feared collision with the British Government.'[2]

Burnes did not discuss any more business with the Maharaja. The last he saw of Ranjit Singh on his visit was when they passed by each other on the road. They shook hands without dismounting. Burnes wrote:

'I never quitted the presence of a native of Asia with such impressions as I left this man: without education, and without a guide, he conducts all the affairs of his kingdom with surpassing energy and vigour, and yet he wields his power with a consideration quite unprecedented in an Eastern prince.'[3]

While Burnes went north-west to prepare the ground in Afghanistan, Wade came back to Lahore to persuade Ranjit Singh

[1]When Burnes left Lahore for Afghanistan, his friend M. Court handed him a detailed guide on those parts with the warning 'En quittant Lahore, dites Adieu a Bacchus pour ne le revoir que dans la belle Europe.'
[2]*Travels into Bokhara*, vol. II, p. 28.
[3]*Ibid*, vol. II, p. 28.

put his signature to a commercial treaty. The Amirs of Hyderabad, Khairpur and Mirpur had been made to sign in April; there was not much Ranjit could do now. On December 26, 1832, he too affixed his seal to the treaty and so renounced his ambitions to extend the Punjabi empire to the sea.

During the months when there was much coming and going of delegations between the British and Ranjit Singh, young French botanist, Victor Jacquemont, arrived at Lahore on his way to Kashmir. His diary[1] of travels across British India into the Punjab and Kashmir gives a picture of the people and their Maharaja. He was an Anglophile and as he travelled up from Calcutta with letters of introduction from one senior English official to another, he came to share their prejudices against Orientals and believe in the rightness of extending the white man's rule over the Asiatics.[2] Like the British officials he met, he believed that Ranjit Singh was a 'sly old fox' who kept his independence by crafty diplomacy rather than by the strength of his army. Compared to Ranjit, 'the most skillful of our diplomats is a complete simpleton', he wrote.[3]

The Maharaja took to the Frenchman from the very start. Jacquemont was a tall, sinewy man with a flowing red beard —and Ranjit Singh liked to see handsome men with beards about him. Jacquemont was surprised to find that the Maharaja had straightaway guessed that he was not an Englishman. When asked how he had found out, Ranjit replied: 'An Englishman would not have changed his posture twenty times: he would have made no gestures while talking; he would not have laughed at the proper times.'[4] Jacquemont was also widely travelled and well-informed—and Ranjit's hunger for information was insatiable. Within a few days of his arrival 'Jackman Sahib Bahadur' became a familiar figure in the Durbar and began to be consulted on all subjects. He wrote: 'Ranjit calls me Aristotle in

[1] The extracts quoted hereafter are taken from *A Journey in India,* by Victor Jacquemont (1835 edition), vol. II.
[2] 'I cannot witness the frightful evils of the present system of governing these people withiout ardently desiring to see the British extend their frontiers from the Sutlej to the Indus, and the Russions occupy the other bank of the river.' Also vol. I, p. 335.
[3] Jacquemont, vol. II, p. 11.
[4] *Ibid,* vol. II, p. 24.

addition to my old titles Aflatoon (Plato) and Socrat (Socrates).'[1]

Jacquemont thawed in the Maharaja's warm embrace of friendship and lavish hospitality. Knowing the Frenchman's tastes, the Maharaja issued orders 'to all dancing girls in the town of Lahore to put on male garments, hold swords and bows in their hands and be decorated with other arms as well and then present themselves'. It is not surprising that Jacquemont liked the life at Lahore, where he 'lived in a little palace of the Arabian Nights Entertainment.' He was treated with great deference. He wrote: 'A battalion of infantry was on duty near me; the drums saluted whenever I put my head out of doors; and when I walked in the cool of the evening, in the alleys of my garden fountains played round me by the thousand: A most splendid fete was given to me; with an accompaniment of Cashmerian dancing girls, as a matter of course; and although their eyes were daubed round with black and white, my taste is depraved enough to have thought them only the more beautiful.'[2]

The wide range of Ranjit Singh's questions impressed the French botanist. 'His conversation is like a nightmare. He is almost the first inquisitive Indian I have seen; and his curiosity balances the apathy of the whole of his nation. He has asked me a hundred thousand questions about India, the British, Europe, Bonaparte, this world in general and the next, hell, paradise, the soul, God, the devil and a myriad others of the same kind.'[3]

Jacquemont's other observations of Ranjit were not so complimentary. 'He is like all people of rank in the East, an imaginary invalid; and as he has a collection of the greatest beauties of Kashmir, and the means of paying for a better dinner than anyone else in this country, he is generally annoyed that he cannot drink like a fish without being drunk, or eat like an elephant and escape surfeit.'[4]

Jacquemont's observations on other subjects are illuminating. What impressed the Frenchman most was Ranjit's humanity,

[1]Durbar records refer to him with the title *Aflatoon-i-Zaman*, Aristotle of the age.
[2]Jacquemont, vol. II, p. 47.
[3]*Ibid*, vol. II, p. 22.
[4]*Ibid*, vol. II, p. 22.

evidenced by the fact that although he was a despot he was
unique in that he had created an empire with so little blood-
shed. And in a country with a tradition of religious intolerance,
Ranjit commanded the loyalties of subjects, a majority of whom
were fiercely opposed to his religious beliefs. The secret, according
to Jacquemont, was Ranjit's basic cynicism towards all religious
systems. 'He is a Sikh by profession, a sceptic in reality. Every
year he pays his devotions to Amritsar and, what is very singular, at the shrines of several Mohammedan saints, yet these
pilgrimages offend none of the puritans of his own sect.'[1]

Jacquemont spent seven months as the guest of the Maharaja.
It is not known whether it was due to riotous living in the
Punjab or to an infection he caught on his way back, but he
developed an abscess of the liver and died soon after in Bombay.

The political fiasco at Rupar had its emotional compensations.
After the 'glorious Sahibs' had departed, Ranjit found his thoughts
straying to a courtesan from Amritsar who was one of the troupe
who had danced before his distinguished guests. Ranjit went to
Amritsar and sent for the girl. Gul Begam came as she was commanded and sang and danced. She was an uninhibited coquette,
unlike the coldly aristocratic women of the royal harem. The
middle-aged monarch fell violently in love with the teenaged
Muslim courtesan and resolved to defy convention by marrying
her (as he had when he had married Mohran). He first went
to the Golden Temple to pray for forgiveness for what he was
about to do; then he publicly announced that Gul Begam was
to be treated as a queen. Her faith would be respected and she
would remain a Muslim. Sohan Lal reports the ceremony of
marriage.

'The Maharaja put on saffron garments and jewellery... Gul
Begam came to the pavilion dressed in yellow garments; her
hands and feet were dyed red in henna and from head to foot
she was bedecked in gold ornaments studded with diamonds...
The Maharaja seated Gul Begam in a chair beside him. Gar-
lands of roses interwoven with pearls were tied about the fore-

[1]Jacquemont, vol. II, p. 25.

head of the Maharaja and a gold nose-ring with a pearl was fixed in the nose of Gul Begam. Gul Begam was renamed Gul Bahar Begum.'[1]

Social censure bothered Ranjit, and his sleep was disturbed by nightmares in which a figure in black (obviously a Nihang) menaced him. Ranjit consulted his astrologers, who interpreted the dream as a portent of danger from the fanatic Akalis and persuaded him to appease their wrath by large charities to the gurdwaras—which the superstitious Ranjit immediately proffered.

Maharani Gulbahar Begam dominated the Maharaja's life for the next few years. She did not veil herself and on ceremonial occasions rode on the same elephant as her husband. It was the last love affair of Ranjit Singh's life.[2]

Even the ministrations of the youthful Gulbahar could not prevent the Maharaja from having a sort of political hangover. The feeling that the English loved him was followed by an unpleas-

---

[1]Sohan Lal, *Daftar* III.

[2]There were many women in the royal harem some of whom had been admitted after some sort of ceremony; others (usually widows) simply took residence in the palace because the Maharaja had cast his mantle over them (*Chaddar andāzi*); and there were yet others who came as maidservants but having caught Ranjit's fancy became his mistresses. The following names appear in the records as having enjoyed some sort of relationship with the Maharaja:

Mehtab Kaur (married in 1796, died 1813). She bore the Maharaja three sons: Isher Singh who died in infancy, Sher Singh and Tara Singh; Raj Kaur (Mai Nakkain) married in 1798, mother of Kharak Singh. Mai Nakkain died in 1818; Mohran (m. 1802); Rattan Kaur and Daya Kaur, widows of Sahib Singh Bhangi of Gujerat (m. 1812). Rattan Kaur was the mother of Multana Singh and Daya Kaur of Kashmira Singh and Peshaura Singh; Chand Kaur (m. 1815); Lachmi, daughter of Desa Singh Sidhu of Gujranwala (m. 1820); Mehatab Kaur (m. 1822); Guddan and her sister Banso, daughters of Sansar Chand of Kangra; Saman Kaur (m. 1832); Gulbahar Begum and Jindan, mother of Dalip Singh. Other names mentioned are Gulab Kaur, Ram Devi, Rani Devi, Bannat, Har Devi and Danno.

In 1852 the British Government were paying a pension to Jind Kalan as a widow of Ranjit Singh. She and her mother had been summoned by Ranjit Singh about 1832 to answer the complaint of one named Abdul Samad Khan who stated that Jind Kalan was betrothed to him but her mother refused to fulfil the engagement. Ranjit Singh cancelled the betrothal and kept Jind Kalan and her mother in his own seraglio. Besides Mohjran, Gul Begam and Jind Kalan three other Mohammedan ranis are named—Teiboo, Junnut Bibi and Gobe.

In an interview given to *Le Voltaire in* January 1889, Prince Dalip Singh stated: 'I am the son of one of my father's forty-six wives.'

ant sensation that their professions of affection were mere sham;
that they meant to thwart his ambitions towards Sindh and were
befriending his worst enemies, the Afghans, in order to strangle
him in the embrace of friendship.

Once Ranjit Singh's confidence in English sincerity was shaken
he did his best to thwart their moves in Sindh and Afghanistan.
He encouraged the Amirs to resist foreign intrusion, commercial
or political. He was not successful as his own intentions were
commonly known, and the aggressive way in which he had begun
to talk of taking Shikarpur did not square with his professions
as a well-wisher of the Sindhians. Nevertheless, Ranjit's overtures gave the Amirs an opportunity of playing the Punjabis
against the English. Ranjit also began to meddle more actively
in Afghan politics. He encouraged Shah Shuja to make another
attempt to recover the Afghan throne and eject the Barakzais with
whom the British were negotiating commercial treaties. He received emissaries from the Court of Herat. He made it known
to the British that the Russians were anxious to treat with him.
He showed marked favour to agents from Nepal. There were
rumours of fresh contact with the Maratha chiefs and the Nizam
of Hyderabad.[1]

Ranjit Singh also pressed for the settlement of his claims to
some towns across the Sutlej. The English Government accepted
his contentions regarding some of the unimportant ones—
Anandpur, Chamkaur, Kiratpur and Macchiwara, but rejected his
case with regard to the most important, Ferozepur. Ferozepur was
only forty miles from Lahore and close to several fords from
which troops could wade across the Sutlej. This was done on
the advice of military commanders, who felt that Ludhiana was
too far off from Lahore to be an effective base for operations.
The excuse was provided by the death of the widow, Lachman
Kaur, who had been in possession of the town, in Septmber 1835.
The Ludhiana Agent decided that her estates lapsed to the English
and not to Ranjit Singh, who had up till then been acknowledged by them as her overlord. British troops moved in and began
to fortify Ferozepur.

The Maharaja sensed the approaching danger: '*pās ā gayā*

---

[1] The Nizam sent Ranjit Singh a bejewelled canopy which Ranjit presented
to the Golden Temple. It adorns the Temple to this day.

—they have come closer,' he remarked. He countered the move by garrisoning Kasur which faced Ferozepur on his side of the Sutlej.

Within a few months of the protestations of perpetual friendship made at Rupar, the two States were preparing for war.

CHAPTER XVIII

BREAKING OUT OF THE BRITISH CORDON

THE BRITISH had entered into diplomatic relations with the Sindhians and the Afghans, leaving the Punjabis only two directions in which they could expand; across the Himalayas up to the borders of China, and into the Pathan country, which was a strip of no-man's land between the Punjab and Afghanistan. The Punjabis first struck across the almost impassable mountain ranges of Kashmir into Ladakh. The Dogra General, Zorawar Singh, who was posted at Kishtawar, exploited a domestic quarrel in the Ladakhi ruling family. He put one of the contenders in possession on payment of Rs 30,000 per annum to the Durbar and occupied some of the strategically-placed forts. In the winter of 1836, Zorawar Singh presented the Maharaja with the *nazrānā* he had brought from Ladakh and asked for permission to push further westwards to Iskardu and make a common frontier with China. Ranjit Singh ordered him to hold his hand for the time being.

Captain Wade registered a strong protest over the action of the Durbar troops and offered asylum to members of the dispossessed Ladakhi family. The Maharaja reminded him of the treaty of 1809 and of the fact that the territory in question was on his side of the Sutlej. Wade ignored the note and warned his government of the danger of allowing the Punjabis to have a common frontier with the Chinese.

While Zorawar Singh was carrying the Punjab's standards into Tibet, Ranjit Singh was taking steps to push his western frontier further westwards. His earlier offer to put Shuja back on the throne had come to nothing because he had not only wanted the Shah to renounce his title to Multan, Dera Ghazi Khan, Dera Ismail Khan, Mankera and Peshawar, but also to send tribute in the shape of gifts of horses, fruit, etc. In addition, there were clauses requiring an absolute ban on the slaughter of kine in Afghanistan and the surrender of the sandalwood portals of the Hindu temple of Somnath which the iconoclast Mahmud had taken to Ghazni 800 years ago. Shuja thought it best to say nothing to the Durbar and try to regain his throne by himself.

Shuja received some support from the Amirs of Sindh. He was assured that there would be a general rising of the tribes in his favour as soon as he crossed over into Afghanistan. But when he entered his country, tribal leaders did no more than reiterate their promise of help without moving out of their fortresses. Dost Mohammed sent his brothers to check Shuja's march towards Kabul. In a brief encounter at Kandahar, Shuja's troops were routed and the Shah came back to Ludhiana and rejoined his 600 wives.

Ranjit Singh came to the conclusion that if he wanted his North-West Frontier really secure and capable of being used as a springboard for an invasion of Afghanistan, he would have to bring it under his direct control instead of leaving it in the hands of Afghan chiefs who paid tribute. Consequently, when Shuja was contending with Dost Mohammed's brothers, Hari Singh Nalwa was instructed to take over the Governorship of Peshawar from the Durbar's Afghan vassal, Sultan Mohammed, and the city was garrisoned with Punjabi troops.

Nalwa left the Maharaja's grandson, Prince Nau Nihal Singh, to administer Peshawar, and occupied himself in taming the semi-savage tribes inhabiting the surrounding country. Pathan tribesmen held the Punjabis, whom they had bullied over the centuries, in utter contempt. Nalwa decided to be absolutely ruthless. Whenever the Pathans resorted to ambushing and sniping (their favourite mode of fighting), he raided their villages and destroyed every home. Within a few months the name of Nalwa became a terror in the tribal territory.[1] He completed the chain of forts, each within sight of the other. Two which stood on the entrance of the Khyber Pass were fortified and placed under the command of the Durbar's ablest of officers—Shab Kadar with a garrison of 1,900 under Lehna Singh Sandhawalia; Jamrud with a garrison of 600 under Maha Singh. Dost Mohammed hurried towards Peshawar. He addressed several rude notes to Ranjit Singh

[1]To this day Pathan women, when they want to frighten their children into behaving well, say: 'Hush child, Nalwa is coming.'

asking him to evacuate the city or taste the steel of the Afghan sabre. Ranjit replied in the same tone, saying he would welcome a trial of strength between the Punjabis and the Afghans.[1]

Dost Mohammed tried to persuade the English to help him. When that failed he resorted to the old trick, the holy war. On January 2, 1835, he had himself invested with the title of *Amir-ul-Mumnin*—Commander of the Faithful—and exhorted Mussulmans to destroy the infidel. He began to suffer from the same *folie-de-grandeur* as Syed Ahmed and fined anyone who called him Sardar instead of Amir; Hindus he mulcted without conscience. His sons led an army of regulars and Ghazis determined to clear the Punjabis out of the North-West Frontier.

The Maharaja sent Fakeer Azizuddin and the American, Josiah Harlan, who had served under the Afghans, to Dost Mohammed. The Amir agreed to receive the envoys and when they arrived, swore: 'Ah! you Kafirs, I have taken you in.' When the Fakeer protested that it was improper to detain foreign envoys, Dost replied that infidels and their agents were beyond the pale of diplomatic convention. But even in detention, Josiah Harlan succeeded in sowing discord among the Afghans. He wrote: 'I divided his (i.e. Dost Mohammed's) brothers against him, exciting their jealousy of his growing power....I induced his brother, Sultan Mohamed Khan, lately deported chief of Peshawar with 10,000 men, to withdraw suddenly from his camp about nightfall. The chief accompanied me towards the Sikh camp, while his followers fled to their mountain fortresses.'[2] Dost Mohammed, continues Harlan, went back to Kabul and in 'bitterness of spirit declaiming against the eruptions of military renown, plunged himself in the study of the Koran'.

Dost Mohammed's disillusionment with worldly success reduced tension on the North-West Frontier. It gave Ranjit Singh time

---

[1]'If out of haughtiness the Maharaja does not pay heed to my request I (Dost Mohammed) will gird up my loins for battle and become a thorn in the courtyard of your rose garden. I will muster an army of crusaders who know nothing except fighting unto death. I will create tumult on all sides and a scene of chaos everywhere.'

To which Ranjit's answer was: 'We have broken the heads of refractory chiefs and put our foes in irons. If Dost, out of avarice and greed, desires to give battle with the small force he has, let him come...' *Lahore Durbar*, pp. 178-9.

[2]*European Adventurers in Nothern India*, p. 257.

to turn to Sindh and try to thwart English attempts to coerce
the reluctant Amirs to align themselves on the British side. The
only chance the Sindhians had of preserving their independence
was to incite their voracious neighbours against each other. They
tried to do this by provoking a tribe known as the Mazaris, who
inhabited the fork between the Indus and the Sutlej, suddenly to
attack isolated Punjabi outposts south of Multan and plunder
villages in the Durbar's domains.

Prince Kharak Singh was ordered to take punitive measures.
He made short work of the ill-disciplined Mazari tribesmen and,
in the summer of 1836, occupied Mithankot and Rojhan. He
wrote to his father asking for permission to proceed to Shikarpur.
Ranjit Singh had ample excuse to take Shikarpur as the Wahabi
fanatic, Nasiruddin, had made it the centre of his campaign
against the Sikhs, but he hesitated to take a step which might
involve him in hostilities with the English. The hesitation proved
fatal to his ambitions in the south.

The English made capital of the Maharaja's nervousness.
MacNaughten, Secretary to the Government of India, advocated
immediate steps be taken to forestall the Punjabis. 'The Government of India is bound by the strongest consideration of political interest to prevent the extention of the Sikh power along the
whole course of the Indus,' he wrote. In August, Wade was sent
to see Ranjit Singh and 'use every means in his power short of
actual menace to keep His Highness at Lahore and to prevent
the further advance of his army'.[1] If the Durbar maintained that
his expedition was punitive, it was to be told that the Amirs
had formally placed themselves under British protection (which
was not true).

Ranjit Singh tried to outmanoeuvre the English. He entered
into an agreement with Shuja undertaking to help him in yet
another bid to recover his kingdom in return for Shuja's renounc-
ing his claim on Peshawar (which was already in Ranjit's hands)
and Shikarpur (which was not). He faced the English with a
threefold argument. He had to punish the people who had instigated the Mazaris; Shuja, who had a valid title to Shikarpur,
had passed it on to him; and in the treaty of 1809 the British
had solemnly sworn not to meddle with the affairs of territories

[1] *Lahore Durbar*, pp. 140-1.

west of the Sutlej. The English agreed that the Durbar had been
wronged by the Mazaris, but refused to recognize its right to
take Shikarpur either as a prize or by virtue of an agreement
with Shah Shuja. And as for the treaty of 1809, they replied
ingenuously, the territories in question were not west of the Sutlej,
but west of the Sutlej plus the Indus, which was not the same
thing.

The Durbar's Ministers were indignant. They exhorted the
Maharaja to make a firm stand and, if necessary, go to war.
They argued that a nation which had so often violated its solemn
promises and which had made systematic expansion a policy,
would sooner or later find an excuse to annex the Punjab. They
vaunted the martial qualities and invincibility of the Khalsa
armies. Ranjit Singh was extremely angry with the English but
he had never let anger be his counseller. After his temper had
subsided, he asked his advisers: 'What happened to the 200,000-
strong army of the Marathas who fought the English?' He tried
through Fakeer Azizuddin to persuade the English to agree to
consider Sindh *Mulk-i-mahfuza*—neutral territory—and obtain an
assurance that a similar policy would not be followed in Afghanistan. Wade evaded the suggestions by delivering sermons on
British policy of preserving peace and spreading civilization.
Ranjit Singh tried to have the question of Sindh postponed till
he had discussed the matter personally with the new Governor-
General, Lord Auckland. He told Wade that his Sardars were
saying to him: 'Look at what the *Sāhib log* are doing! They are
seizing one place and defining boundaries in another.' But Wade
was immovable. At one of the meetings the Maharaja asked the
Englishman the meaning of the words 'welfare and prosperity'
and 'respect and consideration' which the Governor-General had
used in his letter to him. Wade ignored the sarcasm and proceeded to explain the meaning of the words at some length.
Ranjit Singh cut him short: 'I understand too well.' Wade described the end of the interview: 'His Highness betrayed some
impatience; he grasped the hand of the Fakeer and struck the
palm repeatedly.'[1] At last, Ranjit Singh gave in and agreed not
to go farther—*bil fel O bil hal*—for the time being. The debate
on Sindh was closed. But he refused to sign any more treaties

[1]SC$_{17}$ of March 6, 1837.

6. SIKH CHIEFTAINS
(Engraving from a drawing by Prince Alexis Soltykoff, 1842)

7. THE COURT OF RANJIT SINGH: Sher Singh returned from the hunt – Ranjit Singh seated under the umbrella. (Oil painting by Auguste Theodor Schoefft, c.1838) (Photo: Collection of the late Princess Bamber-Sutherland)

on the subject and refused to give up his advance post at Rojhan.

Ranjit Singh had reluctantly written off Sindh; he was in no mood to have his authority challenged elsewhere when trouble restarted on the North-West Frontier. Nalwa's energetic measures, particularly the chain of forts that he had made, gave the Afghans reason to believe that the Punjabis contemplated an invasion of their country. Dost Mohammed gave up the study of the Koran and began to whip up religious sentiments of the tribesmen for yet another Jihad. He decided to strike when he heard that the Durbar was preoccupied with the nuptials of Prince Nau Nihal Singh and Nalwa was ill and confined to his bed in Peshawar.

Dost Mohammed's strategy was to isolate the Punjabi garrisons at Shabkadar, Jamrud and Peshawar and reduce each in turn. The first on the list was Jamrud. It was the most advanced outpost and the weakest link in Nalwa's chain of fortresses. One detachment was sent to keep Lehna Singh Sandhwalia at Shabkadar whilst the main Afghan army, numbering over 25,000 men with eighteen heavy guns, beseiged Jamrud. Maha Singh had only 600 men and a few light guns. Within a few hours the Afghan guns reduced the walls of Jamrud to rubble. Maha Singh's men dug trenches and for four days kept the Afghans at bay with musket fire; then Maha Singh sent word to Nalwa that he could not hold out any longer. (A Sikh woman disguised as an Afghan stole through the enemy's ranks at night to carry the message to Peshawar.) Nalwa got up from his sick bed and made his way to Jamrud.

The news that Nalwa had risen was enough to frighten the Afghans. They raised the siege of Jamrud and, in order to ensure escape in the event of defeat, took up position in the valley of the Khyber. Nalwa drew up his troops in battle formation and waited for the Afghans, who outnumbered him three to one, to attack him. For seven days the armies faced each other. Nalwa realized that the Afghans had no stomach for battle and ordered the troops to advance. The engagement took place on April 30, 1837. The Punjabis drove the Afghans and Pathan tribemen before them without any difficulty and captured eleven enemy guns; their chief problem was to keep their ranks intact while in pursuit. Dost Mohammed's son, Mohammed Akbar Khan, who was watching the battle from an escarpment, saw Nalwa leading the attack well ahead of his men. Mohammed Akbar Khan swooped down on the isolated advance column, poured lead into Nalwa's howdah and, in the confusion which followed this surprise attack, retook all his guns and in addition captured three belonging to the Punjabis. His own personal achievement was the killing of one Sikh soldier.

Nalwa was grievously wounded and was bought back to Jamrud. He knew his end was near. He ordered his officers to keep his death a secret until the troops had driven the Afghans beyond the Khyber Pass. This the Punjabis did with great vigour. Although the Afghans had to give up their plan to recapture Peshawar and Shabkadar and had been forced to retreat ignominiously from Jamrud, they returned to Kabul in absolute jubilation. What if the battle was lost? They had killed Nalwa, whose name alone was worth 'a hundred and twenty-five thousand men.'[1]

An account of the battle and the death of Nalwa was sent by an Englishman, Dr Wood, to Wade,[2] who forwarded it to the Governor-General. He wrote that there had been a great slaughter of the Afghans; amongst those killed was Mohammed Afzal, the eldest son of Dost Mohammed. Dr Wood estimated that the Punjabis lost about 6,000 of their total force of 12,000 men; the Afgans, who outnumbered them, left 11,000 men dead on the field. Of the death of Nalwa, Dr Wood wrote:

'Hari Singh received four wounds: two sabre cuts across his chest, one arrow was fixed in his breast which he deliberately pulled out himself, and continued to issue orders as before until he received a gunshot wound in the side, from which he gradually sank and was carried off the field to the fort, where he expired, requesting that his death should not be made known until the arrival of the Maharaja's reliefs.'

Ranjit Singh was on his way to the Khyber when information of Nalwa's death was brought to him. The Maharaja broke down, beat his breast in anguish and wept bitter tears. By the

[1]The Afghans had really not much to boast of on this action. Although Akbar Khan plumed himself on a transcendent victory. The Sikhs scarcely acknowledged defeat, but their loss in the person of their chief was irreparable.' Masson, vol. III, ch. 16.
[2]PC_{59} of May 29, 1837.

time he reached Jamrud, the last Afghan soldier had vanished from the scene.

Let us turn back a few pages of the Maharaja's diary to see the wedding that had prevented Ranjit Singh from coming to Nalwa's aid in time.

CHAPTER XIX

PRINCE NAU NIHAL'S WEDDING
AND THE FESTIVAL OF HOLI

'BY THE GRACE of Sree Akalurakhjee—Friendly and kind Sir, in consideration of the friendship which promotes unity and sincerity, in these auspicious days marked by a thousand happy omens we wish to complete the picture of our desires by arranging the marriage of our son, Prince Nau Nihal Singh, who is fortune's favourite child, the lustre on the forehead of felicity, the apple of the eye of our dominions, the lord of the glorious garden of sovereignty and the solace of our soul, with the pen of friendship we write to request your Excellency, who is replete with amiable and friendly qualities, to grace this occasion with your presence and so make our joy and happiness limitless.'

Thus ran the Maharaja's invitation to Sir Henry Fane, Commander-in-Chief of the British Army, to attend the wedding of his grandson. Sir Henry was instructed by the Governor-General to accept it as the representative of the Government of India. In Sir Henry's suite was his young nephew, Lt. Henry Edward Fane, who accompanied him as his A.D.C. The young subaltern's diary gives a fairly detailed picture of the ceremonial and a lively portrait of the ageing Maharaja. It reminds one of Milton's lines:

'Where the East, with richest hand, showers
on her kings barbaric pearls and gold.'

The Commander-in-Chief's party, which included Captain Wade, was received by Prince Sher Singh on the western bank of the Sutlej. Young Fane was struck by his looks: 'as handsome a black-bearded gentleman as one often sees, richly dressed in silks and brocade...he had the most beautiful tiara of diamonds, emeralds and rubies I have ever seen; some of the emeralds in particular being enormous'.[1] The Fanes were guests of Sher Singh's and on one occasion were shown the young prince's dressing room. 'It was filled with looking glasses, French scent bottles and little knick-knacks of all kinds, and evidently showed the master to be a dandy of the first water. His fondness for European luxuries is not confined to his toilette.' Sher Singh loved French wines and liked to ride in his English carriage which followed him wherever he went.

On March 5, 1837, the British party arrived at Amritsar and was received by Prince Kharak Singh and Raja Dhian Singh. 'Both he and all his suite literally blazed in jewels, and cloth of gold and silver,' wrote Fane. Dhian Singh, who attracted more attention, was 'superbly mounted on a large Persian horse, who curvetted and pranced about, as if proud of his rider. His bridle and saddle were covered with gold embroidery and underneath the latter was a saddlecloth of silver tissue, with a broad fringe of the same, which covered his horse to the tail; the horse's legs and tail were dyed with red, the former up to the kness, and the latter half-way up, as an emblem of the number of enemies he had killed in battle, and that the blood from them had covered the animal thus far.'

The next morning the party went to call on Ranjit Singh, who was staying in a house outside the city. The Maharaja came on his elephant to receive his guests. Fane's picture of Ranjit is not flattering. 'The lion of the Punjab is a very small, infirm-looking old man of fifty-five (looking ten years older), but still more hale and stout than I expected to have seen him from what we had previously heard. He was dressed very plainly in green cashmere turban, coat and gloves, with single rows of large pearls down the breast, round his neck and on his arms and legs, and a single string of very large diamonds round his arms. The Seikh turban, which so much disfigures the whole of this handsome race, does so particularly with him, and gives his countenance a low expression of cunning, which it would not probably otherwise have. His single eye is bleared and bloodshot, but still shows that wonderful acuteness and determination by which he has been able to subdue the unruly spirit of his people.'

The British party was taken to the Maharaja's enclosure where

[1]Fane, p. 120.

the courtiers had assembled: 'The dresses and jewels of the Raja's Court were the most superb that can be conceived; the whole scene can only be compared to a gala night at the opera. The Minister's son (Hira Singh in particular, the reigning favourite of the day) was literally one mass of jewels; his neck, arms and legs were covered with necklaces, armlets and bangles, formed of pearls, diamonds and rubies, one above the other, so thick that it was difficult to discover anything between them.' The Maharaja was in high spirits. 'The old prince talked away at a great rate, discussed many subjects and asked questions of all kinds, many of them showing his shrewd and calculating character. The size of the Company's army—the number of battles Sir Henry had been in—the number of English offices attached to each regiment—our mode of casting artillery.'

In the afternoon the party were present at the *neundra* the ceremonial of giving presents to the bridegroom. This took place in the house of a Sardar with much nautch and noise. The presents, says Fane, were valued at nearly £17,000.

The bridegroom's party left Amritsar and in the afternoon formed into a procession. There were seventy elephants and 600 horsemen. The Maharaja showered gold and silver coins on the throng of beggars. 'The crowd assembled surpassed belief,' wrote Fane. 'I should say it included from five to six hundred thousand persons, all shoving and fighting to get in the direction—near the Raja's elephant.' On arriving at the bride's residence, the guests dismounted and assembled in a large tent. 'The bridegroom was now introduced for the first time, having his face covered with a veil made of strings of large pearls hung on gold thread. He is a thin, unhealthy looking boy, dreadfully marked with smallpox, but seemed intelligent and well-mannered.'

The actual marriage took place at 9 p.m. as fixed by the astrologers. The guests reassembled in Ranjit's pavilion, where they 'found him seated, as usual, surrounded by his ministers and favourites, perched on a chair, with a highly embroidered gold stool for his knees to rest on. His dress was almost always the same (green cashmere) and, with the exception of the rows of great pearls I before mentioned, and on State occasions the Koh-i-noor, his great diamond, he very seldom wore jewels. He never was the cleanest person in the world, and his dress, I should imagine, was but seldom changed in any part. He has a curious habit of wearing but one stocking, from having had the rheumatism in one of his feet, which he thinks necessary to keep warm.

'The Raja sent round the intoxicating liquor which he drinks, at such a rate (particularly to the General, whose cup he always looked into to see that he really drank) that we were all right glad to get away, and retire to our beds, after one of the most fatiguing days I have ever experienced. The liquor he drinks would kill most people in a week, being, I should imagine, considerably stronger than spirits or wine; so much so as to bring tears into our eyes, even with the smallest quantity; and yet, during our different visits, he seldom drank less than several small glasses full and without any apparent effect.'

An exhibition of the bride's dowry was the next item on the list. Except for elephants, of which there were only eleven, there were one hundred and one animals each of all the other varieties given: cows, buffaloes, camels, horses, bullocks etc. There were five hundred 'of the most beautiful' Cashmere shawls; 'the jewels were many of them very handsome and of great intrinsic value. Among other things was a complete set of native dinner and washing things, all of silver, and beautifully carved.'

At the grand soiree, when the ladies were invited, the whole pavilion was lit with oil lamps and fountains played. 'From the open building where the Court and ourselves sat, the whole scene looked more like an imitation of fairyland at a theatre than anything else, and at times I felt myself beginning to wonder when the spirits were going to appear. No drinks were served in the presence of ladies, but as soon as they retired the old lion was as usual plying the General with liquor and asking questions.'

Two days later Ranjit Singh paid a visit to the English camp and inspected their troops. 'He never ceased asking questions from the moment he entered—"What was the strength of the Indian Army?" "Did we think that Russian interest was doing us much harm in Persia?" "Was it thought that Persia had sufficient power to give effectual aid to Russia in the event of their coming in this direction?" etc, etc. These and many other questions, put with the greatest acuteness, and many of them most difficult to answer, made that generally most dull of all amusements quite the reverse; and though he remained for longer than is generally the case, none, I think, felt bored.' After seeing the presents (one elephant, eight horses, a double-barrelled gun, fifty-one pieces of artillery) Ranjit Singh examined every gun and questioned each gunner minutely.

The next day Sir Henry Fane inspected the Sikh troops. 'Some few were beautifully dressed in chain armour, and looked so like the pictures one sees of warriors in the time of Richard *Coeur de Lion,* that one might almost fancy one's self transported back to the times of the Crusaders; for which all these gentlemen in yellow and all the colours of the rainbow, would make a good appearance as the soldiers of Saladin.

The party were shown the royal jewels, including the Koh-i-noor. And the evenings were as usual devoted to 'nautching, drinking and fireworks'.

Holi, the colourful festival of spring, which was ever Ranjit's favourite, was upon them. The British Commander-in-Chief was persuaded to stay on as the astrologers had pronounced his earlier departure inauspicious. Sir Henry Fane went to the Maharaja's pavilion.

'And a most extraordinary scene it was,' Fane writes. 'We found him (Ranjit) seated, surrounded as usual by his court and, for the first time, the guard of Amazons, some thirty or forty in number, many of them very pretty, armed with bows and arrows, which they drew the moment we made our appearance, in the most warlike style...whether in the presence of an enemy they would be found equally bold, I know not, but in that of the old chieftain they dared to do and say in a way that none of his most favourite courtiers ventured to attempt.'

Holi was a most hilarious affair. 'In front of every chair were small baskets, heaped one above another, full of small, brittle balls, filled with red powder, and alongside them large bowls of thick yellow saffron, and long gold squirts, with which each of us armed ourselves. As soon as we were all seated, the Raja took a large butter-boat kind of article, filled with the said saffron, and poured it on Sir Henry's bald head; while, at the same time, the Prime Minister rubbed him all over with gold and silver leaf, mixed with red powder.

'We were all holding our sides with laughter at the Chief bowing to all this, wondering at the meaning of it, when our mirth (or rather mine) was changed into grief, at having one eye nearly put out by a long-bearded gentleman opposite, who deliberately threw a ball, filled with red powder, into one eye, while another factious youth closed up the other with saffron soup.... Ranjeet himself seemed to enjoy the fun as much as anyone; and though few of the courtiers aimed at him personally, this did not prevent him from taking an occasional shot himself, his being more particularly directed against an Afghan Ambassador, just arrived at his Court from Kandahar. This poor man was dressed in his best, his beard combed and dyed to a nicety, his tucked well under him, and his face drilled to a grave, diplomatic caste. Never having before seen the festival of Holi, he had not the smallest idea what he had to expect, and his look of astonishment at a ball of red shot being shied in his eye, and his horror when his beard was turned to a bright saffron colour, I shall long remember. We turned all our ammunition upon him, and first one eye and then another was closed up, till at length he was fairly beat out of his etiquette, and took to his heels amidst a roar of laughter from all our party.

'The battle raged for more than an hour, during which neither the Commander-in-Chief nor the Amazons came off scot-free; and by the time we all got up to return home, the honourable company of London chimney-sweeps would have turned us out as too dirty for their society.'

Holi was the one festival Ranjit always looked forward to; and he made sure that it was *waddā tamasha* (big fun).

The Maharaja gave farewell gifts to all his English guests. The Commander-in-Chief and the military secretary were invested with the order of the Star of the prosperity of the Punjab *(Kau-Kāb-i-Iqbāl-i-Punjāb)* which the Maharaja had inaugurated that year. Young Fane was almost sentimental about the old Sikh Raja when it came to taking leave. 'I am sure both he (General Fane) and almost everyone present felt sincere sorrow at parting from the good-natured, kind old man, whom we had all begun to consider as an old friend.'

Fane's account of the visit ends with a handsome tribute. 'Runjeet, among his subjects, has the character generally of a kind and generous master, and one of the best princes that has ever reigned in India. As evidence of his being a really good and amiable man, may be cited his kindness to children (two or three of whom he has crawling about the durbar), and the fact of his never having, since he conquered the country, put a man to death for even the most heinous crimes.'

CHAPTER XX

THE ARMY OF THE INDUS

MUCH AS Dost Mohammed tried to claim the battle of Jamrud as an Afghan victory (he heaped public honours upon his son as the victor), nothing could stop the stench of eleven thousand Afghan corpses strewn about the pass of Khyber reaching the nostrils of the tribesmen in the neighbouring hills and valleys. The Durbar's flag still fluttered on the heights of Bala Hissar in Peshawar, at Shab Kadar and on the ruins of Jurud. And now the ghost of the valiant Nalwa haunted the rocky defiles, spreading terror amongst the people.

It was necessary for Dost Mohammed to recover his prestige. At first he tried flattery and wrote to the Maharaja: 'I always regarded myself as established by your authority...I was your servant.' If the Durbar could give him Peshawar, he would pay tribute and there would be no trouble on the frontier. He promised not to turn to the English if the Punjabis agreed to this proposal. But if the request was turned down he would be compelled by circumstances to fight and seek the help of other powers. *Tang āmad bajang āmad*—when one is forced, one goes to battle.[1]

Ranjit Singh expressed surprise at Dost Mohammed's demand for Peshawar. He told the Afghans that the English had signed a treaty with him not to interfere in the affairs of countries west of the Sutlej and added that 'The English, for the firmness of their engagements, the truth of their pledges, adherence to their word, the purity of their intentions and fidelity to claims of long-enduring friendship, are celebrated throughout the world.' Maintenance of peace, warned Ranjit Singh, was not the sole monopoly of the Afghans. If they could force war on him, he too could force it on them. If Dost Mohammed wanted to stay

[1] PC$_{28}$ of September 11, 1837.

peacefully on his throne at Kabul, he had better send a tribute
of horses, dried fruit, etc., to Lahore.

While Dost Mohammed and Ranjit Singh were thus engaged
in verbal warfare, the Governor-General sent Alexander Burnes
to Afghanistan to try and draw Dost Mohammed to their side;
rumours of Russian infiltration into Persia and Afghanistan were
the chief reason for taking this step. 'By the blessing of prudence,
the English and the Sikh nation will be united to the end of time,'
wrote Auckland to Ranjit Singh, and explained Burnes's mission
being purely commercial.

Burnes did not fare too well at Kabul. He had not much to
offer Dost Mohammed and words of flattery (when speaking to
Dost, Burnes always joined the palms of his hands and addressed
him as *gharib-nawaz*—cherisher of the poor) were of little avail
against the Russian Agent, Vektavich, who promised large sums
of money. Dost made Peshawar the price of his co-operation,
which the British could not give him without going to war with
the Punjabis. Auckland had to choose between Dost Mohammed
and Ranjit Singh. He chose Ranjit Singh and decided to seek
his help in ousting Dost and putting Shah Shuja on the throne
of Afghanistan. In April 1838, Burnes's mission was withdrawn
from Kabul[1] and Auckland expressed a wish to meet Ranjit Singh
for an 'exchange of ideas'.

By then the Governor-General was describing the Maharaja
as 'the most powerful and valuable of our friends'.[2]

Ranjit Singh sent a delegation headed by Fakeer Azizuddin
to convey his compliments to Lord Auckland, reiterate the
goodwill of the Durbar towards the British Government and say
that the Maharaja would be delighted to meet the Governor-
General. A return delegation, headed by W. H. MacNaughten,
followed on the heels of Fakeer Azizuddin's and waited on the
Maharaja at Adinanagar. Captain Wade and Dr McGregor were
with this delegation; so also was W.G. Osborne, Military

[1] Masson, who was with Burnes, wrote: 'Thus closed a mission, one of the
most extraordinary ever sent forth by a government; whether as to the singular
manner in which it was conducted, or as to its results. There was undoubtedly
great blame on all sides. The government had furnished no instructions,
apparently confiding in the discretion of a man who had none.' vol. III, ch. 17.
[2]Minute dated May 12, 1838.

Secretary to the Governor-General, whose diary of daily events
in The Court and Camp of Ranjit Singh is most vivid.[1]

Osborne describes the first meeting with the Maharaja: 'Cross-
legged in a golden chair, dressed in simple white, wearing no
ornaments but a single string of enormous pearls round the waist,
and the celebrated Koh-i-noor, or mountain of light, on his arm
(the jewel rivalled, if not surpassed, in brilliancy by the glance
of fire which every now and then shot from his single eye as
it wandered restlessly round the circle)—sat the Lion of Lahore.
On Ranjit's seating himself, his chiefs all squatted on the floor
round his chair, with the exception of Dhian Singh, who remained
standing behind his master. Though far removed from being
handsome himself, Ranjit appears to take a pride in being
surrounded by good-looking people, and I believe few, if any,
other, courts either in Europe or the East could show such a fine
looking set of men as the principal Sikh Sardars.'[2]

Osborne also remarked on the Maharaja's curiosity and range
of interests: 'It is hardly possible to give an idea of the ceaseless rapidity with which his questions flow, or the infinite va-
riety of subjects they embrace. "Do you drink wine?" "How
much?" 'Did you taste the wine which I sent you yesterday?"
"How much of it did you drink?" "What artillery have you
brought with you?" "Have they got any shells?" "How many?"
"Do you like riding on horseback?" "What country's horses do
you prefer?" "Are you in the army?" "Which do you like best,
cavalry or infantry?" "Does Lord Auckland drink wine?" "How
many glasses?" "Does he drink it in the morning?" "What is
the strength of the Company's army?" "Are they well disciplined?" etc.'[3]

The delegates saw a lot of Ranjit in the next few days. They
were present at the durbar in the mornings, inspected troops at
parade, sat beside the Maharaja watching his Kashmiri beauties
in soldiers' uniform dancing, and drank out of his gold goblets.
'The more I see of Ranjit, the more he strikes me as an
extraordinary man,' wrote Osborne. 'Cunning and distrustful

[1]Quotations from Osborne are taken from a reprint of The Court and Camp
by Susil Gupta Ltd in 1952.
[2]Osborne, p. 29.
[3]Ibid, p. 31.

himself, he has succeeded in inspiring his followers with a strong and devoted attachment to his person with a quick talent at reading men's minds, he is equally adept at concealing his own; and it is curious to see the sort of quiet indifference with which he listens to the absurd reports of his own motives and actions which are daily poured into his ears at the durbar, without giving any opinion of his own, and without rendering it possible to guess what his final decistion on any subject will be, till the moment of action has arrived. Though he is by profession a soldier, in religion he is in reality a sceptic, and it is difficult to say whether his superstition is real, or only a mark assumed to gratify and conciliate his people.'[1]

After two days of complimentary speeches and entertainment, MacNaughten introduced the business by reading out Auckland's letter outlining the plan to restore Shah Shuja. Auckland was keen that the Durbar should undertake the expedition entirely on its own; but if it did want the English to co-operate, they were willing. Osborne records the reactions of the courtiers: 'Dhian Singh here showed manifest tokens of disapprobation; and though not daring to make any remark, could not refrain from expressing, both by his countenance and sundry ominous shakes of the head, his dissatisfaction at the idea of any alliance with us.'[2]

Ranjit Singh ignored his Prime Minister's views and agreed in principle to back the venture. He was strong enough to do so, having at the time 31 regiments of infantry, 9 regiments of cavalry, 288 pieces of artillery of various calibres, 11,800 irregular sowars.[3] When the formal audience was over, his ministers asked him to consider his decision. Only two, Fakeer Azizuddin and Bhaia Ram Singh, were for co-operation with the English; all the others led by Dhian Singh were against it. The debate continued behind the scenes.

Ten days later, the Maharaja and the delegates left Adinanagar and proceeded to Lahore. The Englishmen were received in the

[1] Osborne, p. 35.
[2] Ibid, p. 38.
[3] Shahamat Ali, pp. 23-35. According to Shahamat Ali the cost of maintaining this large fighting force as Rs 1,27,96,482, i.e. more than one third of the State's income. Besides this, the jagirdars furnished 9 regiments of infantry, 5 regiments of cavalry, 87 pieces of artillery and 6,460 irregular sowars.

Shalamar Gardens where they were joined by Alexander Burnes and Dr Ford, who had just returned from Kabul, Burnes incited Ranjit Singh by repeating words he alleged Dost Mohammed had used in relation to the Maharaja : 'I can't do that brute any real harm, but I will torment him a good deal yet before I have done with him.' The trick worked and Ranjit Singh expressed willingness to join the English against Dost Mohammed. The English delegation promptly got the draft of the treaty ready. Dhian Singh pleaded with the Maharaja not to be hasty and reconsider his decision. Ranjit began to waver. 'The old lion has turned sulky, and refuses to sign the treaty, wishing to stipulate for all sorts of concessions which cannot be granted, and thus reference to headquarters is rendered necessary,' wrote Osborne.

Behind the scenes Fakeer Azizuddin and Bhaia Ram Singh took up the issue with Dhian Singh. Their argument was that if the Durbar held back the English would most certainly undertake the expedition on their own and put a man entirely beholden to them on the throne of Afghanistan. It was in the Durbar's own interest to see that a minion of the English was not in power on its western frontier. The reasoning appealed to Ranjit Singh. On the morning of June 29, writes Osborne, 'we received a visit from old Fakeer Azizuddin, who gladdened our hearts by informing us that we might commence our preparations for a return to Simla as the Maharaja had at last made up his mind to put his name to the treaty without any further delay.' The expedition was to be a joint Anglo-Punjabi venture.

MacNaughten's party enjoyed Ranjit's hospitality for another fortnight. The monsoons had converted the dry, dusty countryside to a verdant green. It was a time for drinking, dancing and merry-making. But the doctors forbade Ranjit Singh to take alcohol and for once he listened to their advice. It did not depress him; nor says Osborne, did the news of a military reverse on the frontier, which reached him about that time. 'A trifling defeat now and then is useful as it teaches both men and officers to be cautious.' When Osborne asked him the reason for such self-assurance, Ranjit Singh told him that his confidence rested on the conviction that the Sikhs were the bravest nation in the east.

MacNaughten proceeded to Ludhiana to get Shah Shuja's

signature to the treaty. Shuja signed without any hesitation. He wanted to regain the throne of Kabul on any terms. And all said and done, a treaty was a mere scroll of parchment and a signature only a means to an end.

Ranjit Singh was determined to make his interview with Auckland an even bigger *tamāshā*[1] than the one at Rupar. There was a happy prelude to the meeting. The Maharaja's youngest wife, the comely Jindan (who later played a tragic role in the downfall of the kingdom) bore him a son—his seventh. The boy (born according to Sohan Lal under the evil combination of Pisces and Pisces) was named Dalip Singh.

The meeting was scheduled to take place at Ferozepur in the last week of November 1838. Ranjit Singh was to inspect the force the British would send; and the Governor-General would see the Durbar's contingent which was to join the British. It was to be a review of what came to be known as the Grand Army of the Indus.

A month before the meeting, the ostensible reason for the campaign ceased to exist. On October 22, 1838, the Persians raised the siege of Herat and Perso-Russian danger of infiltration into Afghanistan was removed. The English nevertheless adhered to their plans to take Afghanistan. If the country had to be saved from the Russians, why could it not be saved from the rest of the world as well? Why the Durbar did not change its policy is still an enigma. Presumably the argument that prevailed was the old one, viz, it was better to have a person who was under some obligation to the Durbar as ruler of Afghanistan than one who was a mere puppet of the British.

The Army of the Indus was to invade Afghanistan from two directions. The Punjabi force under the command of Colonel Sheikh Basawan was to force the Khyber Pass. Shah Shuja's son, Prince Taimur, with Afghans and Pathans, was to accompany

[1]The preparations by the Lahore Durbar were on a gigantic scale. Provision was made for 100,000 chickens, 20,000 maunds of wheat, 700 maunds of wine: the ration for the Governor-General's party was estimated at 4,000 chickens and 15,000 eggs per day. All the celebrated courtesans of the Punjab were invited to attend.

There are many eye-witness accounts of this meeting: from the Durbar end, Sohan Lal's; from the English, one by young Lieut. Fane, another by Osborne and a third by Lord Auckland's sister, the Hon. Miss Emily Eden. Emily was as gifted a gossip-writer as she was a painter. This narrative borrows from all these accounts.

the Punjabis with Wade as liaison officer. The British force was
to go through Sindh and advance on Kabul through Kandahar
and Ghazni; Shah Shuja was to accompany the British. The two
armies were to meet at Kabul.

The Aucklands saw something of the esteem in which Ranjit
Singh was held by people in the British protected part of the
Punjab. At Ludhiana the Governor-General inspected howitzers
which were to be presented to Ranjit. The guns had the star of
the Punjab with Ranjit's profile engraved on them. The Governor-General's sister, Emily Eden, wrote in her diary: 'Captain
E. says that thousands of Sikhs have been to look at these guns,
and all of them salaam to Runjeet's picture as if it were himself.'[1]

Fakeer Azizuddin received the Aucklands at Ferozepur. When
Lord Auckland said he was looking forward to meeting the
Maharaja, the Fakeer answered: 'The lustre of one sun (Ranjit)
has long shone with splendour over our horizon; but when two
suns come together, the refulgence will be overpowering.' The
English party smiled at the compliment. 'What force is the
Maharaja bringing with him?' asked Lord Auckland—and when
the Fakeer looked nonplussed, added that he only wanted to see
the Punjabis on parade. '*Inshāllāh*'—if God wills'—replied the
Fakeer much relieved.[2]

The first meeting was finally fixed to take place on November 29. Ranjit Singh spent the morning in prayer and gave a
large sum in offering to the Granth Sahib before he set out from
his camp. Fane gives a vivid description of the procession and
meeting: 'The crowd was what one might expect from the meeting
of upwards of one hundred elephants within the space of as many
yards, and the crush, of course, awful; elephants trumpeting,
gentlemen swearing, and each one trying how he could best poke
out his neighbour's eye with the corner of his howdah; while
the confusion was not a little heightened by the cannon firing
within three yards of one, and frightening our elephants.

'But all this was a mere trifle to what was to come. At the
entrance of the Governor-General's tent, where all dismounted,
the scene of confusion and riot was what I never before saw in

[1]Emily Eden, *Up the Country*, vol. I, p. 127.
[2]*Journal of Upper Hindustan*, French, 1854, p. 80.

India or elsewhere. In consequence of no good or proper arrangement having been made, everyone, whether belonging to the suite of the Governor-General or the Commander-in-Chief, or not, and also those of the Maharaja, and upwards of two hundred army officers, all anxious to see the durbar, crowded in together, each pushing, hustling, and elbowing his neighbour, till at last it was found necessary to bring in two companies of Europeans, and clear a street for the passage of those entitled to sit in the durbar. This was at last effected, though not without difficulty, and the select few found their appointed places.

'I being one of these, stationed myself behind the General's chair, where I remained the whole of the durbar. It was, as usual with Runjeet, somewhat long, from his having so many questions to ask; but after some three-quarters of an hour he got up and proceeded to examine the presents. These, as usual, consisted of guns, pistols, swords and *kingcobs*. After looking at these for some time, and putting his solitary eye as close as possible to each article, he walked into the next tent to examine two beautiful nine-pound howitzers, both in reality, and in his estimation, the most valuable part of the gifts: they were brass nine-pounders, beautifully inlaid and carved, with a medallion of his own head in the centre of the barrel. These were given him with harness and everything, even to the most minute articles, complete and ready for service, with one hundred shrapnel shells. They also gave the old gentleman a very good oil-painting of Her Majesty Queen Victoria; upon the giving of which a royal salute of one hundred guns was fired in honour of it. I do not think he quite understood it, but he seemed to think Her Majesty made a very decent nautch girl.'[1]

Emily Eden, who had painted the portrait of Queen Victoria, describes Ranjit Singh as being 'exactly like an old mouse, with grey whiskers and one eye'.[2] He wore no jewels whatsoever and his dress was of the commonest red silk. 'He had two stockings on at first; which was considered an unusual circumstance; but he very soon contrived to slip one off, that he might sit with one foot in his hand, comfortably.' With Ranjit Singh were Hira Singh, 'a very handsome boy...loaded with emeralds and pearls',

[1] Fane, vol. I, p. 320.
[2] *Up the Country*, vol. I, p. 284.

and his father, Dhian Singh, who was 'uncommonly good looking'. The children of soldiers who had fallen in battle were
always allowed in court. 'They were crawling about the floor,
running in and out between Runjeet and the Governor-General.'
When the introductions and the inquiries about health were over,
the presents (including the portrait of the Queen) were exhibited.
'His strongest passion is still for horses: one of these hit his
fancy, and he quite forgot all his state, and ran out in the sun
to feel its legs and examine it.'[1]

The next day Auckland returned the Maharaja's call. There
was the same scene of confusion of elephants, horses, cheering
crowds, the crash of bands and firing of cannon. Ranjit gave
presents to every member of the Governor-General's party.

In the evening Ranjit gave a reception where business was to
be discussed. The secret conference was not to be so secret. Fane,
who was present, writes: 'The usual scene was going on; half-
a-dozen sets of nautch girls were dancing and screaming in the
front, with no one attending to them; fireworks blazing and
shooting in all directions; and the Maharaja seated in his chair,
with the great men on either side, as perfectly unconcerned as
if he had been there all his life.' There was little to argue since
the whole affair had already been settled. Ranjit was willing to
collaborate with the British to restore Shuja. He gave a categori-
cal 'No' to the proposal that a British Resident should be stationed at his Court at Lahore.

They got down to pleasanter business. Nautch girls were presented to the English guests. The three most talented were
Khairan, Paro and Kaulan—the last being famed for her great
beauty. While they sang and danced, the *gadwais* (cup bearers)
poured out their special preparation of 'emeralds, grapes and
oranges'—which the guests were told was 'good for digestion'.
Ranjit Singh pressed the drink on the abstemious Auckland[2] who
took it so as not to hurt his host's feelings. But Emily couldn't
take 'that horrible spirit....one drop of which actually burnt the
outside of my lips' and being on Ranjit's blind side poured it

---

[1]*Up the Country*, vol. I, p. 286.
[2]At an earlier meeting with MacNaughten Ranjit Singh had asked whether
the Lord Nawab Sahib was a good drinker. MacNaughten replied in the
affirmative just to watch the fun.

on the carpet when he was busy talking to her brother. Ranjit was impressed with the Englishwoman's capacity for country liquor as he refilled her goblet many times himself.

The Maharaja loved talking of wine as he did of horses. 'He said he understood that there were books which contained objections to drunkenness, and he thought it better that there should be no books at all than that they should contain such foolish notions,' wrote Emily. She was taken by Ranjit. 'He has made himself a great King; he has conquered a great many powerful enemies; he is remarkably just in his government; he has disciplined a large army; he hardly ever takes away life, which is wonderful in a despot, and he is excessively beloved by his people.'[1]

There were more visits and return visits, exchange of presents and inspection of troops. The Aucklands were taken to Amritsar to see the Golden Temple. Emily, who was with Ranjit Singh, wrote, 'There is something rather touching in the affection his people have for him. The other day, in going through the city, it struck us all, the eagerness with which they called out "Maharaja!" and tried to touch him, which is easy enough in these narrow streets, and the elephant's reaching to the roofs of the houses.'[2]

From Amritsar the party proceeded to Lahore which was 'very dirty and not odoriferous'. The ceremonies and festivity were resumed with greater vigour till Ranjit himself could stand it no more. Emily's diary of December 24, 1838, records: 'The Maharaja is ill—he has cold and fever—so all parties, and etc. are put off.' On Christmas Day, his condition took a turn for the worse. 'Dr D. has seen him twice. ... He thought his voice very indistinct, and I fancy the danger is another stroke of palsy—he had one some years ago.'[3]

The Aucklands went to bid farewell to their host on December

[1]*Up the Country*, vol. I, pp. 298-9.
[2]French was most impressed with the scenes of splendour in Amritsar. In his diary of December 12, 1838, he quoted:
  In gaudy objects, I indulge my sight
  And turn, where eastern pomp gives gay delight
  See the vast train in various habits drest
  By the bright scimitar and sable vest.
[3]*Up the Country*, vol. II, pp. 25, 31-2.

28, 1838. Ranjit Singh was 'wonderfully better' but still confined to bed. He embraced the Governor-General and gave his party more presents: his own picture set in diamonds and pearls; a sword, matchlock and belt all bejewelled for the Governor-General. There were shawls for Emily and her sister. The Governor-General in return gave the Maharaja a bunch of grapes made of emeralds and a ring with a very large diamond. Ranjit embraced his visitor once more and bade him God-speed. 'He asked if the Governor-General had any request to make to him; and the Governor-General said only one more, that he should occasionally wear the ring he was going to put on his finger, and he produced the ring, made of one large diamond...it nearly covered Runjeet's little finger, and it was quite odd to see the effect it had on the old man. He raised himself quite up, and called for a candle to put behind it, and seemed quite taken by surprise.'

CHAPTER XXI

THE LAST CHAPTER

'HE WAS A pearl without any flaw or stain of any kind,' said Fakeer Azizuddin, speaking of Ranjit Singh's physical constitution. 'He enjoyed unusually good health, took regular exercise every day, slept well, had an excellent appetite; his functions were natural.'

This is not surprising because Ranjit Singh was extremely punctilious in his habits—he rode in the morning and evening, ate at fixed hours, took a mid-morning siesta, and when he did not have to entertain, he retired early to bed. The only indiscretion he allowed himself, and which undoubtedly impaired his health, was alcohol, and in later life, laudanum in larger and larger doses. The brandies specially prepared for him (curiously enough by the same man who mixed his gunpowder[1]) were of an unusual potency having been brewed from raisins and fortified with ground pearls.[2] The savouries which went with this liquid fire were 'fat quails stuffed with spice'. He often drank to excess, particularly on festivals like Holi and Diwali. And he could never resist alcohol during the rains. As a young man he was able to hold his liquor without any visible ill-effect. Later on, the same amount of drink made him very sick: he remained out of sorts and his inflamed eye told the tale of bacchanalian indiscretions for several days after. His liver was affected and lowered his resistance to disease. Ranjit Singh's first serious illness

[1] The Hungarian homeopath Dr Martin Honigberger.

[2] 'Brandy in which were the strongest sauces compounded from the flesh of every animal, beef excepted, pearls and jewels, musk, opium, plants of various kinds, all mingled together into a beverage, which must be nearly as strong as alcohol itself. This devil's drink I had myself tasted the evening before, and found the flavour good enough, but the following morning my spirits were exceedingly depressed.' Baron Hugel, *Travels in Kashmir and the Punjab*, p. 298.

was in the summer of 1826 when he had a virulent attack of malaria. On Hakim Azizuddin's advice he sent for Dr Murray from Ludhiana. The doctor stayed in Lahore for seven months. By the winter Ranjit Singh shook off the ill-effects of the fever and was once more able to lead an active, vigorous life spending four to five hours in the saddle. He continued to enjoy excellent health for the next nine years

On the night of August 17, 1835, Ranjit Singh had a mild stroke which paralysed his face and right side; he could not speak for many hours. He told Dr W.L. McGregor who had been summoned to attend on him how the attack came on. The doctor conveyed the information to the Resident of Ludhiana in the following words:

'The Maharaja retired to rest in a chamber where his body was freely exposed to a free circulation of cool air, the body being at the time in rather a profuse state of perspiration. In the middle of the night, he woke suddenly and found himself unable to move his tongue so as to articulate and his mouth distorted to a considerable degree. His attendants were alarmed at these symptoms and various remedies, chiefly aromatics, were prescribed by Fakeer Azizuddin. By the end of these, the Maharaja was soon able to articulate a little. His health likewise suffered a visible change. There was a loss of appetite, some heaviness about the head, heat on the palms of the hands and soles of the feet; thirst, frequently urgent, a general despondency and depression of spirits.'[1]

---

[1]The version given by Fakeer Azizuddin to Baron Hugel is somewhat different. 'He (Azizuddin) informed me, that on a very sultry day, just before the rainy season set in, which in the past year was preceded by heats which were unusually great, the Maharaja had ridden the whole day on horseback, and had greatly exhausted and overheated himself. With his usual carelessness with regard to food, he took nothing that day but water melons, of which he partook very freely. A heavy storm fell in the afternoon, the rain poured down in torrents, and the piercing wind from the mountains of Kashmir suddenly lowered the temperature to a degree inconveniently cold. The Maharaja rode for a long time, and at a foot's pace through this storm, until he reached a hut. There, however, the walls afforded him little protection against the wind, and he sat in his wet clothes, the draughts of air penetrating to him, and of course contributing to chill his frame. He did not reach his tent until nightfall, and nothing could persuade him to take any medicine, or use any sort of remedy. A violent pain in the stomach occasioned him very disturbed sleep; and when he would have called for assistance, his tongue felt heavy in his mouth, and he found his left hand quite powerless. When a

Ranjit Singh was not a good patient. He consulted dozens of physicians and lent a willing ear to quacks who promised miraculous cures. He particularly disliked the bitter medicines the English doctor prescribed. 'The Maharaja has much aversion to the use of internal medicines; so that I experienced extreme difficulty in treating him,' complained Dr McGregor. He also refused to change his daily routine. Even after a night disturbed by high fever he would go out in the morning in his palanquin either to the river or some orchard; and on his return he attended durbar to hear petitions and newswriters' reports and give orders. He only stopped work when he was utterly exhausted or seized with another bout of fever. Dr McGregor was however able to impose some discipline on his wayward patient and within a month, the Maharaja was well on the way to recovery and was able to allow the doctor to return to Ludhiana.

Baron Hugel, who met Ranjit Singh in 1836, wrote that the Maharaja was considerably bowed by disease and his speech was so much affected by paralysis that it was not an easy matter to understand him. He was easily fatigued by walking and leant on an attendant's arm. He said to Baron Hugel: 'I begin to feel old; I am quite exhausted now.'[1]

Early in 1837 Ranjit Singh had a second stroke of paralysis. This time the whole of his right side was affected and its effects persisted for nearly six months. The Maharaja was never the same person again. He was no longer able to mount his horse himself and had to be lifted into the saddle. An accident which took place on July 24, 1838, showed how weak he had become. He was out taking the morning air when an elephant which had run amok attacked his palanquin. The litter bearers and the guards ran away. Ranjit Singh was unable to get out himself and the elephant smashed the glass windows of the palanquin. He was saved from being trampled to death by Attar

---

servant came and saw him in this state, he called immediately for Aziz-ud-Din, who found him with his face much drawn up, and next to speechless. I could not understand what means were employed to restore him, but according to the Hindu custom, musk was probably administered in large doses. He was brought back to Lahore and became somewhat better, and Dr McGregor being called in from Ludhiana, he was placed under his care.'
[1]Baron Hugel, *Travels in Kashmir and the Punjab*, p. 327.

Singh Sandhawalia who diverted the elephant's attention by attacking it with his sword.

The third stroke was brought about by the strain of festivities in honour of Lord Auckland's visit. On the eve of the Christmas of 1838 he was taken violently ill and for the next five days he hovered between life and death. He rallied by the New Year and was taken back to Lahore.

The stroke at Ferozepur completely deprived the Maharaja of his power of speech and he had to communicate by signs. The only courtiers who could interpret the sign language were Bhaia Ram Singh and Fakeer Azizuddin—particularly the latter whose devotion to his sick master is said to have been greater than that shown by a son to his father. Even the most unintelligible stammer meant something to him. To catch the words the Fakeer would put his ear close to Ranjit's mouth. If he understood, he expressed joy exclaiming: 'eysh', 'eysh'. If he did not, he shook his head and admited humbly: *Nami fahmam*—'I did not follow.' The Maharaja tried all over again: with his speechless tongue, his one hand and his single eye.

The winter rain and the biting cold of January did not do the Maharaja much good. He kept indoors in an overheated room taking medicines that the native doctors gave him and having himself massaged with almond oil. His cold became heavier and he developed a rasping cough. His spirits were further dampened by the news of the death of his friend, M. Allard, on the North-West Frontier.[1] The weather became milder in February and the Maharaja was able to be in the sun. His health improved and he began to summon courtiers to his bedside.

The Maharaja went to Amritsar to pray for his health. He gave away large sums to charity: cows with gilded horns, elephants with gold or silver howdahs, images of gold and silver. The chief recipients were Brahmins, but shrines of all religious denominations, Hindu, Muslim and Sikh received their share. Although by the month of March 1839, the Maharaja was reported by the local newswriters to be enjoying better health, there was no real improvement and once more the Agent at

[1]The news of Allard's death is recorded by Sohal Lal in his diary of January 30, 1839. It reads: 'Allard Sahib bade farewell to the mortal world and packed up the baggage of existence on account of incurable constipation.'

Ludhiana was asked to send an English doctor. Drs. Murray and Steele came to Lahore.

Dr Steele wrote of his surprise at the wretched surroundings in which the Maharaja was living: 'His house is situated close on the edge of a filthy canal from which roads are constantly wetted and the surrounding grounds kept in a swampy state. It is in an atmosphere sufficient to create disease among the most healthy. He sleeps in a small tent adjoining which (within ten yards) there is a small patch of rice cultivation. This is constantly under water. I needn't say that the smell arising from the damp earth and confined air is anything but pleasant.' The room in which the Maharaja rested during the day had no windows and consequently no fresh air. 'In addition to the constant unpleasant exhalation from the damp floor and walls, the room is constantly crowded with his followers,' wrote Dr Steele. On the doctor's insistence, the Maharaja was removed to a healthier locality.

Dr Steele made a thorough examination of the Maharaja for a week and dispatched a confidential report to be transmitted to the Governor-General. 'Is the Maharaja likely to live long?' he queried at the end of the report. 'I think "not long". He is in that state that the least unfavourable accidental occurrence in the form of disease may be decisive and likely to be so. He may live for a short time, perhaps for a few months or even a year, but that latter period I think, improbable, although I consider that he has still some remaining energy and the natural powers of his constitution to be great and his rallying powers, from what I have heard, to be extraordinary.'

The summer's heat made Ranjit Singh more restless than ever; by the end of May, he had no doubt in his mind that his days were numbered. Fifty Brahmins were employed to pray for his recovery; Fakeer Nuruddin was ordered to distribute ten maunds of bread to the poor every day and large numbers of cows, horses and elephants and quantities of gold and silver were given away to holy men and shrines.

By June 1839 the Maharaja had six European doctors—three sent by the Governor-General and three of his own beside a large number of *hakeems* and *vaids* attending on him. He preferred to take the medicine given by the homeopath Dr Martin Honigberger—drops of nightshade mixed with sugar and his favourite brandy—to the bitter mixtures prescribed by the English physicians. Dr Honigberger pleaded with him to shift to the fort where the air was more salubrious. The astrologers who were consulted pronounced against a move before June 13; so the Maharaja stayed where he was and after a few days began to ignore even the homeopath by trying all kinds of medicine,[1] drinking ice-cold water and taking opium in the afternoon.

The evening of June 10 was particularly hot and still. At night a violent storm burst on Lahore, tearing two of the city gates and one of the fort's from their hinges and uprooting a large number of trees. Ranjit Singh could get no sleep because of the noise and a persistent cough. After midnight his temperature rose and his feet began to swell. The fever abated by the morning but was followed by a discharge of blood with the motions.

On June 13 Ranjit Singh was taken into the fort. The *Lahore Akhbar* reported:

'After sunset, at the hour pointed out by the astronomers, the Maharaja entered the Summam Burj. He moved very slowly in his palanquin and on his entering the wall of the city there was a salute of guns and volleys from the regiments at Anarkalee.'

The Maharaja ordered the following items to be given away in charity: "11 cows with horns covered with gold, 25 satin dresses, 10 gold silver images, 5 golden deer and as many of silver, 2 horses, 1 elephant, 2 diamond rings, 11 coral strings and 2,000 rupees in cash to Brahmins. He also had himself weighed five times against grain and it was given to the Brahmins.'

The fresh air of the elevated Musummum Burj cheered Ranjit Singh's drooping spirits. He told his elder son, Kharak Singh, that 'he was much better and that if he remained so for a fortnight, he would no longer feel ill'.

---

[1]Sohan Lal records in his diary of April 22, 1839, of a French doctor prescribing a medicine which would act like gunpowder on the paralysis. It was tried on a paralysed elephant driver with success. It did not cure the Maharaja. He took oxide preparations (*Kushta*) made of mica, pearls, cardamom and *tabasheer* which Rajah Dhian Singh brought for him and claimed was over 100 years old. This too had no effect.

That evening there was a heavy shower of rain and the temperature dropped. The Maharaja however passed a sleepless night and complained that 'he felt pain now and then in his eyes'. Next morning a general proclamation was issued to officers in various cities ordering them to see that all slaughter of animals—goats, sheep, kids, etc.—in the Punjab be stopped forthwith.

Neither prayers nor charities helped the ailing Maharaja. Five days later he developed palpitations of the heart and on Fakeer Nuruddin's advice put agate on his person. It was prepared from 'two *mashas* of green stone called *subza* ground down in million of tears'.

The end did not seem far off. In the early hours of the morning of the 20th the Maharaja was once again seized with fever and had a discharge of blood from his nose. He also felt great pain in his knees. He sent for his astrologers and asked them to predict what fate held in store for him. Pandit Mudsudan observed that the continuance of liberal grants would have the best effect. The Maharaja added the extra feeding of his horses to his already varied charity. But he was not one to humbug himself and told his son that it was not good enough to be 'better one day and ill another'. On the advice of Fakeer Azizuddin he decided to entrust the government to Kharak Singh with Raja Dhian Singh as his Chief Minister.

Next morning Prince Kharak Singh and Raja Dhian Singh reviewed the troops and received nazars from the officers. Later in the day Kharak Singh held a durbar at Musummum Burj where the proclamation of succession drafted by Fakeer Azizuddin was read out. Raja Dhian Singh was installed as Chief Minister with the sonorous title of *Nāib-i-Sultanat-i-Oozma, Khair Khwāh-i-Summeemee-i-Koobra, Vazir-i-Azāro-Mukhtār Kool, Rājāh Dhian Singh Bahādur*—the second in the great kingdom, the sincere well-wisher of great prosperity, the principal minister, the Chief Wazir, the omnipresent manager, Raja Dhian Singh.

The investiture was carried out just in time. The next day the Maharaja had a relapse while in Court. 'He lay down on his bed and no one was allowed to speak. The Ministers were greatly distressed. Koonwer Khurruck Singh and Raja Dhian Singh sent their guards to the doors and fort gates...'

The angel of death hovered about the Musummam Burj. In the traditional Hindu manner the Maharaja was laid down on the floor to die in the lap of Mother Earth which had given him birth. There was still some fire in his debilitated frame, and despite the prognostications of his physicians that he would not last more than a few hours, he rallied and had to be put back on his bed again. But life continued to ebb. On the afternoon of the 24th he had another setback and 'at the idea of departing from all his worldly wealth ordered his treasures and jewels to be brought forth. Cows with gilded horns, a hundred caparisoned horses and five of the best breeds such as the *Kubootrah*, the *Nandhuree*, the *Nageena* and others, all equipped in gold and jewelled saddles, four elephants with gold and silver howdahs, a golden chair and bedsteads, plates, strings of pearls, swords, shields, gems and innumerable other valuables were given in alms to be distributed in all parts of India and at all sacred Hindu shrines and temples.' The newswriter computed the value of gifts given away on the one day to be about two crore of rupees. The same day the Maharaja sent for the Koh-i-noor and desired that it be presented to the temple of Jagganath at Puri. He was dissuaded from doing so by his courtiers who represented that it was far too valuable—worth the revenues of all India—and that there would be no one to buy it from the Brahmins.

The Maharaja's last act was that of a dying soldier. He summoned his courtiers to his bedside and gave away his weapons; swords, shields, lances, pistols and matchlocks with his own hands. The courtiers wept loudly as they took the gifts; the Maharaja tried to console them but broke down many times himself. At the end of the ceremony he washed himself with Ganges water.

On June 26 the Maharaja lost consciousness. Kharak Singh summoned a special durbar at which he confirmed his father's grants to the estate-holders and the ministers and senior officials made overtures of mutual concord. The ministers said that they should observe strict unanimity similar to that of British councils for the safety of the State and the preservation of Koonwar Khurruck Singh and Koonwar Naonihal Singh's right from foreign encroachments. Raja Dhian Singh demanded in a tone of defiance which betrayed his nervousness: 'Who will dare to look at us with an unfriendly eye?'

All hope of recovery was abandoned. Dhian Singh ordered the carpenters to prepare a bier worth Rs. 5,000. Despite this, during the few minutes the Maharaja regained consciousness the sweet-tongued Azizuddin assured his master that he would not die for another four or five years.

The end came on the evening of June 27, 1839.[1] The *Lahore Akhbar* described the poignant scene. 'The death of the Maharaja being known, the Ranees, Koonwer Khurruck Singh, Raja Dhian Singh, Jumadar Khooshal Singh and others raised their voices in lamentation, tearing their hair, casting earth on their heads, throwing themselves on the ground and striking their heads against bricks and stone. This continued during the night by the side of the corpse. Every now and then looking towards the corpse their shrieks were shriller.'

Precautions were taken against civil disturbance and incursion from abroad. A large quantity of ammunition was distributed to the troops and specific orders issued to the officers posted along the Sutlej ferries to keep the boats on the western bank, leaving only one for the use of passengers crossing the river.

During the night the body of the Maharaja lay in state on the floor with oil lamps burning on all sides; and all night the wailing and the lamentation went on. Raja Dhian Singh, who was more emotional than the rest, announced his intention to burn himself on the Maharaja's funeral pyre. Kharak Singh and the principal Sardars placed their turbans at his feet to make him change his mind. But nothing would dissuade four ranis and their seven maidservants from their resolve to immolate themselves as Satis. Rani Guddan, daughter of Raja Sansar Chand of Katotch, thought it the most appropriate occasion to obtain an oath of loyalty to the State. She took Raja Dhian Singh's hand, placed it on the breast of the corpse and made him swear never to betray Kharak Singh or his son Nau Nihal Singh, and always to be attentive to the welfare of the State. In the same way she made Kharak Singh swear that he would not be led away by misrepresentations of interested parties against Raja Dhian Singh. 'The torments of

---

[1]By a curious coincidence exactly forty years to the day after he had entered Lahore as a victor. (The dates are calculated according to the Bikrami calendar.)

hell due for the slaughter of a thousand cows were to be visited on him who should violate this oath.'

The next morning the Maharaja's body was bathed with the water of the Ganges and placed on a sandalwood bier designed like a ship; its sails were made of silk and brocade. Ministers and courtiers paid their last homage by placing shawls on the bier. The funeral procession left the fort with the four ranis and their maidservants, who were to burn themselves walking immediately behind the cortege. They were dressed in their bridal costumes and jewels. Every now and then they took off a bangle, a necklace or an earring and flung it into the midst of the throng of beggars or gave it to someone in the parties of hymn-singers or the Brahmins chanting mantras. The cortege passed through the narrow streets of the city crammed with mourners and came to the garden at the foot of the massive wall of the fort—not far from the temple marking the site of the martyrdom of Arjun, the fifth Guru of the Sikhs. A newswriter describes the scene that followed in these words:

'Having arrived at the funeral pile made of sandalwood, the corpse was placed upon it. Rani Guddan sat down by its side and placed the head of the deceased on her lap; while the other ranis with seven slave girls seated themselves around—with every mark of satisfaction on their countenances.'[1] The last prayers were said by members of all communities, Hindus, Muslims and Sikhs. Brahmins performed their prayers from the Shastras; Sikh priests recited passages from the Granth Sahib; and Mussalmans accompanied them with their 'Ya Allah, Ya Allah'.[2] The prayers lasted nearly an hour. 'At the time fixed by the Brahmins, Koonwar Khurruck Singh set fire to the pile and the ruler of the Punjab with four ranees and seven slave girls was reduced to ashes. A small cloud appeared in the sky over the burning pile and having shed a few drops cleared away. No one saw a hope of relief but in resignation. Raja Dhian Singh attempted four times to jump into the burning pile, but was withheld by the multitude.... The heart is rent in attempting a description of the distress and lamentations in the palace amongst the ranees and amongst the citizens of every age, sex and religion.'[3]

[1]*Lahore Akhbar*, June 1839.
[2]Honigberger, *Thirty-Five years in the East*, p. 102. Also *Umdat-ut-Tawarikh*, Daftar III, p. 156.
[3]*Lahore Akhbar*, June 1839.

'The consuming of his pile occupied two days,' writes Honigberger; 'on the third, some of the bones and ashes of each of the bodies were collected in the presence of the Court only, and separately placed in urns.' The citizens of Lahore paid their final farewell to the ashes of their monarch and his consorts. 'Upon the procession leaving the fortress, it traversed the streets and bazaars, the ministers and some of the principal Sardars on foot, with numerous others mounted on their elephants and horses. Thousands of persons were assembled in the streets, bazaars, and on the tops of houses, by whom flowers were thrown upon the palanquin.... Upon the arrival of the procession outside Delhi Gate, a final and profuse royal salute was given by the thundering of cannons from the fort and ramparts of the city.'[1]

The ashes were conveyed by slow stages to be immersed in the Ganges at Hardwar. All along the 300-mile route people came to pay their homage; princes with expensive shawls and salutes of guns; peasants with flowers and their tears.

[1]Honigberger, *Thirty-Five years in the East*, pp. 103-4.

Table 1

THE FAMILY OF RANJIT SINGH

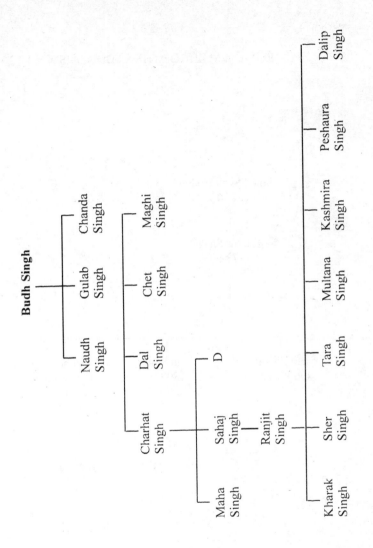

Table 2

ROYAL FAMILY OF THE SADDOZAIS

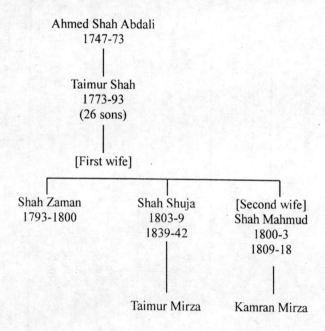

Ahmed Shah Abdali
1747-73

Taimur Shah
1773-93
(26 sons)

[First wife]

Shah Zaman
1793-1800

Shah Shuja
1803-9
1839-42

[Second wife]
Shah Mahmud
1800-3
1809-18

Taimur Mirza

Kamran Mirza

Table 3

THE BARAKZAI FAMILY

Payandah Khan
(given title Sarfraz by Taimur)

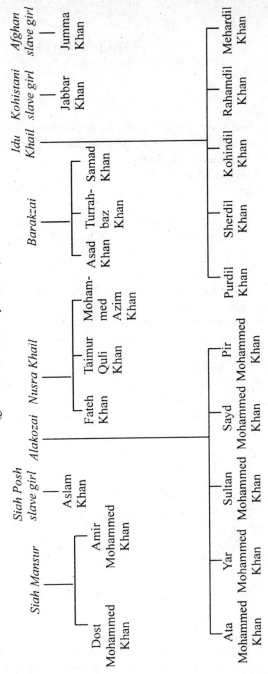

Siah Mansur

Dost Mohammed Khan — Amir Mohammed Khan

Siah Posh slave girl

Aslam Khan

Alakozai

Nusra Khail

Fateh Khan — Taimur Quli Khan — Mohammed Azim Khan

Ata Mohammed Khan — Yar Mohammed Khan — Sultan Mohammed Khan — Sayd Mohammed Khan — Pir Mohammed Khan

Barakzai

Asad Khan — Turrahbaz Khan — Samad Khan

Idu Khail

Purdil Khan — Sherdil Khan — Kohindil Khan

Kohistani slave girl

Jabbar Khan

Rahamdil Khan

Afghan slave girl

Jumma Khan

Mehardil Khan

BIBLIOGRAPHY

PERSIAN

Amar Nath, Dewan, *Zafar Namah-i-Ranjit Singh*, Lahore, 1928.
Ghulam Husain Khan, *Siyar-ul-Mutakherin*,1785. Translated by Raymond and Briggs.
Kamwar Khan, *Tazkirat-us-Salatin*, M.S. 1723.
Kanhaya Lal, *Zafar Namah-i-Ranjit Singh*, Mustafii Press, Lahore, 1876.
Sohan Lal Suri, *Umdat-ut-Tawarikh*, 5 vols., Lahore,1889. (Partly translated by V.S. Suri. S. Chand & Co, Delhi.)

GURMUKHI

Gyan Singh, Gyani, *Panth Prakash*, Amritsar, 1880. *Tawarikh Guru Khalsa*. Amritsar.
Kahan Singh, *Gur-Shabd Ratnakar Mahan-kosh.*
    Encyclopaedia of Sikh Literature, 4 vols. Patiala, 1931.
Karam Singh, *Maharaja Ranjit Singh.*
Kohli, Sita Ram, *Maharaja Ranjit Singh*, Delhi, 1953.
Prem Singh, *Maharaja Ranjit Singh. Baba phula Singh Akali. Khalsa Raj de Usariya.*
Ratan Singh Bhangu, *Prachin Panth Prakash*, Amritsar, 1914.

ENGLISH

Ali, Abdul, *Notes on the Life and Times of Ranjit Singh*, London Historical Records Commission.
Ali, Shahamat, *History of Bahawalpur*, John Murray, 1848. *Sikhs and Afghans*, John Murray, 1847.
Andrew, W. P., *The Indus and Its Provinces: Their Political* and *Commercial Importance*, W.H. Allen, London.
Archer, Major, *Tours in Upper India and in Parts of the Hima-layan Mountains*, London, 1833.
Atkinson, James, *The Expedition into Afghanistan*, Allen & Co, London, 1842.
Auckland, Lord, *Private Letters, 1836-42*. Mss. British Museum, London.
Barr, Wm, *Journal of a March from Delhi to Peshawar and from thence to Kabul including Travels in the Punjab*, James

Maddon, London, 1844.

Bingley, Capt A. H., *Sikhs*, Govt Printing Press, Calcutta, 1918.

Boolchand, Dr, *The North-West Question of Indian History 1798-1830*, Calcutta University, 1940.

Boulger, D.C., *Lord William Bentinck*, Clarendon Press, Oxford, 1892.

Burnes, Alexander, *Travels into Bokhara*, 3 vols., John Murray, London, 1834. *Sindh and Afghanistan*, Calcutta, 1839. *Correspondence* (privately printed). *Reports and Papers: Political, Geographical and Commercial*, Calcutta, 1838. *On the Political Power of the Sikhs beyond the Indus*, Calcutta, 1839.

Caror, Olaf, *The Pathans*, Macmillan, London, 1958.

Chhabra, Dr G.S., *Advanced Study in the History of the Punjab*, 2 vols., Sharanjit, Ludhiana, 1961.

Chopra, Gulshan Lall, *Punjab as a Sovereign State, 1799-1839*, Lahore, 1928.

Connolly, A., *Journey to the North of India*, 2 vols., Richard Bentley, London, 1838.

Correspondence of Sir George Russel Clerk, 1831-43, Historical Interpretation P.G.R.O.

Court, Henry, *History of the Sikhs*, Lahore, 1888.

Cunningham, J.D., *History of the Sikhs*, John Murray, London, 1849.

Douie, Sir James, *The Punjab, North-West Frontier Province & Kashmir*, Cambridge, 1916.

Dunbar, Janet, *Golden Interlude*, John Murray, London, 1955.

Eden, Emily, *Up the Country*, 2 vols., Richard Bentley, London, 1866.

Elphinstone, Mountstuart, *An Account of the Kingdom of Cabul*, 2 vols., 1839.

Falcon, R.W., *Handbook on Sikhs*, Pioneer Press, Allahabad, 1896.

Fane, H.E., *Five Years in India*, 2 vols., London, 1842.

Farooqi, B.A., *British Relations with the Cis-Sutlej States, 1809-23*, P.G.R.O., 1941.

Forster, W., *A Journey from Bengal to England through North India, Kashmir, Afghanistan and Persia into Russia, 1783-84*, 2 vols., London, 1798.

Francklin, W., *Military Memoirs of George Thomas*, Calcutta, 1803.

Fraser, J. Baillie, *The Military Memoirs of Lt-Col James Skinner*, 2 vols., Smith Elder & Co., London, 1851.

Fraser-Tytler, Sir Kerr, *Afghanistan; A Study in Political Developments in Central Asia*, Oxford University Press, 1953.

French, Charles J., *Journal of a Tour in Upper Hindustan*. Prepared during the years 1838 and 1839, published 1854.

Ganda Singh, *Ranjit Singh*. Death Centenary Volume. Edited by Ganda Singh, Amritsar, 1939.

Gardner, A., *Memoirs of Alexander Gardner*, London (re-edited 1898).

Garrett, H.L.O. and G.L. Chopra, *Events at the Court of Ranjit Singh*, P.G.R.O., 1935.

Gordon, J.H., *The Sikhs*, Blackwood, London, 1904.

Grey, C., *European Adventurers of Northern India 1785-1849*, Punjab Govt, 1929.

Griffin, Lepel H., *Ranjit Singh*, Oxford, 1905. *The Rajas of the Punjab*, Lahore, 1870.

Griffin and Massey, *Chiefs & Families of Note in the Punjab*, 2 vols. and Appendix, 1909.

Gupta, Hari Ram, *Cis-Sutlej Sikhs, Vol. II, 1769-1799*, Minerva, Lahore, 1944. *Trans-Sutlej Sikhs, Vol. III, 1769-1799*, Minerva, Lahore, 1944.

Geographical, Statistical & Historical Account of the Country between the Sutulege and Jumna, Oriental Press, Calcutta, 1839.

Geographical Memoirs—Territories ceded by Shuja to Ranjit, 1839.

Harlan, J., *Memoir of India & Afghanistan*, Philadelphia, 1842. *Central Asia 1823-41*, Luzac & Co., London, 1939.

Havelock, H., *Narrative of the War in Afghanistan in 1838-39*, London, 1840.

Honigberger, J. M., *Thirty-Five Years in the East*, H. Bailliere, London, 1852.

Hough, Major Wm, *Political & Military Events in British India in 1756-1849*, 2 vols., 1853.

Hugel, Baron Charles, *Travels in Kashmir & the Punjab*, Johan Petheram, London, 1845.

Hutchison and Vogel, *History of the Punjab Hill States*, 2 vols., Govt Printing Press, Lahore, 1933.

Ibbetson, D.C., *Punjab Castes*, Govt Printing Press, Lahore, 1916. Imperial Records Office-Foreign Department (unpublished records).

Jacquemont, Victor, *Letters from India Describing a Journey in the British Dominions of India, Tibet, Lahore & Cashmeer*, 2 vols., Edward Churton, London, 1835.

Kacher, Hansraj, *The Punjab 1792-1849*, Moon Press, Agra, 1916.

Kaye, J.W., *The Life & Correspondence of Charles Lord Metcalfe*, 2 vols., Smith Elder & Co., London, 1858. *History of the War in Afghanistan*, 3 vols., R. Bentley, London.

Khushwant Singh, *The Sikhs*, Allen & Unwin, London, 1953.

Kiernan, V.G., *Metcalfe's Mission to Lahore 1808-9*, Lahore, 1943.

Kohli, Sita Ram, *Catalogue of Khalsa Durbar Records*, 2 vols., Govt Press, 1927.

Latif, Syed Mohammed, *History of the Punjab*, Central Press, Calcutta, 1891. *Lahore—Its History, Architectural Remains & Antiquities*, Lahore, 1892.

Lawrence, Major H. L., *Adventures of an Officer in the Punjaub*, 2 vols., H. Colburn, London, 1846.

Malcolm, Sir John, *A Sketch of the Sikhs*, London, 1812.

Masson, Charles, *Narrative of Various Journeys in Baluchistan, Afghanistan and the Punjab*, 3 vols., R. Bentley, London, 1842.

McGregor, W.L., *History of the Sikhs*, 2 vols., James Madden, London, 1846.

Mohan Lal, *Journal of a Tour through the Punjab, Afghanistan, Turkestan, etc.*, Longman Greens, London, 1834.

Moorcroft and Trebeck, *Travels in the Himalayan Provinces of Hindustan and the Punjab, in Ladakh and Kashmir, in Peshawar, Kabul, Kundu and Bokhara*, 2 vols., John Murray, London, 1837.

Murray, Wm, *History of the Punjab*, 2 vols., William Allen, London, 1846.

Nair, Lajpat Rai, *Fakir Azizuddin*, Ilmi Markaz, Lahore. *Sir Wm Macnaughten's Correspondence Relating to the Tripartite Treaty*, P.G.R.O., Lahore, 1942.

Narang, Sir Gokul Chand, *Transformation of Sikhism* (5th Edition), New Book Society, 1960.

Orlich, Leopold Von, *Travels in India including Sind and the Punjab*, 2 vols., Longmans, London, 1845.

Osborne, W.G., *Court & Camp of Ranjit Singh*, London, 1840.

Panikkar, K.M., *The Founding of the Kashmir State*, Allen & Unwin, London, 1953.

Payne, C. H., *A Short History of the Sikhs*, Nelson & Sons, London.

Prinsep, H.T., *The Origin of the Sikh Power in the Punjab*, Calcutta, 1834.

Punjab & N.W. Frontier of India by an Old Punjaubee, London, 1878.

Punjab Government Records Vol. I (Delhi Residency & Agency 1807-57), Lahore, 1911.

Punjab Government Records Vol. II (Ludhiana Agency 1808-15), Lahore, 1911.

Ramakrishna, L., *Les Sikhs*, Paris, 1933.

Ross, David, *Land of the Five Rivers*, London, 1893.

Seagrim, D., *Notes on Hindus and Sikhs*, Pioneer Press, Allahabad, 1895.

Sethi, R.R, edited by, *Lahore Durbar, 1823-40*, P.G.R.O., 1950.

Shastri, Prakash, *Organisation Militaire des Sikhs*, Librairie Russe, Paris, 1932.

Shungloo, K., *Metcalfe Mission* (unpublished thesis, Punjab University).

Sinha, N.K., *Rise of the Sikh Power*, Calcutta, 1946. *Ranjit Singh*, Calcutta University, 1933.

Smyth, Major Carmichael, *History of the Reigning Family of Lahore*, Calcutta, 1847.

Steinback, Lt-Col, *The Punjaub: Being a Brief Account of the Country of the Sikhs*, Smith & Elder, London, 1845.

Stulpnagel, C.R., *The Sikhs*, Lahore, 1870.

Suri, V.S., *Some Original Sources of Punjab History*.

Swynnerton, The Rev Charles, *Romantic Tales from the Punjab*, Constable & Co, London, 1903.

Teja Singh and Ganda Singh, *Short History of the Sikhs*, Orient Longman, India, 1950.

Temple, R.C., *The Legends of the Punjab*, 3 vols., Bombay Education Society.

Thompson, Edward, *Life of Charles, Lord Metcalfe*, London, 1937.

Thorn, Major Wm, *Memories of the War in India Conducted by General Lord Lake, Major General Sir Arthur Wellesley, Duke of Wellington*, T. Egerton, Military Library, Whitehall, 1818.

Thornton, T.H., *History of the Punjab*, 2 vols., London, 1846.

Trotter, L.J., *Earl of Auckland*, Oxford, 1893.

Trevaskis, H.K., *The Land of the Five Rivers*, Oxford, 1928.

Vigne, G.T., *Travels in Kashmir, Ladakh, Iskardo, etc.*, London, 1844. *A Personal Narrative of a Visit to Ghazni*, London, 1840.

Wade, C., *Report on the Punjab & Adjacent Provinces Forming the Territories of Maharaja Ranjit Singh Together with a Historical Sketch of that Chief*. Mss.

Wolff, Rev. Joseph, *Travels & Adventures*, 2 vols., Saunders Otter & Co., London, 1860-1.

INDEX